THE
TRAFALGAR CHRONICLE
Dedicated to Naval History in the Nelson Era

New Series 5

Journal
of
THE 1805 CLUB

The 1805 Club

Edited by
JUDITH E PEARSON, SEAN HEUVEL & JOHN RODGAARD

In association with The 1805 Club

Seaforth
PUBLISHING

Text copyright © individual authors 2020

First published in Great Britain in 2020 by
Seaforth Publishing,
A division of Pen & Sword Books Ltd,
47 Church Street,
Barnsley S70 2AS

www.seaforthpublishing.com

British Library Cataloguing in Publication Data
A catalogue record for this book is available from the British Library

ISBN 978 1 5267 5962 7 (PAPERBACK)
ISBN 978 1 5267 5963 4 (EPUB)
ISBN 978 1 5267 5964 1 (KINDLE)

Pen & Sword Books Limited incorporates the imprints of Atlas, Archaeology, Aviation, Discovery, Family History, Fiction, History, Maritime, Military, Military Classics, Politics, Select, Transport, True Crime, Air World, Frontline Publishing, Leo Cooper, Remember When, Seaforth Publishing, The Praetorian Press, Wharncliffe Local History, Wharncliffe Transport, Wharncliffe True Crime and White Owl.

Designed and typeset in Times New Roman by Mousemat Design
Printed and bound in India by Replika Press Pvt Ltd

CONTENTS

President's Foreword – Admiral Sir Jonathon Band — 5

Editor's Foreword – Judith E Pearson, Sean Heuvel & John Rodgaard — 6

Articles on the 2020 Theme: Portrayals of the Georgian Navy in Art, Film, and Literature

Representations of Horatio Nelson in the Visual Arts: Heroic Portraiture Versus Historical Reality from a Medical Perspective – Gerald Stulc — 9

William Beatty, Arthur Devis and the Death of Lord Nelson in Early Nineteenth-Century Literature and Art – Andrew Venn — 33

Nelson in Caricature and Cartoon – Peter Turner — 44

Tobias Smollett and the Early Georgian Navy – Anthony Bruce — 62

Beyond Lady Barbara: Women as Portrayed in British Naval Fiction – Linda Collison — 74

The Rise of the Fouled Anchor: The Visual Codification of the Royal Navy During the 1700s – Lily Style — 87

Spain and American Independence: The Best-Kept Secret of the Georgian Age – Chipp Reid — 93

Biographical Portraits

Sir Andrew Pellet Green: Vice Admiral Thomas Fremantle's Protégé – Charles Fremantle — 105

Commander Sir James Pearl – Sean Heuvel — 114

Captain John Houlton Marshall – John Rodgaard and Lisa Heuvel   121

Captain Ralph Willett Miller – Gerald Holland   137

Articles of General Interest

The Popham Code Controversy – Chris Coehlo   141

Cornwallis, a Woman Named Cuba, and the Caribbean – Barry Jolly   156

A Second Naval War: The Immediate Effects of the American War
on Royal Navy Operations, June 1812–July 1813 – Samantha Cavell   167

Contributors' Biographies   *175*

Notes   *179*

The 1805 Club   *200*

Colour Plate Section between pages 128 and 129

President's Foreword

With its 2020 issue, the *Trafalgar Chronicle* stands at the threshold of its fourth decade. The journal has now transitioned to a new team of editors in Dr Judith E. Pearson, Dr Sean Heuvel, and Captain John Rodgaard USN, Ret. These three come from varied academic backgrounds and experience and are well-qualified for the task. They will most certainly carry on the fine work of the previous editor, Captain Peter Hore RN, Rtd. Judy, Sean, and John live in the US, where over 100 members of the 1805 Club now reside; almost a quarter of the club's membership.

The central theme for the current issue is the portrayal of the Georgian Navy era in art, literature, and film. The contributions by writer–historians are impressive, demonstrating the enduring influence of that era in portraits, caricatures, and films of Nelson and the Royal Navy, as well as mythological depictions, nautical symbolism, and historic novels about the Age of Sail. The writers and editors have drawn from their experience, education, and talents in diverse fields such as military/naval history, medicine, the fine arts, and journalism to bring forth a quality product. Much of the content is new research that has not been published elsewhere. Some of it revises and expands on what most readers already know about the era of the Georgian Navy. You cannot read this issue without finding something that is intriguing, surprising, memorable, and noteworthy!

The editors have also decided that this issue and future issues of the *Trafalgar Chronicle* will continue to include biographic portraits of Nelson's contemporaries, articles about technological advances in naval warfare of the era, battles at sea and their aftermaths, and the monuments and artefacts that help us to remember the Georgian era of the Royal Navy and Nelson. The theme for the upcoming 2021 issue will concern the Georgian Navy's encounters with indigenous cultures and enslaved populations.

The *Trafalgar Chronicle* is a vital aspect of The 1805 Club's mission to preserve the naval history and memorials of the Georgian era and Nelson's memory through conservation, education, research, and commemorative events. My hearty kudos (or should I say 'Bravo Zulu'?) to the editors and my heartfelt thanks to the writers who contributed so generously to this year's volume.

ADMIRAL SIR JONATHON BAND GCB DL
Former First Sea Lord
President of the 1805 Club

Editor's Foreword

As the *Trafalgar Chronicle* embarks on its fourth decade, we are delighted to take the helm from Captain Peter Hore RN, Rtd, the previous editor from 2015 to 2019. While all three of us have published books and articles and possess broad experience in writing and editing, for each of us this is a first experience in editing a scholarly research journal. In fact, as we look over the list of editors of the past issues, we feel honoured and humbled to be included in the pantheon. Captain Hore has generously given us his blessings and guidance as we undertake this new adventure. We are committed to maintaining his high standards.

The theme for this 2020 issue is portrayals of the Georgian Navy in art, literature, and film. As proposals and submittals began arriving over the past year, we have felt astonished and excited by the quality of material we have received, the acumen of the authors, and the depth of their diligent research. Because our theme concerns the arts, we also received, to our amazement, almost 100 illustrations – some familiar to our readers and some quite rare.

Our feature article is by Captain Gerald Stulc, Medical Corps, US Navy Ret. As a civilian, Captain Stulc is a retired cancer and trauma surgeon. His paper explores how paintings, drawings, and films have depicted Nelson's ailments and battle injuries. Dr Stulc brings his medical knowledge to bear in discussing Nelson's bouts with viruses and fevers as well as head trauma, impaired vision in one eye, a wound to his abdomen, the loss of his right arm and the circumstances of his death. We learn that the many depictions of Nelson seldom squared with medical reality. Yet, not only his victories but his injuries as well made him a hero in the eyes of his countrymen, who lionised him in death.

Complimenting Dr Stulc's article, historian Andrew Venn examines narratives and paintings of Nelson's death. He sifts through the eyewitness accounts written by those who witnessed Nelson's death and compares the paintings of West and Devis, who both portrayed his final moments. Venn sees Devis' painting as being much closer to reality. West, however, compensated for his inaccurate illustration with a more masterful, allegorical painting of Nelson's ascension to immortality.

Cartoonist and writer, and the new editor of The 1805 Club's *Kedge Anchor*, Peter Turner casts a light-hearted glance at the many ways Nelson's image has been captured in caricature and cartoon – sometimes in a flattering manner and sometimes not.

Writer and educational consultant Anthony Bruce describes how Royal Navy surgeon's mate Tobias Smollet drew on his real-life-at-sea experience to expose the dismal state of medicine in the Georgian Navy through his 1748 novel, *The Adventures of Roderick Random*. While the novel was published a generation before Nelson's time, we can surmise that Nelson and his contemporaries encountered similar conditions aboard Royal Navy ships, minus, perhaps, the disreputable characters who swaggered through Smollett's novel.

For her article, novelist Linda Collison studied depictions of women in historic novels about the Georgian Navy. Such novels, some based loosely on real-life accounts, suggest that women played a much more pervasive role in naval operations than history admits. While it is well known that most wives tended to hearth and home while their men were away at sea, some wives joined their husbands to brave the perils of shipboard life. They served food, mended clothes, worked as powder monkeys and, during battle, as nurses. Some women even gave birth at sea and some were wounded or died in battle or from yellow fever. Of course, readers might also encounter the occasional female spy and the usual prostitutes as well, just for a change of pace.

Emma Hamilton expert and direct descendant of Nelson and Hamilton, Lily Styles gives readers a treat: a discussion of the fouled anchor as a decorative motif. Introduced in 1758 on buttons on Royal Navy officers' uniforms, the fouled anchor soon found a place on fine china and textiles, as well as becoming an emblem in the US Navy.

Journalist/author and fellow 1805 Club North American member Chipp Reid delivers a must-read article on the 'best-kept secret of the Georgian age': the alliance between the Spanish Armada and the French Navy that helped Americans win their war for independence. Mr Reid applied his knowledge of Spanish to locate nearly 'impossible to find' evidence that the Spanish provided money, supplies, and munitions to the revolutionary cause. He also reveals how English-speaking historians may have biases about Hispanics, resulting in inaccurate portrayals of Spanish historical figures and the role they played during the American War.

As we planned, this issue of the *Trafalgar Chronicle* also offers articles that focus on historic figures, battles at sea, technological advancements of the Nelson era, discoveries of artefacts, and the preservation of monuments and historical sites. Fellow 1805 Club member Charles Fremantle, a prolific writer and frequent contributor, provides an article on Sir Andrew Pellet Green, a protégé of Mr Fremantle's ancestor, Vice Admiral Thomas Fremantle. We also have three biographical summaries on Commander James Pearl (by Sean

Heuvel), Captain John Houghton Marshall (by John Rodgaard and Lisa Heuvel), and Captain Ralph Willet Miller (by Gerald Holland); all North Americans who became officers in the Georgian era Navy.

Naval historian Chris Coelho travelled from his home in the US to his birthplace in Buenos Aires for research on Sir Home Popham, a controversial figure, and some would say a scoundrel, who, nevertheless, reinvented the signal flag system of the Royal Navy. Popham's system was in effect when Nelson raised the famous signal at Trafalgar: England expects every man to do his duty.

Admiral Sir William Cornwallis has been portrayed in his retirement years as a devout bachelor, living the quiet life as a country gentleman. Few naval historians would guess that, in his 'wild' youth, while stationed in the Caribbean, Cornwallis fathered at least three illegitimate children with women of colour. Barry Jolly of the Milford-on-Sea Historical Society conducted research on the Jamaica Church of England Parish Register in the International Genealogical Index to discover the details and bring them to our readers.

North American 1805 Club member Dr Samantha Cavill, history professor at Southeastern Louisiana University, writes about the effects of the War of 1812 on Royal Navy Operations; particularly how the demands of war with America created massive problems for the Royal Navy in terms of logistics, expenditures, ships, personnel, and supplies; especially since Britain was concurrently engaged in war with France. Students of the War of 1812 will find a wealth of information and statistics in this article that will enrich their understanding.

Working with authors such as these, our first year as editors of the *Trafalgar Chronicle* has been rich and rewarding. To our readers: we welcome your comments, questions, ideas, and suggestions about this issue and future issues. If you like to write and conduct historic research about all manner of things pertaining to the Royal Navy and other navies of the Georgian era, send us a proposal or get on our mailing list of potential contributors. The theme for the 2021 issue will be Georgian Navy encounters with indigenous cultures and enslaved populations.

Tell your friends and colleagues about the *Trafalgar Chronicle*. Our publisher, Seaforth Publishing, is happy to issue new subscriptions to individuals as well as organisations, universities, institutes, and libraries. Contact us at tc.editor@1805Club.org.

Judith E. Pearson, Ph.D. Burke, Virginia
John Rodgaard, Captain USN, Ret. Melbourne, Florida
Sean Heuvel, Ph.D. Williamsburg, Virginia

May 2020

Representations of Horatio Nelson in the Visual Arts:
Heroic Portraiture Versus Historical Reality from a Medical Perspective

Gerald Stulc

Vice-Admiral Horatio Nelson (1758–1805), 1st Viscount Nelson, 1st Duke of Bronté, KB, was already a celebrated hero among the British populace by the time of the Battle of Trafalgar of 21 October 1805. Upon his death at age forty-seven at the hands of a sniper in that battle, he achieved mythic proportions that persist to this day. In perpetuating his heroism and his subsequent legacy, particularly in times of war and danger to Britain, the visual representation of Nelson among his countrymen necessitated a traditional rendering and reworking of the man in epic proportions. His representation in the visual arts – paintings, engravings, and film – is examined as it pertains to the expected heroic image versus what is known from reports of his physical and medical, and to a point, emotional conditions. The depictions of any given civilisation's heroes traditionally portray them often as literally larger than life, perfect in physical form, domineering and victorious, whether it be of Ramses II, Octavian, or the Zeus-like sculpture of a bare-chested George Washington.

Nelson entered service with the Royal Navy inauspiciously in 1771 at the age of twelve. He soon found that he suffered from seasickness, which would become a chronic illness often treated with peppermint. In support of the East India Company, he was sent to the Indies and Bombay in 1773. In 1775, he became ill with malaria, which was so severe that he nearly died. A coffin was prepared for him in the expectation that he would not survive the voyage back to Britain. In his febrile delirium, he experienced the vision of a glowing orb associated with the premonition that he was destined to become a hero.

Nelson recovered, but while at Portsmouth in June 1777 he collapsed, apparently from another malarial attack. By 1780, he had been promoted to post-captain, and was part of Major-General John Dalling's expedition to Central America against its Spanish colonies. During his trek up the San Juan River, Nelson began to experience chest pains, diagnosed as 'gout', a probable

Captain Horatio Nelson, Jean Francis Rigaud 1781. (National Maritime Museum)

recurrence of his malaria. In subsequently besieging the Spanish Fort of San Juan, he was one of the first of his men to fall ill, either from typhoid or yellow fever ('yellow jack'), or, less likely but asserted, poisoning from drinking water into which the highly toxic fruit of the manchineel tree had fallen.

Nelson commanded the land force, which was able to capture Fort San Juan shortly after he became ill. His first full portraiture was painted by Francis Rigaud in 1781, after Nelson had spent a good part of the remainder of 1780 recovering from a probable recurrent bout of malaria or yellow fever while in Costa Rica. The fort forms the background for the slender and rather unremarkable young man in the naval uniform of captain, his hands resting victoriously upon his sword. Despite his gaunt appearance, his visage and piercing gaze are directed squarely at the viewer, a look of authority and self-assurance. The dawning day suggests the trials and triumphs to come that are his destiny. Apart from two episodes of a severe febrile illness, in this portrait he is unmarked by trauma at the early age of twenty-three.

Nelson was of medium height for his time, between 5ft 5in and 5ft 6in. Later full-length portraits depict Nelson with long legs, which seem disproportionate compared to his actual height, and in several depictions, he is portrayed as taller than the surrounding men. Nevertheless, his body habitus remains lanky, consistent with his illnesses but not necessarily with middle age. The portrait of Nelson by Guy Head, c1798–1800, standing next to a boy aboard ship shows, once more, a disproportion between the head and body height, suggesting a taller person. In this case, even the face bears little resemblance to Nelson, and raises the question of whether the artist painted this directly from the subject. The known ratio of femur length to height ranges from 1:3.33 to 1:3.66. The length of the thigh in this painting is not in keeping with his known height, nor is his head in proportion to a man of medium height.[1] However, it is in keeping with a figuratively larger-than-life personage.

Nelson continued to suffer from various illnesses and symptoms after the expedition to Central America, leading to a speculation that he was somewhat of a hypochondriac. While in London in May 1781, he complained that his left arm and leg were troubling him, the fingers of his left hand white and swollen with loss of feeling. These features are not compatible with malaria or yellow fever, but may indicate peripheral neuritis as a chronic complication of typhoid fever.[2] By 1782, Nelson was posted to a North American station. The transatlantic voyage of approximately eight weeks had resulted in lack of fresh vegetables and the onset of scurvy affecting Nelson and the crew. Nelson's gingiva (gums) became spongy with the resultant loss of many of his teeth, a result of lack of Vitamin C. His cheeks were consequently sunken, a feature noted to greater or lesser degrees in his subsequent portraits.[3, 4] Additionally, by 1783 at the age of twenty-five, Nelson's hair was already turning white due in part to his recurring febrile crises.

During his posting to the West Indies in 1784, Nelson had a recurrent attack of malaria, sweating so profusely amidst that climate that he shaved off his hair for comfort, wearing a wig for the time being. Three years later, on the voyage from the West Indies to Britain, he developed a febrile illness serious enough that a keg of rum was set aside to preserve his body should he succumb. With the onset of peace by the time he returned, Nelson went on half pay and began domestic life, with his wife Fanny Nisbet. Still, Nelson longed for a command and for action.[5]

Horatio Nelson, Guy Head, 1798–99. (National Portrait Gallery)

In 1793, Nelson was recalled to service following Revolutionary France's annexation of the Austrian Netherlands and declaration of war. Nelson sailed in command of the third-rate HMS *Agamemnon* (64) with Hood's fleet to Toulon. He was shortly thereafter sent to Naples with dispatches requesting reinforcements for Hood. After the fall of Toulon, Nelson undertook coastal raids along Corsica and the interruption of enemy shipping. Upon his suggestion, a naval bombardment and land siege on Bastia took place.

On 19 April 1794, while inspecting installed shore batteries at the siege of Bastia, he received a 'sharp cut' to the back. He had barely escaped death when a heavy shot from the town battery threw up a massive shower of earth, which fell on him. However, he sustained the first of his major and famed injuries later, at the siege of Calvi, on 10 July 1794, when shot hit a sandbag near where Nelson stood. The spray of sand and small rocks peppered the right side of his face, injuring his eye, probably with penetration of the globe, and causing multiple superficial facial lacerations that bled liberally. The left eye may have been affected, as well.[6]

After seeking medical attention, Nelson returned to the fight, later writing that, 'I got a little hurt this morning.' The resulting eye injury, likely a severe corneal abrasion versus a hyphema (collection of blood behind the cornea) or retinal detachment, eventuated in mydriasis (dilation of the pupil) and scarring of the cornea, giving it a milky, opaque appearance. The pupil remained as large as his iris. Nelson lost partial sight in that eye, but not the eye itself, and was able to discern light from dark through it.[7-9]

In 1797, he wrote to his friend, Commissioner Hope, stating that the Navy Board – in charge of naval medical affairs – did not believe that he was blind in that eye, meaning that a cursory exam belied a significant eye injury. Consequently, he sought additional evidence to support his claim. On 12 October 1797, he was examined for a second opinion by the Company of Surgeons in London, whereupon he was given a disability pension and a medical certificate stating loss of vision in the eye proportional to the loss of an eye or limb.[10, 11] However, the *Times* of 10 April 1804 claimed that he was 'weaker' in the right eye, but 'not blind in either eye'.[12]

Subsequent depictions of Nelson do not reveal the clouding of the pupil of his eye, though there may have been mild divergence of the globe from the left eye and drooping of the right upper eyelid, perhaps subtly portrayed in several depictions. By the mid-nineteenth century, it became increasingly common to portray Nelson as wearing an eyepatch, despite the fact that he never did.[13] However, by January 1801, Nelson's doctor became determined to protect the sight in the left eye. Nelson wrote or signed letters, and read during much of the day below decks with only a single candle for light. His doctor instructed him to bathe the left eye in cold water every waking hour, and forbade letter writing and the ingestion of alcohol. His doctors, including his surgeon at the Battle of Trafalgar, William Beatty, were certain that Nelson would eventually lose all sight in that eye. Nelson was given a green eyeshade, made by Emma Hamilton, with which to protect his good eye from sunlight. This shade was attached to the front of his cocked hat as a visor.[14] It may have been for that reason that Nelson continued to wear his hat transversely rather than in the more current fashion of wearing of it lengthwise from front to back (or fore and aft).

Contemporary portraits by Lemuel Abbot, William Beechey, Arthur Devis, and John Hoppner do not suggest any significant opacification or injury to the right eye. Regardless, it became *de rigueur* in twentieth-century cinema to follow established convention, and depict Nelson with an eyepatch or swathing scarf. The silent 1921 movie, *Lady Hamilton*, presented actor Conrad Veidt as Nelson not only wearing a wide black bandage, but across the wrong eye.

In the 1926 silent movie, *Nelson*, Cedric Hardwicke portrayed Nelson also wearing a dark wrap across his left (wrong) eye, which he removed before he was about to meet Lady Hamilton. Both eyes are intact, but Lady Hamilton refers to the loss of his 'left eye and right arm' in acknowledging his sacrifice to his country. In 1941, at the time the United Kingdom faced its greatest threat of

1921 movie *Lady Hamilton*, Conrad Veidt as Nelson.

invasion since Napoleon, Laurence Olivier portrayed Nelson in *That Hamilton Woman*. The morale-boosting film was meant to instil a sense of patriotism and courage made more dramatic by exaggerating Nelson's loss of sight in one eye. Olivier intermittently wears an eyepatch over his right eye, the upper eyelid drooping. Actor Peter Finch, in the 1973 movie *Bequest to the Nation*, wears an eyepatch over his right eye in his final hours aboard *Victory* on the day of the Battle of Trafalgar, perpetuating the myth. Of note, the figurehead of Nelson from HMS *Trafalgar* in the historic Portsmouth dockyard was repainted in 2011, in accordance with historians'

1926 movie *Nelson*, Cedrick Hardwick as Nelson.

recommendations to accurately portray the decorations on his uniform; in addition, the pupil of the right eye was painted over to make it appear opacified.

Perhaps the most accurate on-screen portrayal of Nelson from a medical aspect is to be found in the BBC television miniseries of 1982, *I Remember Nelson*. Kenneth Colley is featured as a weary Admiral Nelson sans

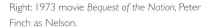

Above: 1941 movie *That Hamilton Woman*, Laurence Olivier as Nelson.

Right: 1973 movie *Bequest of the Nation*, Peter Finch as Nelson.

eyepatch but displaying the prominent and somewhat hypersensitive forehead scar sustained in 1798 in the Battle of the Nile, a disfigurement absent in most representations prior to that TV series.

1982 BBC TV Miniseries *I Remember Nelson*, Kenneth Colley as Nelson.

Serving under Admiral Jervis, then-Commodore Nelson sustained the facial scar when he intercepted a Spanish fleet sailing toward the Atlantic port of Cadiz intending to join the French fleet. In the ensuing Battle of Cape St Vincent on Valentine's Day, 14 February 1797, Nelson aggressively and against orders broke toward the van of the Spanish fleet. His ship attacked the third-rate *San Nicholas* (80), which had already struck its colours, and then utilised the surrendered ship in order to board the adjacent Spanish first-rate ship of the line, the *San Josef* (114). During the boarding of the surrendering *San Nicholas*, the *San Josef* opened fire with its guns. Nelson sustained blunt trauma to his lower abdomen by a wood splinter from one of the shots. According to Captain Ralph Miller of the third-rate HMS *Captain* (74), Nelson 'would have fallen had not my arms supported him'.[15]

Nelson wrote to Sir Gilbert Elliot a day after the battle, 'Among the slightly wounded is myself, but it is only a contusion and of no consequence, unless an inflammation takes place in my bowels, which is the part injured.' A week later, Nelson wrote to his uncle, William Suckling, 'My hurt at the moment was nothing, but since, it has been attended with a suppression of urine, but the inflammation has gone off, and I am nearly recovered.' In a subsequent letter to Lady Hamilton dated November 1804, Nelson wrote, 'My cough is very bad, and my side, where I was struck on the 14th February is very much swelled; at times a lump as large as my fist, brought on, occasionally, by violent coughing.'[16]

It appears that he minimised the severity of his injury, implied by the incongruity between Captain Miller's account of Nelson requiring support after being struck, and Nelson's initial letters afterwards. The trauma was sufficient to preclude normal micturition (urination) for several days, suggesting a perivesicular hematoma (blood collection alongside the bladder) and/or swelling of tissues in the abdominal wall musculature. The resulting bleeding and inflammation would have been enough to decrease the capacity of the bladder. This may well have been compounded by dehydration due to initial blood loss and a reflex slowing of bowel function with resulting inability to take sufficient fluids by mouth. Alternatively, bleeding and clots within the bladder may have been just as responsible.

The injury weakened and disrupted the normal abdominal wall musculature such that, with time, the defect resolved into a ventral hernia (abdominal rupture). The persistence of his cough in 1804 would have caused a temporary increase in intraabdominal pressure, aggravating a significant-sized hernia with the potentially serious complication of an incarceration (trapped bowel within the hernia), necrosis (loss of blood circulation) of the intestine and death. There are no known records concerning whether Nelson wore a corset or truss afterward to support the weakness and contain herniation through the defect. The presence and location of the defect would have been concealed by his uniform, and likely not appropriate for rendering had it been clearly visible.

Despite the severity and acuteness of the blunt abdominal trauma, illustrations of his swashbuckling capture of the *San Josef* (later renamed the *St Joseph*), and accepting the sword of surrender from its captain naturally fail to disclose any evidence of incapacitation. It seems the incident was unknown except to those near Nelson at the time, and his most immediate friends. A similar painting by Westall done a year after Nelson's death shows a vigorous and long-limbed Nelson attacking the Spanish sailors.

The Battle of Cape St Vincent, Nelson Capturing the San Jose, George Jones, 1829.
(ArtUK.org; Ashmolean Museum of Art and Archaeology)

Nelson Accepting the Sword of Surrender, The San Jose, Battle of Cape St Vincent, Daniel Orme, 1766–c1832. (National Maritime Museum)

Several months later, Nelson, now a Rear Admiral of the Blue, was stationed off Cadiz, Spain. Learning of a Spanish treasure ship's recent arrival at the Canary Island of Tenerife, Nelson planned an ill-advised and failed amphibious assault on the main city of Santa Cruz on 24 July 1797. As he stepped ashore, a musket ball struck his right arm above the elbow, shattering his humerus. Lieutenant Josiah Nisbet (Nelson's stepson) improvised a tourniquet with his silk kerchief, as Nelson had sustained a compound (open) fracture of the bone with transection of the main (brachial) artery. The tourniquet likely saved Nelson's life. He was rowed back in the prevailing darkness to his flagship, the third-rate HMS *Theseus* (74).[17]

Within the gloomy confines of the cockpit, lit by a single lantern, the able surgeon Thomas Eshelby and his assistant Louis Remonier amputated Nelson's arm successfully. Nelson bore the surgery without complaint, but afterward remarked on the discomfort of cold steel against his flesh. From thereon, he ordered all his squadron surgeons to heat their instruments prior to their use. It is said that Nelson resumed giving commands within an hour of his amputation, his pain somewhat allayed by opium.[18, 19, 20] In the 1806 melodramatic painting by

Richard Westall of Nelson's wounding, there is no evidence of haemorrhage from a nearly severed arm – in spite of a crude tourniquet – and the mutilated limb is delicately hidden from the sensibilities of the viewer. Nelson, ever the warrior, still holds his sword, now in his left hand, and is dressed in military finery.

The loss of his right arm became a signature badge of courage and duty for Nelson among the British populace. Nelson by now was revered as a major

Nelson Wounded at Tenerife, 24 July, 1797, Richard Westall, 1798.
(National Maritime Museum)

hero. He was to endure considerable pain in the stump until December of that year, when the ligature used to tie off the brachial artery during amputation came away in his dressings. Nelson experienced immediate relief of pain, afterwards, giving thanks in the Church of St George in Hanover Square.[21] Evidently, under the duress of surgery performed in the early hours under poor lighting, the median nerve, which runs closely alongside the artery, was incorporated into the ligature. Nonetheless, Nelson would suffer from phantom

Rear Admiral Horatio Nelson, Lemuel Francis Abbott, 1799.

Admiral Nelson, Lemuel Francis Abbot, 1797.

limb pain for the remainder of his life, a common and still not completely understood neurophysiological phenomenon following amputations.[22] This complication certainly added to the strain from chronic and recurrent illnesses Nelson endured, as well as the general stress of command.

One of the most recognisable images of Nelson was painted by Lemuel Abbott shortly after the amputation of his arm. Despite the trauma, probable localised infection and inflammation, chronic pain, and phantom limb syndrome, Nelson appears remarkably robust, the cheeks rosy. Of note, the tattered right sleeve hangs down as if the limb was still present, though buttoned to the front of the jacket. The gold sleeve stripes are clearly positioned such that they, at first glance, appear to be buttons following the line of jacket closure, giving the illusion that the right arm remains. Yet, on closer inspection, the tattered sleeve is a subtle reminder of recent sacrifice.

Interestingly, as with the wounding and loss of sight in his right eye, the arm that underwent amputation was not always rendered on the correct side in subsequent portraits and illustrations. In William Heath's painting, *The Cockpit, Battle of the Nile*, Nelson is shown after he has sustained an injury to the right forehead, but is seen to be leaning against his right arm for support while men rush to his assistance. It is the left arm that is missing in this image. In *Apotheosis of Nelson* by Scott Pierre Lagrand, Nelson is borne as a demigod toward heaven after his death by the major Greek deities. He is extending his right arm to Britannia in farewell, the ostensibly missing left arm hidden from view by Zeus. Importantly, both paintings were created several years after Nelson's death. Apparently, the message trumped anatomical accuracy.

The Cockpit of HMS Vanguard, William Heath, c1817.

On 1 August 1798, Nelson complained of a 'damn toothache' prior to the Battle of Aboukir Bay in Egypt. This was conceivably due to his previous bout of scurvy. In the battle that followed that day, Nelson was struck above his right eye by langridge (shot consisting of scrap iron packed into a casing), resulting in a flap (avulsion) laceration to the forehead involving his eyebrow.[23] He was attended to by Surgeon Jefferson, and noted to be 'pale and concussed', bleeding profusely from a likely tear to the supraorbital/supratrochlear arterial plexus (an artery traversing the forehead, temple, and eye socket). Nelson was convinced he had been fatally wounded. The wound was tightly bandaged, but Nelson experienced a 'splitting, splitting, splitting' headache', and stated that, 'for 18 hours my life was thought to be past hope … I am weak in body and mind, both from this cough and the fever.'[24]

Attributed to Guy Head, allegedly one of Nelson's favourite portraits, c1800.
https://www.wikiart.org/en/lemuel-francis-abbott/rear-admiral-sir-horatio-nelson-1799

Horatio Nelson, Friedrich Heinrich Füger, oil on canvas, 1800. (National Portrait Gallery)

From the force of such a blow and avulsion laceration, it is probable that he sustained a concussion – a traumatic brain injury (TBI) – to the prefrontal cortex, possibly even a skull fracture.[25] He developed a fever and headache for eighteen hours afterwards. While in Palermo, Sicily, a year later, Nelson complained of depression, headaches and nausea, indigestion, irregularity of his heartbeat (palpitations), and breathlessness, leading him to believe he was experiencing heart attacks. His behaviour also became arguably capricious, demonstrating more insubordination toward Lord Keith while in the Mediterranean, while at the same time consorting with Lady Hamilton. He became involved in the controversial trial and execution of the Italian admiral and revolutionary, Francesco Caracciolo, who was hanged on 30 June 1799, on Nelson's orders, for treason against the King of Naples. Any true behavioural changes as suggested by these incidents could be related to permanent injury to the frontal portion of the brain responsible for behaviour and inhibitions.

Regardless, portraits of Nelson by Füger and by Head around 1800 show no trace of an avulsion scar to the right forehead. Nelson thereafter would comb a lock of his hair over the scar. However, a painting by Beechey in 1801 clearly shows the scar as a disruption of the right eyebrow resulting from inaccurate approximation of the hairline. Interestingly, in 2017, one of several paintings of Nelson by Leonardo Guzzardi, c1799, was rediscovered. While restoration proceeded, a rough overpainting of the right forehead was removed, revealing the original depiction of a ragged and still livid irregular scar of the right

Detail, Horatio, 1st Viscount Nelson by William Beechey, 1801.

forehead, with a discontinuous eyebrow and depression of the scar. It appears that similar 'cosmetic' retouching had been done to other of Guzzardi's portraits of Nelson, perhaps being found in the succeeding Victorian and Edwardian periods not befitting the expected image of Britain's principal paladin. This painting was found in the collection of art dealer Philip Mould.[26]

Detail, Horation Nelson by Leonardo Guzzardi, 1799.

Furthermore, an engraving by Gillray of Nelson conquering the 'plagues' of Egypt two months after the Battle of the Nile clearly shows a fresh, irregular laceration of his forehead, still bleeding, though on the incorrect side. Of further note, the majority of later portraits of Nelson depict him from the left side, whether by the artist's or subject's choice, and as if to intentionally minimise the right facial scar, eye opacification, and the loss of limb.

The blow to the head may have resulted in Nelson suffering excruciating headaches for the remainder of his life. Moreover, in the Battle of Copenhagen in 1801, Nelson was thought to be suffering from 'heatstroke', associated with nausea and vomiting. He expressed a conviction that he was near death. While at Gibraltar in 1802, Nelson wrote to Emma Hamilton that he was suffering from seasickness, a toothache, fever, dysentery, a 'heavy cold', and recurrent numbness in his left hand.[27] His prior infectious illnesses or injuries cannot explain the etiology of his left-sided paresthesias, nor is there evidence of loss

Detail, engraving, *Extirpation of the plagues of Egypt*, James Gillray,
Published by Hannah Humphrey; engraving, published 6 October 1798.

of function in his hand that would suggest an impingement of a nerve in his cervical (neck) spine or carpal tunnel syndrome. The symptoms came on intermittently years before his blow to the head. Regardless, there was never a mention of visible changes to the hand, loss of motor function, nor of permanent deformity that could have been represented pictorially.

At the same time, Nelson's scandalous affair with Emma Hamilton was widely publicised in the press and illustrated in satirical engravings. The engraving, 'A Mansion House treat', shows Emma drawing on a long-stemmed pipe in her mouth, while Nelson smokes an even longer pipe ejecting profuse white smoke with an obvious phallic connotation, the pair meanwhile exchanging double entendres. Despite the absence of his right arm, Nelson is shown as a randy and vigorous man in prime health.

By the time of the Battle of Trafalgar in 1805, Nelson, aged forty-seven, had been ravaged by acute and chronic infectious diseases, sustained several life-threatening injuries including possible traumatic brain injury, and laboured under the stress of command mandated by the imminent threat of an invasion of Britain by Napoleon.

Comparable to Guzzardi's unflattering portrait, the painting of Nelson completed in the same year by Devis shows the culmination of these abuses. The face is sunken and care-worn, with heavy eyelids and dark circles beneath

Detail, *A Mansion House treat – or smoking attitudes*, London, 1800, Artist unknown.

the eyes, a distant stare to them. The cheeks and lips remain blushed, whether true or not. The body is lean, somewhat unusual for privileged middle-aged men who tend to gain girth at this point – unlike Guzzardi's portrait that suggests a slight paunch. If so, then Nelson had lost weight in the intervening six years since Guzzardi's painting. The shoulders appear more narrowed from other portraits, augmented only by the epaulettes of an admiral. Once more, the left side of the subject is presented to us, muting the loss of the right arm. The green visor attached to the front of his hat to protect the sight in his left eye also serves to conveniently hide the disfigurement of the right side of the forehead and eyebrow. Our attention is drawn more to the various decorations on his left breast, the uniform embellishing the otherwise weary, chronically ill man within. Nelson wrote around this time, 'Wounds received by Lord Nelson: His eye in Corsica, His belly off Cape St Vincent, His arm at Teneriffe, His head in Egypt … Tolerable for one war!'[28]

On 21 October, a clear Sunday morning, Nelson's fleet had caught up to Villeneuve's combined French and Spanish fleet breaking out from a blockade of Cadiz, and sailing toward the Mediterranean after failing to clear the English Channel in preparation for Napoleon's invasion troops. As is well known, Nelson was shot in the heat of battle by a French marksman from the *Redoubtable*'s mizzentop, the ship's shrouds entangled with those of *Victory*. The musket ball entered the chest near the left shoulder just below the collarbone, carrying a part of his epaulette and cloth from his jacket into the tract of the missile. The musket ball passed obliquely through the left lung and transected the sixth and seventh thoracic vertebrae, causing paralysis from the nipple level down.[29]

During their previous circuit of the quarterdeck while the battle raged, Nelson and Captain Hardy were witness to the death of their secretary, Warrant Officer John Scott, who was cut in two by cannon shot. On their next circuit, at 1.30pm, Nelson had just approached the pool of blood from the recently transected Scott when he himself was shot from above. Nelson fell into the puddle, supporting himself with his left hand. Initially, Hardy and those in

Portrait of Admiral Lord Nelson KB,
Arthur William Devis, 1805.

Portrait of Vice-Admiral Lord Nelson,
Leonardo Guzzardi, 1791.

proximity believed the blood to be Nelson's. Besmirched with Scott's blood, Nelson was carried to the cockpit of *Victory*, where he was undressed, covered with blankets, and attended to by his staff and Dr William Beatty until death ensued three hours later. Nelson's demise resulted from bleeding within the chest, but, as importantly, his autonomic nervous system had been irreparably damaged by the spinal injury, which could have otherwise compensated for a conceivably survivable blood loss.

A month after Nelson's death, engraver Josiah Boydell offered a prize for the best painting of the event. Arthur William Devis was apparently released from debtors' prison for the explicit purpose of entering the competition to pay off his debts. Devis was allowed a week aboard *Victory* to gain material for his painting. His major competitor was the famous American expatriate, Benjamin West. West created a more idealistic painting of Nelson's death, inaccurately having Nelson die on the quarterdeck rather than below decks, and with Hardy present (he was not). West, and later Maclise, painted a symbolic patch of blood on the deck next to Nelson, but Nelson's uniform is immaculate.

Devis also took artistic liberties with his *Death of Nelson*, though accurately portraying the moment of death adjacent to the cockpit deep within the ship's bowels. The gloomy space, however, is shown as much larger than in reality in order to accommodate all the principal characters associated with Nelson's last moments. Hardy is also pictured next to Nelson, though he was not actually present at the moment of death. Notably, Nelson's pillows are adjusted behind his head in a manner suggesting a halo; the saintliness of the dying hero of Trafalgar. He is correctly shown propped up to assist his breathing, as his left

Detail from *The Death of Nelson*, by Daniel Maclise, 1859–64. (Walker Art Gallery)

lung was collapsed and compressed by bleeding within the chest. But, there is no evidence of a gunshot wound to the left supraclavicular area, unlike West's painting in which an assistant is holding a compress dressing against the wound, and that of Armitage adding a blood stain on the pillow. (Devis' painting is shown on page 34; West's painting is shown on page 40. Armitage's painting is not shown).

Actually, such a wound would have been contused but relatively small and with little external bleeding, all the bleeding occurring internally from transected pulmonary blood vessels. The sentiments and composition of the painting serve to express the nascent Romantic notions of the time, while representing the event as accurately as possible. Boydell thought so, as well, selecting Devis's painting over West's for the prize. West had gone to considerable lengths to create his own painting of Nelson's demise, having interviewed more than fifty men who had participated in the battle. In the end, he admitted that it was still a depiction 'of what might have been, not of the circumstances as they happened'.[30]

Following his death and funeral at St Paul's, Nelson was lionised as the man who had given his life to defend Britain against French invasion, though Napoleon had by then withdrawn his invasion troops from the coast, sending them east to new threats culminating in the Battle of Austerlitz. The monument in Trafalgar Square of Nelson and the one in St Paul's attest to Nelson's elevation to the pantheon of greats by his grateful countrymen. Innumerable images were created afterwards, especially on commemorative objects related to his funereal ceremonies. Every form of visual art was used to preserve and propagate his legacy to the point of the mythological. By the twentieth century, these arts included cinema, television, and popular art.

The representations of Nelson mandated heroic depictions of his exploits, sacrifice, and physical characteristics corresponding to the level of deification he attained. Paradoxically, his most visible physical infirmities had to be emphasised to underscore the sacrifices he made without diminishing from a visual perception of indomitability. The significant loss of a limb and disfiguration of an eye were far more compelling than a disfiguring scar of the forehead and eyebrow, loss of teeth, frailty from chronic illnesses, or a pouching abdominal hernia. Moreover, the graphic presence of a useless stump could be genteelly concealed by the flap of an empty sleeve or a tattered sleeve simulating the presence of a limb. The injury to the right eye was either disregarded, the face shown from the left aspect, or dramatically concealed by a scarf or patch, the injury again implied rather than seen.

A First World War poster, 'England Expects, 1805–1915,' showed Nelson as an embodiment of duty and patriotism. When the United Kingdom survived the

1805 "ENGLAND EXPECTS" 1915

ARE YOU DOING YOUR DUTY TO-DAY?

Nelson in a First World War poster.

horrific losses consequent to the First World War and faced invasion once again from Germany during the Second World War, it was only natural to use the new art of cinema to appropriate one of its greatest champions to sustain morale and create patriotic fervour. Any physical or moral infirmities contrary to a culture's veneration and mythology regarding its heroes are necessarily contrary to how that culture optimally views itself. Thus, Nelson was portrayed as robust despite the loss of limb and eye, long of limb and virile, even in satire, commensurate with a historical and culture-wide tradition of portraying a nation's champions in art and literature as the idealisation of its highest values and expectations. Among the general public, particularly outside of the UK, the image of the one-armed admiral wearing an eyepatch and an empty-sleeved eighteenth-century naval uniform is the epitome of that Age of Sail and a stereotypical representation of the best of the Royal Navy of the Georgian era, a romantic idealism without recourse to the grim realities of everyday service and danger in that era.

The author wishes to acknowledge the kind assistance and use of presentation materials of M. K. H. Crumplin, MD (Eng & Ed) FRHistS, per email correspondence, September through November 2019.

Nelson in conflict with a Spanish launch, 3 July, see colour plate 1

Apotheosis of Nelson, Scott Pierre Legrand, c1805–18, see colour plate 2

William Beatty, Arthur Devis and the Death of Lord Nelson in Early Nineteenth-Century Literature and Art

Andrew Venn

The death of Lord Nelson at the Battle of Trafalgar captivated the imaginations of the public from the moment the news was announced in November 1805, with people eager to gain as much information as possible about the demise of a national hero. The scene was the subject of numerous written accounts and works of art, all looking to capture accurately the essence of the moment. Perhaps the most famous and authoritative account of the events that happened in *Victory*'s cockpit came from William Beatty, the ship's surgeon. Beatty's *Authentic Narrative of the Death of Lord Nelson*, published in 1807, provided a running account of events leading up to the battle, following through to Nelson's fateful injury and subsequent death a few hours later.[1] Beatty's account has shaped perceptions of the death of Nelson ever since, serving almost as a full synopsis of all that occurred on the day.

Of course, however, Beatty was far from the only eyewitness of Nelson's last moments, and several other eyewitness accounts from other key individuals present exist. The most prominent of these come from *Victory*'s chaplain, Alexander Scott, and the ship's purser, Walter Burke. Despite the existence of these accounts, and their prominence following Trafalgar in 1805, they have been largely forgotten over time in favour of Beatty's *Authentic Narrative.* But how exactly did this come to be?

This article will scrutinise these different accounts, each written soon after Nelson's death, picking apart both the intentions of their respective authors and the credibility of their descriptions of proceedings. Ultimately, a judgement will be made over each account's impact on the legend of the death of Nelson and our perceptions of events to this day.

Similarly, Arthur Devis' 1807 painting *The Death of Nelson, 21 October 1805*, has proven to be the work of art that most reflects the scene in the cockpit on that fateful day.[2] The latter section of this article will examine the context surrounding Devis' decisions when creating this artwork and how he was influenced by key witnesses, including Beatty, while obtaining information. Like Beatty's account, Devis' work will also be compared with its

The Death of Nelson, 21 October 1805, oil on canvas by Arthur William Devis, 1807. The figures surrounding Nelson include Scott to the left and Burke, Hardy and Beatty to the right.
(National Maritime Museum)

contemporaries, namely Benjamin West's various efforts to capture the essence of the scene. Along with the written accounts, these works of art are a valuable source when examining how perceptions of the death of Nelson have developed over time, providing a visual representation to go with the details of what has been written.

Surgeon William Beatty

The Battle of Trafalgar was the first major action in which surgeon William Beatty had served.[3] Although he was not directly involved in combatting the combined fleet, the battle would have a long-lasting impact on Beatty and his legacy. The role he played in Nelson's last moments and his 1807 *Authentic Narrative of the Death of Lord Nelson* ensured that the Ulsterman would forever be connected in history to the apotheosis of the late admiral.

After authenticating an earlier account published in late 1805 (covered in part II of this article), Beatty felt the need to publish his own version of events to clear up any confusion and uncertainty as to what actually happened. The

Authentic Narrative was far more comprehensive than any of the previous accounts published, covering many aspects of the battle and its context in detail.

In the preface entitled *To the Public,* Beatty addresses his reasoning behind publishing his narrative. He states his authority from the very start, suggesting that he felt 'called upon' and that a 'short statement of facts' was required. Beatty also expresses how he felt compelled to separately release the narrative, originally intended to form part of Clarke and McArthur's *Life of Lord Nelson*, due to time constraints and the public's eagerness for information.[4] As the senior medical officer present in *Victory*'s cockpit, it seems that it was fate that Beatty would be the one to ultimately produce a detailed account of Nelson's wound.

Sir William Beatty, circa 1770–1842, oil on canvas by Arthur William Devis, c1806. Beatty commissioned Devis to paint this portrait. (National Maritime Museum)

Throughout the text, Beatty refers to himself as 'the surgeon', distancing himself from events.[5] He did this possibly to give the account more weight and to remove any notion of his personal attachment to Nelson. Instead, Beatty comes across as a professional man of medicine and a reliable narrator, establishing his authority and giving the overall text an air of accuracy. He includes a detailed explanation of the wound itself, along with the physical effects that Nelson was suffering, and even a history of the admiral's pre-existing wounds and health complaints.[6] Furthermore, the use of the word 'authentic' in the title of the piece gives the impression that Beatty views this work as the definitive account of Nelson's death.

In an early passage of the narrative, Beatty recalls how he desired to warn Nelson of the danger posed by wearing the 'stars' of his orders of merit on his coat. He suggests that the Reverend Dr Alexander J. Scott, *Victory*'s chaplain, and Warrant Officer John Scott,[7] Nelson's secretary, told him that his advice would have no effect, and Beatty later states that he ultimately did not get the chance to warn the admiral.[8] Similar concerns over Nelson's orders of merit were revealed in several other accounts, with different individuals each claiming that they endeavoured to warn Nelson of the danger. In some versions, Nelson is portrayed to have flagrantly ignored the advice, whereas other versions follow a pattern of events similar to Beatty's account.[9]

In contrast to the medical descriptions, the passage in which Beatty describes the actual scenes in the cockpit reads almost like a play, as if the surgeon was writing a dramatisation intended for the stage.[10] Of course, most accounts describe this pivotal moment in such a manner; however none in as much vivid detail as Beatty. Despite such thorough description, questions can be raised from a few comments that Beatty makes, such as when he dictates that he was ordered by Nelson that his duties lay elsewhere with the other wounded patients. Beatty says that he was not constantly by the admiral's side, and therefore suspicions can be raised over how much of his narrative was based on first-hand witness, and how much he pieced together using second-hand accounts. Even if Beatty had been close to Nelson in his last moments, the crowded, infernal conditions of *Victory*'s orlop would have made it near impossible to focus on nearby conversations. It can be inferred therefore that Beatty relied on the experiences of Burke and the Reverend Dr Scott for the details he could not personally provide. However, if this was the case, then key elements of his account, such as Nelson's last words, which Beatty recalls as 'Thank god I have done my duty', would not have been different from those dictated by Burke and Scott.

It must also be considered that Beatty was writing some time after the battle, and therefore memory must have played a role in his ability to recall events. Undoubtedly, Trafalgar had a profound psychological consequence on all involved, let alone those who witnessed the death of a man who was revered as a hero of the Royal Navy and the British people. Of course, it cannot be confirmed precisely which elements of Beatty's account he witnessed and which elements were based on second-hand information. Nevertheless, it was Beatty's account that had a profound effect on perceptions of the death of Nelson, much more so than the other early accounts that exist.

Another point to consider is Beatty's intention when writing this article. It is hard to say whether Beatty was publishing this account purely to provide the public with information, or if he was also looking for personal fame. Beatty had already been appointed Physician of the Channel Fleet in 1806, and perhaps was looking for a way to further elevate his career. The *Authentic Narrative* was Beatty's first published work, and would also prove to be his last.[11] In the preface, Beatty states that he published the narrative as a standalone effort due to Clarke and McArthur's biography of Nelson not yet being completed. However, it could be inferred that Beatty chose to publish his narrative individually to get his name out there in the public domain. Regardless of

Beatty's true intentions, the publication of the *Authentic Narrative* did serve to elevate Beatty's status, with him becoming one of the most well-known figures of *Victory*'s Trafalgar crew, behind Nelson and Hardy.

Other Accounts

Several other accounts came before Beatty's *Authentic Narrative*, each adding different elements to the overall public perception of Nelson's death. The first published accounts in the days following the news reaching Britain were inaccurate imaginings of the events, rather than first-hand accounts, which served the purpose of quelling the curiosity of the public. These accounts included inaccuracies such as the bullet entering through the centre of one of the orders of merit worn on his chest. Others claimed that Hardy tried to warn Nelson of the shot, or that he did not fall at all.[12] Of course, most of these early claims were later rectified, but it is impossible to say if some have survived to this day. One of these common misconceptions that we know has survived is that Nelson was wearing his full dress uniform, making him an easy target for French sharpshooters. In reality, Nelson was wearing a frock coat, with replicas of his orders of merit. In fact, it is highly likely that the shot was not specifically aimed for Nelson at all, as the French were using smooth-bore muskets rather than rifled weapons, a point brought up by Beatty in his *Authentic Narrative*.[13]

An article published in the 9 December 1805 edition of the *Morning Chronicle* featured a brief report of Nelson's last moments, supposedly from an officer who served alongside the admiral.[14] The article perpetuates the myth that Nelson was wearing full dress uniform, suggesting he refused advice to take off his medals, even when asked by those around him. The article also incorrectly states that Beatty removed the musket ball while Nelson was still alive. Adding to the heroic image of Nelson, this account finishes by recounting his last word as 'Victory!', exclaimed as his lungs filled with blood.

Another point of contention in the same article is the description of the operations of *Victory*'s Royal Marines during the battle. It mentions that Captain Charles Adair had sought permission from Nelson for his marines to head up to the fighting tops to combat *Redoubtable*'s musketry. It is stated that Adair was killed in action while making his way up the shrouds towards the tops. This is in direct contradiction to Beatty, who states in his narrative that Nelson forbade the use of small arms in the fighting tops due to the risk involved with sparks igniting the ship's sails.

It has been suggested that this account came from John Pasco, signal lieutenant aboard *Victory*. This is plausible, as Pasco was likely in the cockpit for Nelson's last moments, having been injured by enemy grapeshot early on in the battle.[15] However, this raises the question as to why Pasco suggests that Beatty removed the musket ball while Nelson was still alive. Having remained aboard *Victory* for the voyage to Britain following the battle, it is highly likely that Pasco would have been aware of Beatty's autopsy and subsequent removal of the ball. It has never been confirmed whether Pasco did have a hand in this article, but regardless, its credibility is severely diminished by the several known inaccuracies.

Purser Walter Burke also contributed to the legacy of Nelson with his account, which was published both in the *Morning Chronicle* on 10 December 1805 and in A. Y. Mann's 1806 book dedicated to the events of Lord Nelson's funeral.[16] Burke seems to centre his account on himself and his own experiences. This includes some elements not featured in other accounts, such as Nelson communicating to Burke and asking him to raise his legs. Burke describes Nelson's last words as 'I have done my duty, I praise god for it!' This is not too dissimilar from the 'Thank God I have done my Duty' that is commonly attributed to be the admiral's last words.

Burke and Beatty later combined to authenticate a joint account, published in both the *Morning Chronicle* on 28 December 1805 and in volume 15 of *The Naval Chronicle* in 1806, the latter also including the surgeon's brief medical description of the wound.[17] The article falsifies the claim made in earlier reports that Captain Hardy picked up Nelson, correctly stating instead that it was two seamen who carried their commander-in-chief below decks. This account, along with Burke's earlier effort, is notable for the complete lack of a mention of Alexander Scott, who remained by Nelson's side until his death. It also mentions how Nelson ordered Burke to go and summon Hardy from the quarterdeck, and Burke leaving the admiral's side to do so. This is something that Burke neglected to mention in his earlier account, and also contradicts Beatty's *Authentic Narrative*, which suggests that Burke remained by Nelson's side throughout. This account gives Nelson's last words as 'God be praised!', which again differs from Burke's earlier account.

These early accounts neglected to mention Alexander Scott, a key figure whom Beatty suggests played a prominent role. The *Authentic Narrative* lists Scott as one of the few men to whom Beatty disclosed the true nature of Nelson's wound, and several exchanges between the admiral and Scott are featured. Although Scott did not publish an account of his own, a private letter written to politician George Rose, whom Nelson mentioned to Scott in his dying moments, provides another excellent insight into what happened. Scott recalls in the letter how Nelson asked him to remember him to Mr Rose and that he (Nelson) made a will, leaving Horatia and Lady Hamilton to his country. Scott also recalls Nelson's last words as 'God and my country'. The letter was published in an 1842 biography of Scott and reveals how the events of Trafalgar haunted him for years afterwards.[18]

Scott's influence can also be seen in an early biography of Nelson, *The Life of the Right Honourable Horatio Lord Viscount Nelson* by James Harrison.[19] This was the first detailed account of the battle, pre-dating Beatty's *Authentic Narrative*. Harrison's frequent references to Scott suggest he had a part to play in the account, as do the details that he mentions that were not picked up by Beatty. There are, however, several inaccuracies in this account, including that the shot that struck Nelson came from *Bucentaure* and that Hardy tried to warn Nelson that someone was aiming for him. Harrison also states that Scott supported Nelson's pillow, and that he left for a few moments to get Captain Hardy. Harrison is potentially confusing Scott for Walter Burke here, as it has been said in multiple accounts that Burke was the one who supported Nelson's back, while Scott rubbed his breast for circulation. Burke also states in his account that he was the one who supposedly left Nelson's side to get Hardy, whereas Beatty suggests that Scott remained by Nelson's side until his death. Harrison mirrors Beatty's *Authentic Narrative* by stating the admiral's last words to be 'Thank god I have done my duty.'

Each of these accounts adds a different element to the overall narrative of the death of Nelson and, when combined, provide a comprehensive picture of most of what occurred. When judged alongside Beatty's *Authentic Narrative,* each of these standalone pieces pale in comparison when it comes to the level of detail. However, it is intriguing to compare each of these accounts and their reliability. Pasco's supposed account is the least reliable of these, due to the inaccuracies that have been proven through other sources. Burke's two accounts suggest he was more focused on claiming the limelight than accurately telling the story, as he refers to himself quite a lot more than to the other figures present. There are also several inconsistencies between his accounts, making it hard for either to be seen as reliable, especially when considering that they were published only a few weeks apart. Scott's contributions provide a valuable insight, and are somewhat under-appreciated. Nevertheless, several inconsistencies remain when comparing Scott's work to Beatty's *Authentic Narrative*, which raise questions as to which is the more reliable source. Due to the depth of detail and the authority he asserts, Beatty's account has remained the go-to source for historians ever since.

Artwork Depicting Nelson's Death

Another way in which Nelson's death was brought to life was through artwork. The most notable early eighteenth-century paintings came from Arthur Devis and Benjamin West, whose paintings followed a number of early efforts that varied in their degree of accuracy. Once again, the slowly emerging revelations of the main details surrounding Nelson's death led to various speculative efforts in which the artists relied mostly on their imaginations. Very few early efforts depicted Nelson in the cockpit, with most placing his dying moments on the quarterdeck.[20] Perhaps the most well-known work of this type comes from Benjamin West.

West, much admired for his 1770 painting *The Death of General Wolfe*, tried his hand at recreating the scene of Nelson's demise in a similar style to his earlier work.[21] Supposedly, Nelson greatly admired West's painting of Wolfe, and even spoke to the artist himself of his desire to be painted in a similar way if he were to die in battle.[22] Somewhat controversially, West chose to depict Nelson dying in action on *Victory*'s quarterdeck in his first effort, *The Death of Nelson* (1806).[23] West chose the quarterdeck as the setting for this particular piece instead of *Victory*'s orlop as he wanted to portray Nelson's last moments with dignity, surrounded by his crew in the heat of battle, rather than miserably succumbing to his wounds in the depths and darkness of the cockpit. He did not deem it appropriate for such a national hero to be seen dying in an undignified manner. However, unlike *The Death of General Wolfe*, this painting was not as well received by the public, who craved accuracy over sentimentality.[24]

The Death of Nelson, oil on canvas by Benjamin West, 1806. West's first effort incorrectly places the dying Nelson on *Victory*'s quarterdeck. The body of Marine Captain Charles Adair can be seen to the left of the painting. (Walker Art Gallery)

Arthur Devis' *The Death of Nelson, 21 October 1805* (1807) has over time emerged as the work that both accurately captures the scene in the cockpit and the sombre, yet triumphant, mood of Nelson's last moments. Devis spent a few weeks aboard *Victory* in late 1805, during the ship's journey around the English coast from Portsmouth to the Nore. This was a vital experience for the artist, who could not only get an accurate picture of the surroundings for his artwork, but also hear first-hand accounts from those involved. He made several sketches of the area in which Nelson breathed his last, and supposedly even made a model that he could refer to in his studio. It is also likely that Devis would have had the opportunity while aboard *Victory* to sketch the likenesses of those present in the scene of his painting.[25] It is here that Beatty's influence over our perceptions of the death of Nelson re-emerges. It is said that one of Devis' main contacts while on board *Victory* was the surgeon. Devis even assisted Beatty with his autopsy of Nelson's body, sketching the musket ball once Beatty had removed it from the admiral's torso. Beatty also managed to commission Devis to paint his portrait, which he did in 1806.[26]

Devis depicts Nelson bathed in a pool of light, surrounded by Hardy, Burke, Scott and Beatty among others. Although he wanted to represent the scene as accurately as possible, Devis does use artistic licence in a few ways. The pool of light around Nelson gives connotations of divinity, making him appear as a god-like figure, surrounded by his disciples. Devis has also increased the height of the deck, as the 6ft 4in Captain Hardy is standing fully upright, whereas in reality *Victory*'s orlop is much more cramped. The painting was made part of the Naval Gallery at Greenwich hospital in 1825.[27] A print of the painting was also present on *Victory*'s orlop until recently, displayed beside the spot where Nelson died. The painting's appeal has lasted for generations.

Realising his mistake, Benjamin West attempted to paint the scene again, this time accurately placing Nelson in the cockpit. *The Death of Lord Nelson in the Cockpit of the Ship 'Victory'* (1808) is similar to Devis' effort, depicting a more intimate scene with only the key figures present.[28] However, this painting was only tepidly received as it was deemed to have not captured the spirit of the moment.

West also produced an effort in the year before, titled *The Immortality of Nelson* (1807).[29] This was a much more abstract representation, depicting the deceased Nelson ascending to immortality. This painting was used in the biography of Nelson written by Clarke and McArthur, which also featured Beatty's *Authentic Narrative*.[30] In the painting, Nelson's body, again bathed in a pool of white light, is delivered to Britannia by Neptune. It is this sort of painting that contributed to the apotheosis of Nelson and his ascendance from national hero to god-like status.

The Death of Lord Nelson in the Cockpit of the Ship 'Victory', oil on canvas by Benjamin West, 1808. West's second effort accurately depicts Nelson in *Victory*'s cockpit, in a similar fashion to Devis's painting. (National Maritime Museum)

The Test of Time

Beatty's *Authentic Narrative* remains the most complete and comprehensive version of events surrounding the death of Nelson, despite the questionable nature of some of its particular elements. It has stood the test of time as the undisputed leading account, surpassing other versions of events such as those by Burke and Scott. Ultimately, by writing such a comprehensive and authoritative account, Beatty cemented his place in history and his long-standing association with the death of Nelson. It should be considered when dealing with this account, as with all first-hand accounts, that caution should be taken with regard to its overall reliability. Of course, we can never be fully sure which parts are accurate and which parts stray from the truth, but one thing is for sure: if it wasn't for individual eyewitnesses such as Beatty, Burke and Scott, we would be reliant on highly questionable accounts from third-party sources, and for that we should be grateful.

Likewise, Arthur Devis' *The Death of Nelson, 21 October 1805* has stood the test of time to emerge as the leading visual representation of events in *Victory*'s cockpit, largely due to Devis' accuracy and attention to detail. Compared with the efforts of Benjamin West, who tried to capture the romanticism of the moment, Devis managed to both capture the mood of the scene and maintain a level of accuracy. Beatty's *Authentic Narrative* and Devis' painting, combined, have led the way in shaping perceptions of Nelson's death, and making his last moments remembered through generations. Both are the leading works in their respective fields, and both are by now synonymous with Nelson's death at the Battle of Trafalgar. In particular, Beatty's version of Nelson's last words, 'Thank god I have done my duty', have emerged as the accepted phrase, compared with all the other versions in earlier accounts.

Immortality of Nelson, see colour plate 3

Nelson in Caricature and Cartoon

Peter Turner

This article is intended to be simple entertainment, and is not in competition with the more serious, learned and informative articles in this publication. The purpose of this article is to show how caricature artists and cartoonists portrayed Nelson in the late eighteenth and early nineteenth centuries, as a form of news, commentary, amusement and entertainment.

When the seed of the idea for this article first germinated, it looked as if it would present a number of early caricatures of Nelson, with a few later cartoons, and a few pithy remarks on each. But then reality set in: firstly, the subject is huge, much too big for a short article in this publication and needing a book, or books, of its own (a recent example being *Broadsides: Caricature and the Navy 1756–1815* by James Davey and Richard Johns, published in 2012,[1] which was useful in the preparation of the first part of this article); secondly, the informed reader will already have seen most of the illustrations available, and, finally, the reproduction of most of those images, in good quality, high definition suitable for publication, became a minefield of copyright and licensing that would have required a greater expenditure of research, time and money than this author was willing to allocate.

So, being a cartoonist and facsimilist, this author decided to revert to the original purpose of these few examples, which was/is to entertain, by taking the Nelson elements of those famous caricatures and some cartoons and reproducing them approximately in the style of the originals, thus avoiding copyright problems, and by making a short mention of the artists and the originals and where to find them, which would satisfy the more curious. The purpose of these representations is neither to copy nor parody, nor to criticise the original artists but to acknowledge their contribution to our heritage and to remind ourselves of their efforts in an era before cameras and Photoshop.

Caricaturists developed their art from a strong English tradition of graphic satire and their work started to appear with the additional freedoms of the press during the seventeenth century, flourishing towards the end of the eighteenth century. A period of many wars and radical politics coincided with advances in the methods and machinery of printmaking, and the more readily available abundance of colouring materials made the process simpler and bolder.

Newsprint and print shops, and the means of distribution of their products, flourished and, as they became more affordable, the caricatures appealed to a ready audience across the nation.

Nelson has more faces than a clock factory, but nobody today can be certain about what he really looked like. We will not solve that little problem from caricatures or cartoons. Relatively few of these artists actually met him and there were no cameras to photograph him, so we have to rely on the wildly variable skills of the many artists who made portraits of him. But few of these were done from life; most were done from, at best, memory of a brief meeting or glimpse or, more often, from imagination. And as for the caricaturists, they mostly did not move in the same circles as senior naval officers and their aim was to send a pictorial message, not to make a portrait. So we know Nelson from caricatures and cartoons (and some portraits) only by his uniform and regalia – or even simply because the artist tells us who it is. Some portraits are so bizarre that we can consider them caricatures. Formal portraits will consequently be mostly avoided in this article.

As already stated, the purpose of this article is to entertain you. Please be so.

Peter Turner *pinxit* after *Commodore Nelson receives the Spanish Admiral's sword on the deck of the San Josef – 14th February 1797* by Daniel Orme, engraved by John Rogers. An example of the nineteenth-century print from which this image was produced is held in the St Vincent College collection and can be seen at: https://www.stvincent.acuk/Heritage/1797/battle/SanJosef.html

We begin our consideration of Nelson's caricatures with a 'portrait', despite the title of the article and despite the promise to avoid them in the foregoing introduction, in order to at least give a nod to chronology, because the first images of Nelson to hit the public gaze were in the aftermath of the Battle of St Vincent, in 1797. At this stage in his yet-to-be famous life, the only images seem to have been so-called portraits.

Peter Turner *pinxit* after *Extirpation of the Plagues of Egypt; – Destruction of Revolutionary Crocodiles – or – The British Hero cleansing ye Mouth of ye Nile* by James Gillray. An example of the print from which this image was produced is held by Royal Museums Greenwich and can be seen at: https://collections.rmg.co.uk/collections/objects/108968.html

An image of Nelson accepting the surrendered sword of the captain of the Spanish ship *San Josef* has been chosen, in which he can be seen without the future trappings of glory and honour that later caricaturists came to rely upon so heavily. He had yet to earn them. In fact, this image was painted in 1799 but not published until 1853 and is from a print of a painting by Daniel Orme, engraved by John Rogers, and published by J. F. Tallis. A quick perusal on the internet will produce at least half a dozen copies of this painting, in which Nelson could have been depicted as anyone, the painter having been unlikely to have ever seen him.

Daniel Orme (1766–c1837) was born in Manchester but moved in 1785 to London, where he lived until 1814, during which time he studied at the Royal Academy. He became a painter and engraver in London. Orme made a career out of painting historical scenes of great current events and great men doing them. In 1814 he moved back to Manchester. John Rogers (fl1808–88) was a prolific printmaker, engraver of landscapes, portraits, and figures.

Our second example is the much more familiar one of Nelson getting control of the crocodiles after the Battle of Aboukir Bay in 1798, at which juncture Nelson really hit the publicity machine running. The original caricature is called '*Extirpation of the Plagues of Egypt; – Destruction of Revolutionary Crocodiles; – or – The British Hero cleansing ye mouth of ye Nile*' and was by James Gillray, first published in 1798. Newspapers were hungry for illustrations of Nelson, but, of course, he was still away in Naples, so the caricaturists set their imaginations to work.

From the depiction of Nelson in this example, one cannot help wondering whether Gillray actually had Beethoven sit as his model. Maybe not. But, clearly, Gillray had little idea of what Nelson looked like (and a hook, for goodness sake!) or even of what a naval officer's uniform looked like, not to mention what crocodiles look like – at that time even fewer people had seen a crocodile than had seen Nelson, probably. But, as stated previously, the important thing for Gillray was to send a message to the viewer of the print.

James Gillray (c1756–1815) was a British caricaturist and printmaker well-known for his etched political and social satires, with most of his famous works being completed from 1792 to 1810. Gillray is regarded as being one of the two most influential cartoonists of his day because of his ability with drawing and with observing what was ridiculous in the social and political life of the great and good, and of lowly citizens, too. Born in Chelsea, London, Gillray commenced adult life by learning letter engraving, but wandered for a time with a company of strolling players, eventually returning to London and enrolling as a student in the Royal Academy, supporting himself by engraving. His caricatures are mostly in etching, some are also aquatints, and some use stipple technique. None are strictly engravings, although often described as such. Gillray is distinguished amongst the caricaturists in history by the fact that he is a more accomplished artist; his sketches really are works of art. The themes are robust and poetically astute in their intensity of meaning, forthright, in keeping with the style of their day, and are valued today for their historical information. Prints from Gillray featuring Nelson are reasonably kind, when compared with some of his sharper observations of others. In *Extirpation of the Plagues of Egypt* he celebrates Nelson's victory at the Battle of the Nile, with crocodiles in French tricolour colours representing the captured and sunk ships. Nelson in this print is aggressive and vigorous, albeit mutilated by his wounds, and wielding a heavy club of 'British Oak', representing the fleet.

Peter Turner *pinxit* after *The Hero of the Nile* by James Gillray, published by Hannah Humphrey, 1 December 1798. An example of the print from which this image was produced is held by The National Portrait Gallery and can be seen at:
ttps://www.npg.org.uk/collections/search/portrait/mw62277/Horatio-Nelson-The-Hero-of-the-Nile8968.html

Peter Turner *pinxit* after *The Gallant Nellson* (sic) *bringing home two Uncommon fierce French Crocadiles* (sic) *from the Nile as a Present to the King* by Isaac Cruikshank, published by Samuel Fores, 7 October 1798. An example of the print from which this image was produced is held by Royal Museums Greenwich and can be seen at:
https://collections.rmg.co.uk/collections/objects/128024.html

In *The Hero of the Nile* Nelson is shown more as he was in life: a frail man of small stature but standing on deck, proud in his full dress uniform with all his decorations and regalia, which seem to be in danger of overwhelming him by their size and splendour; especially the chelengk received from the Sultan of the Ottoman Empire after his victory at the Nile, with which he adorned his hat ever after. This caricature by Gillray pokes gentle fun at a man who, by then, was as well-known for his vanity as for his skill as a fighting admiral. Anyone who is familiar with the name James Gillray is probably familiar with the name Hannah Humphrey, his usual publisher and print seller. Humphrey (c1745–1818) was the sister of engraver William Humphrey and first had a shop in The Strand, then in New Bond Street, then in Old Bond Street, and finally in St James' Street. She began publishing prints in the 1770s and established her first shop in c1779, where she sold historical and portrait prints. In 1791, Gillray started to work almost exclusively for Humphrey and she became London's foremost print seller. Gillray lived with her for his working life, although no confirmation of the status of their relationship is certain. There

(left) Peter Turner *pinxit* after *John Bull taking a lunch – or Johnny's purveyors pampering his appetite with dainties from all parts of the world* by S. W. Fores, printed by Charles Williams 1 November 1798. An example of the print from which this image was produced is held by the British Museum and can be seen at:
https://research.britishmuseum.org/research/collection_online/collection_object_details/collection_image_gallery.aspx?assetId=91976001&objectId=1466882&partId=1

(right) Peter Turner *pinxit* after *John Bull taking a luncheon: – or – British cooks, cramming old grumble-gizzard, with bonne-chére* by James Gillray, published by Hannah Humphrey, 24 October 1798. An example of the print from which this image was produced is held by the British Museum and can be seen at:
https://research.britishmuseum.org/research/collection_online/collection_object_details.aspx?assetId=91976001&objectId=1466882&partId=1

is a story that they were nearly married, more than once, which apparently is just that – a story. Humphrey is believed to be depicted in Gillray's print '*Twopenny Whist*' and her St James' Street shop is believed to be in the background of his '*Very Slippy Weather*' print. Crowds of people are reported to have gathered when one of Gillray's prints was newly displayed in Humphrey's shop window.

Yet another face of Nelson is given in *The Gallant Nelson bringing home two uncommon fierce French Crocodiles from the Nile as a present to the King* by Isaac Cruikshank. In this caricature, we can see Nelson more as he would probably have seen himself: confident, happy and fully in control of the situation – of course, he must have had self-doubts, but they were not shown in this example.

In the original, Nelson has his crocodiles, who bear the heads of anti-war politicians Fox and Sheridan, shedding 'crocodile tears' of remorse, chained and secured. Nelson is telling them they are being taken to his king, and an admiring member of the public comments in the background. The '*Gallant Nelson*' print was published by S. W. Fores (1761–1838), who began publishing in 1783 and who operated from Piccadilly, London, from 1795.

Fores produced coarser and more contentious caricatures, along with his contemporary, Thomas Tegg of Cheapside, who catered to the flourishing lower end of the trade. Sometimes both of them produced their own cheaper versions of popular caricatures by Gillray and others, which is why the duplication of ideas seems apparent occasionally. One example of such duplication is *John Bull Taking a Lunch – etc.*, by Fores and *John Bull Taking a Luncheon: – etc.*, by Gillray, in which we see two more faces of Nelson.

When the original print of *Mansion House Treat* was first published, the characters depicted would have been instantly recognisable, with the Lord Mayor (Staines) entertaining the Prime Minister (Pitt), William Hamilton, Emma Hamilton and Lord Nelson, all smoking Egyptian tobacco brought home to them by Nelson – i.e., by winning the Battle of the Nile. But none of that was the deeper point being made by Cruikshank, who was teasing out the point that Nelson's pipe was bigger and more vigorous than those of the others. Perfectly innocent, if you read it to be; perhaps risqué if you prefer. Nelson is therefore offered in a rather flattering manner as being somehow more alive and it did no harm to his reputation at the time.

Isaac Cruikshank (1764–1811) was born in Edinburgh and grew up in New North Kirk parish in Edinburgh after his family moved there, having been dispossessed because of his father's role during the Jacobite rising of 1745. He moved to London in 1783, where he married Mary MacNaughton in 1788, and with her he had five children, of whom two sons, Isaac Robert Cruikshank

Peter Turner *pinxit* after *A Mansion House Treat, or Smoking attitudes!* by Isaac Cruikshank, published by Samuel Fores, 18 October 1800. An example of the print from which this image was produced is held by the British Museum and can be seen at:
https://research.britishmuseum.org/research/collection_online/collection_object_details.aspx?objectI
d=1506565&page=1&partId=1&peoA=96375-1-9&people=96375

(1789–1856) and George Cruikshank (1792–1878), also became artists. Isaac Cruikshank was noted for his dislike of Napoleon. Cruikshank and James Gillray, together with Thomas Rowlandson, are credited with developing the satirical figure of John Bull. Cruikshank was a prolific creator of prints, averaging fifty per annum between 1793 and 1800. He, Gillray, and Rowlandson are considered to be the masters of The Golden Age of Caricatures. Cruikshank died prematurely in 1811 as a result of a successful drinking competition – successful in that he won it, but somewhat less successful in that it killed him. This event launched his son, George, on a lifetime campaign for temperance.

With that, and before we leave the Nile, we must mention Rowlandson's most famous caricature of Nelson, in *Admiral Nelson recreating with his Brave Tars … etc.* in which he is depicted celebrating the Nile victory with his men aboard the third-rate HMS *Vanguard* (74). Clearly telling the observer that, for

Peter Turner *pinxit* after *Admiral Nelson recreating with his Brave Tars after the Glorious Battle of the Nile* by Thomas Rowlandson. An example of the print from which this image was produced is held by the Royal Museums Greenwich and can be seen at:
https://collections.rmg.co.uk/collections/objects/128027.html

all his greatness, Nelson was still one of the crew, and a cheerful young man (remember, when he commanded at the Battle of the Nile, Nelson was not yet forty years old).

Thomas Rowlandson (1756–1827) was born in Old Jewry, in the City of London, to William and Mary Rowlandson, but was moved to Richmond, North Yorkshire, by his bankrupt father in 1757. His Aunt Jane is believed to have provided both the funds and accommodation that allowed Thomas to attend school in London. While still a schoolboy, Rowlandson 'drew humorous characters of his master and many of his scholars before he was ten years old', covering the margins of his schoolbooks with his artwork. At about that age he started attending the Soho Academy. When he was sixteen he became a student at the Royal Academy and spent two years studying in Paris, where he studied drawing human anatomy and caricature, returning to take classes at the Royal Academy, then based at Somerset House. He made frequent tours to the

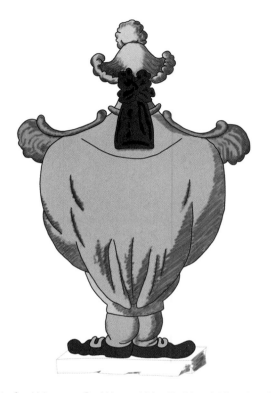

Peter Turner *pinxit* after *Nelson as a Greek Vase*, published by Hannah Humphrey 8 May 1801. An example of the print from which this image was produced is held by the Royal Museums Greenwich and can be seen at: https://collections.rmg.co.uk/collections/objects/128010.html

Continent later in life, increasing his portfolio of sketches of life and character. On the death of his aunt, he inherited £7,000 with which he indulged in a life of dissipation and was known to sit at the gaming table for thirty-six hours at a stretch. He was rescued from ruin and poverty through the friendship and role model of Gillray, who most likely encouraged him to make a living from caricature. Rowlandson's success started with the publication, in 1785, of prints of his drawing of Vauxhall Gardens, which clearly demonstrates his skill as a draughtsman and artist.

Rowlandson was a prolific artist who earned well, selling many prints, in many different styles, including pornography. He died at 1 James Street, Adelphi, London, after a prolonged illness, on 21 April 1827 and was buried at St Paul's, Covent Garden, aged seventy years.

Our penultimate contemporary caricature of Nelson is again by Gillray, depicting our hero as a Greek vase, implying that he is another one of William Hamilton's collection. In a way, truth overtook the parody, as the image held by Royal Museums, Greenwich, was one of the collection of prints made by Sir William Hamilton. In the collection, this caricature is attributed to H. Humphrey, but the style is entirely that of Gillray (compare with the image he produced of the Prince of Wales at https://www.victoriagal.org.uk/england).

Inevitably, we reach the end of caricatures contemporary with Nelson after the Battle of Trafalgar, when the nation went into mourning for their hero and the caricaturists went into a frenzy. Gillray, who throughout Nelson's public life had both celebrated and criticised him, managed to produce this sympathetic parody, with everything exaggerated, including Britannia striking a typical Emma Hamilton 'attitude', and the claim for Nelson's immortality – a prediction that may have proven to be prescient, at least until now.

Peter Turner *pinxit* after *The Death of Admiral Lord Nelson – in the Moment of Victory!* by James Gillray, published by Hannah Humphrey 23 December 1805. An example of the print from which this image was produced is held by the National Portrait Gallery and can be seen at: https://www.npg.org.uk/collections/search/portrait/mw62724/The-death-of-Admiral-Lord-Nelson—-in-the-moment-of-victory-Horatio-Nelson-Sir-Thomas-Masterman-Hardy-1st-Bt

We now move into the present day, with the poster illustration produced by Ralph Steadman for the Nelson Exhibition held at the National Maritime Museum from 1995 to 2000.[2] In his inimitable style, Steadman depicted Nelson as a proud, haughty, brave and somewhat ridiculous figure, while reminding us of many facets of his character by means of adjectives, demonstrating why we all love and revere Nelson, and why he can survive such an image.

Contemporary artist Ralph Idris Steadman was born in Wallasey, Cheshire, but was brought up in Abergele in North Wales after his family moved there during the Second World War, where he attended the local grammar school, not very happily. His father was a commercial traveller and his mother was a shop assistant. Steadman's keen hobby of making model aeroplanes, and his need to do homework before indulging it, taught him how to work very fast. He started work at De Havilland, where he learned draughtsmanship, and then joined the Royal Air Force to do his national service. When he left the RAF, he started earning his living as a cartoonist, but then attended East Ham Technical College and the London College of Printing to further develop his skills.

Peter Turner *pinxit* after *Lord Nelson* by Ralph Steadman. An example of the print from which this image was produced is held by the Royal Museums Greenwich and can be seen at:
https://leadinglives.rmg.co.uk/casestudies/popupdata/activitycards.pdf

Steadman's career evolved into an often controversial pattern, with many considering him too cruel in his depiction of national figures, and some of his work deemed unpublishable. He usually refuses to sell his original artwork and has reputedly said, 'If anyone owns a Steadman original, it's stolen,' and has consequently kept possession of the vast bulk of his production. Steadman continues to entertain many, and offend a few, and a travelling retrospective exhibition of his work opened in 2018.

This next illustration is reproduced from a greeting card produced by Elizabeth Passerieux, in which we see a Nelson somewhat more sympathetically treated than he was by Steadman, though still looking rather more like a stereotypical French aristocrat than a salty English hero.[3]

Peter Turner *pinxit* after *Lord Nelson* by Elizabeth Passerieux. An example of the print from which this image was produced is available from *Etsy Inc* and can be seen at: https://www.etsy.com/hk-en/listing/498994426/original-prints-ink-and-watercolors-lord?ref=landingpage_similar_listing_top-4

Peter Turner *pinxit* after *Turning a Blind Eye* by Eric Smith. An example of the print from which this image was produced is held by the US Naval Institute and can be seen at: *https://www.navalhistory.org/2016/03/25/salty-talk-turning-a-blind-eye*

Elizabeth Passerieux, who is based in Virginia Beach, Virginia, in the US, is a mixed-media artist and illustrator whose studio there is called Blashy Gallows. She interned for a time at the Virginia Museum of Contemporary Art and currently has a day job with a stone countertop company, when she is not working in traditional and digital illustration at her own studio. She considers education to play a vital role in life and is also always open to commission work. Her style, created for this example in ink and watercolour, is quite unusual and distinctive and she uses it to great effect in her more typical illustrations of folklore and nature.

Eric Smith from Annapolis, Maryland, in the US, is a political cartoonist who featured in the *Capital Gazette* for nearly four decades before he retired, and still does from time to time. He is now 'on the grown-up side of the podium', as he puts it, teaching American government at the US Naval Academy.

This image of Nelson, by Smith, is rather surprising, from a navy man, in that it shows Nelson using the right arm, which he did not possess, to hold a telescope to the eyepatch, that he never used (although admittedly the cartoon's point would be lost without it). The reader will be unaware, though, that the original image shows Nelson in a pink – yes, PINK! – uniform. A good excuse for this black and white interpretation, if ever there was one. Another surprise, given the anomalies, is that this illustration is used by the US Naval Institute in their Naval History Blog – just for fun, one assumes.[4]

Gary Brown is based in Bristol, UK, and must not be confused with the similarly named Scottish cartoonist of quite different style. Brown has created

Peter Turner *pinxit* after *Lord Nelson* by Gary Brown. An example of the print from which this image was produced is held by CartoonStock Limited and can be seen at:
https://www.cartoonstock.com/cartoonview.asp?catref=gbrn163

a very full portfolio since first being published in 2008, concentrating on his preferred emphasis on the facial characteristics of his subjects, who are public figures, both contemporary and historical. He has our hero looking very confident and resolute, despite having given him such a diminished stature (typical of Brown's products), but, at least, back in a proper (cartoon) uniform and without the apocryphal eyepatch.[5]

Moving away from the usual media of illustrations of Nelson, we turn next to ceramics, firstly with a set of delft tiles designed by Paul Bommer, artist, printmaker and illustrator. The Nelson tile is one of a series of limited-edition delft tile designs produced for the annual 2012 Full Fathom Five exhibition (A Celebration of the Nautical World) at Hornsey's at The Gallery in Ripon, North Yorkshire, by five designers, including Bommer.[6] This is another example of Nelson represented sympathetically and looking happy and confident, within the limits of the available technique for these products.

Paul Bommer is a graduate of the National College of Art & Design in Dublin who worked until quite recently in the East End of London but has now relocated to the north Norfolk coast, seeking space and new inspiration. In his work we can recognise an irreverent humour together with a love of history and style, captured with a deft line. He also works on limited edition screen prints and other decorated ceramics.

And finally, after all the various degrees of lampooning Nelson, perhaps while respecting him, we end up with a bizarre, but *so* cute, ceramic figurine of Nelson that featured in the Bunnykins collection created by Royal Doulton – this piece in 2005. Lord Nelson Bunnykins[7] was designed by Caroline Dadd, who is currently the Design Director at Origin Studios in Stoke-on-Trent, UK, after working through the 1990s as a designer and design manager at Royal Doulton.

This little figurine stands just 4¼in high, and it has proven to be quite a collectors' item – a quick internet search produced examples available with a price difference of four times, so beware!

Peter Turner *pinxit* after *Admiral Lord Horatio Nelson. A National Hero and Norfolk's proudest son. 'Kiss me Hardy'* by Paul Bommer. An example of the print from which this image was produced is held by the Royal Museums Greenwich and can be seen at:

http://paulbommerarchive.blogspot.com/2012/

So, what can we conclude from these few illustrations, and all the thousands of others not selected and commented upon? First of all, as the opening comments asserted, we do not know for sure what Nelson looked like in life, but it is certain that he cannot have looked like every one of the characterisations published over the years. Secondly, it seems that the vast majority of illustrations of Nelson are more flattering than otherwise. He is constantly used as a model for many artists using many and varied media. We love him. We in The 1805 Club must be reassured that, even in these sea-blind times, our fellow countrymen and women of many countries still see the virtues in Nelson as a role model, as a brave, resolute, and considerate leader of men – men who were happy, no, *keen*, to follow him. We must be grateful that a navy man is so revered, and not regret that so few others are remembered. The 1805 Club is here to rebalance things, where possible.

Peter Turner *pinxit* after *Lord Nelson Bunnykins* designed by Caroline Dadd, produced by Royal Doulton in 2005. An example of this rare figurine is available from Pascoe & Company and can be seen at:
https://www.pascoeandcompany.com/media/catalog/product/cache/1/image/550x550/040ec09b1e3 5df139433887a97daa66f/N/E/NELSON-BUN-365_3.jpg

Tobias Smollett and the Early Georgian Navy

Anthony Bruce

The Scottish author and satirist Tobias Smollett (1721–71) was one of Britain's earliest novelists and one of the first to describe a naval surgical operation. The only major eighteenth-century author to have witnessed combat at first hand, in *The adventures of Roderick Random* (1748), his first and most successful novel, Smollett drew on his own naval service as a surgeon's mate to produce the first significant fictional account of life on board a British warship.[1] According to George Orwell, who described Smollett as 'Scotland's best novelist', *Roderick Random* gave 'not only an unvarnished account of the Cartagena expedition, but an extraordinarily vivid and disgusting description of the inside of a warship, in those days a floating compendium of disease, discomfort, tyranny and incompetence'.[2] The apparent realism of his descriptions of the unreformed Georgian Navy led some early historians to treat them as fact rather than fiction, but more recently the significance of his work has been reappraised.[3]

Although he was not the first author to satirise the different naval characters to be found at sea, the vivid caricatures he created were to have an enduring influence on later novelists.[4] His second novel, *The adventures of Peregrine Pickle* (1751),[5] also included several memorable naval officers but they were based on land rather than at sea. Although many of his contemporaries claimed that his naval characters represented real people, Smollett issued several denials, the first of which was included in the preface to the first edition of *Roderick Random*.

Smollett was born in 1721 in Dunbartonshire, Scotland, into a prominent local family whose fortunes were in decline.[6] At the age of fourteen he entered Glasgow University and probably attended classes in anatomy and medicine while also being apprenticed to two surgeons in the city. In the summer of 1739, a change in financial circumstances forced him to leave for London, where he pursued his ambition to write for the stage. However, early setbacks meant that he had to seek alternative employment and the declaration of war against Spain in October 1739 (soon known as the War of Jenkins' Ear), provided him with an opportunity to join the Royal Navy. In March 1740, he was granted a warrant authorising him to serve as a surgeon's second mate and entered the third-rate HMS *Chichester* (80), with a complement of some 600 men.[7]

In October 1744, *Chichester* left for the Caribbean as part of a squadron of thirty ships under the command of Rear Admiral Sir Chaloner Ogle, who had orders to support Vice Admiral Edward Vernon in an expedition to occupy the Spanish stronghold of Cartagena on the Caribbean coast of what is now Colombia.[8] In the Bay of Biscay, severe storms scattered the squadron, split *Chichester*'s mainsail and swept two men overboard. Based in the surgeon's mates' cockpit, Smollett cared for the sick and suffered at least one major illness himself. Ogle's squadron joined up with Vernon's fleet in Jamaica and the combined force anchored off Cartagena early in March 1741. It is not certain whether Smollett was still on *Chichester* by this point as he may have transferred to another warship serving at Cartagena.[9] The Spanish were heavily outnumbered by Vernon's force, which consisted of 120 ships and 27,000 men, including 8,000 soldiers under the command of General Thomas Wentworth. The army succeeded in occupying the fortifications guarding Bocachica, the narrow entrance to Cartagena Bay, after a 'terrible cannonading' by the navy, but made no further progress in capturing the city.

Vernon's attempt to take the castle of San Lázaro, which dominated the city, ended in defeat when deadly grapeshot and musket fire from the Spanish defenders caused heavy British casualties.[10] A decision to renew the attack depended on the navy reinforcing the army, but Admiral Vernon was not willing to agree. There were thousands of sick and wounded soldiers and seamen for Smollett and his colleagues to treat and an epidemic of yellow fever significantly increased the death toll. Smollett was back in Britain by September but remained on *Chichester*'s payroll until February 1742. He later returned to the Caribbean but early in 1744 he was living in London, where he established himself as a surgeon and resumed his literary career.

In 1744, Smollett drafted a factual *Account of the expedition against Carthagene, in the West Indies besieged by the English in the year 1741*,[11] although it was not published until 1756. Written at a time when Vernon's version[12] of events was generally accepted, he discussed the reasons for the expedition's failure, including the lack of cooperation between the army and navy and the failings of the two commanders: Vernon was a 'man of weak understanding, strong prejudices, boundless arrogance, and overboiling passions', while Wentworth was 'wholly defective in point of experience, confidence and resolution'. In 1758, one of Vernon's captains, Charles Knowles, now a vice admiral, alleged that Smollett had libelled him when he criticised his conduct as commander of the abortive expedition against Rochefort in 1757.[13] Smollett pointed out that the problem at Cartagena and at Fort Fouras (a potential target of the Rochefort expedition) was the same: the commanders' reluctance to allow their ships to approach closely enough to their targets because they claimed the water was too shallow.

Smollett published *The adventures of Roderick Random* in January 1748 at a time when the pamphlet war about Cartagena was still in progress. He drew on his still unpublished *Account*[14] as well as on a pamphlet defending General Wentworth, *A journal of the expedition to Carthagena* (1744).[15] The novel, which is set in the 1730s and 1740s, tells the story (in the first person) of Roderick Random, whose parents were a Scottish gentleman and a former housekeeper. After his mother dies and his father disappears, he is sent away to school, where he suffers at the hands of an abusive tutor who denounces him to his grandfather. Without the financial backing of his paternal family, Roderick relies on the occasional support of his maternal uncle, Tom Bowling, a naval officer. After leaving university, he spends some time in London before embarking on a series of adventures across the globe, including service on the warship *Thunder* and on a privateer. The novel concludes on a positive note when Roderick is reunited with his long-lost father in Buenos Aires; he inherits some funds, enabling him to marry.

The naval chapters begin in London with Roderick discovering how to obtain a medical appointment in the navy. He meets 'Beau' Jackson, a former surgeon's second mate, who tells him that he will need to obtain a statement of qualifications from the Company of Barber Surgeons at Surgeon's Hall and submit it to the secretary of the Navy Board. He would need to pay several different fees and a bribe (amounting to 'a three-pound twelve piece') to the 'rapacious' secretary; the support of an influential patron would also be necessary. The cost of equipment was an additional financial burden. Jackson had borrowed the money for his equipment and had an option to borrow further amounts, an arrangement that was necessary when officers' pay was received in the form of a 'ticket' rather than in cash. The ticket was normally sold at a significant discount to its face value.

At Surgeon's Hall, Roderick is led into a large room, 'where I saw about a dozen of grim faces sitting at a long table,' and asked questions about his nationality and surgical practice, revealing the panel's prejudices and questionable understanding of medicine.[16] After he receives his qualifications, the Navy Board secretary confirms that he is qualified as a second surgeon's mate but informs Roderick and his friends that there are no current vacancies. When Roderick asks about future opportunities, 'he surveyed me with a look of ineffable contempt, and pushing us out of his office, locked the door without deigning us another word'.[17] Unlike Smollett, Roderick is unable to obtain an appointment because he has no money or influential patrons.

With no naval appointment in prospect, Roderick is 'reduced to a starving condition', but is soon seized by a press gang near the Tower of London, an area where disembarked sailors who had just collected their back pay were

A caricature of a naval press gang in action near the Tower of London, an etching by Samuel Collings, 1790. (Royal Museums Greenwich)

targeted.[18] During the eighteenth century, impressment was widely used to meet the navy's wartime manpower requirements, with press gangs routinely using violence to coerce their victims, as Roderick soon discovers.[19] When he defends himself with his cudgel, he is quickly overwhelmed: 'after an obstinate engagement, in which I received a large wound on my head, and another on my left cheek, I was disarmed, taken prisoner, and carried on board a pressing tender.'[20] Roderick's experiences on the tender – a 'claustrophobic hell'[21] – give him a foretaste of what to expect when he is assigned to a warship. The commanding officer will not permit his wounds to be dressed and a fellow prisoner steals from him. In the meantime, he recollects that 'loss of blood, vexation and want of food, contributed, with the noisome stench of the place, to throw me into a swoon'.[22] He is revived by a draught of flip (a mixture of beer and spirits) provided by honest Jack Rattlin.

Roderick is then transferred to the third-rate HMS *Thunder* (80), commanded by Captain Oakum, who is 'coarse, ignorant, inhuman, aloof from crew and fellow officers alike, susceptible to flattery but oblivious to the dictates of humanity'.[23] He quickly comes into conflict with Crampley, the malicious and bullying first mate – a 'tarpaulin' later promoted to captain of a sloop-of-war – who hits him several times with a 'supple jack' and reports him to Oakum, who places him in irons. Oakum is later replaced by Captain Whiffle, an effeminate gentleman captain, who 'appeared in every thing the reverse of Oakum, being a tall, thin, young man … a white hat, garnished with a red feather, adorned his head, from whence his hair flowed upon his shoulders, in ringlets tied behind with a ribbon'.[24] He rarely ventured from his cabin and would see members of the crew only if they obtained his permission in advance.

Once on board, Roderick is assigned to Dr Atkins, the surgeon, a 'good-natured indolent man', who orders him to serve as a medical orderly ('Loblolly Boy'). He works with the surgeon's mates (Morgan, an affable Welshman, and Thomson, his best friend, who treats his wounds) in making and administering medicines. The mates have their quarters in the cockpit, a 'dismal gulph', which is situated under the lower gun-deck. It is accessible only by 'divers ladders to a space as dark as a dungeon, which … was immersed several feet under water, being immediately above the hold'.[25] The second mate occupies 'a square of about six feet, surrounded with the medicine chest, that of the first mate, his own, and a board, by way of table … it was also inclosed with canvas nailed round to the beams of the ship, to screen us from the cold'.[26]

The cockpit is dominated by an 'intolerable stench of putrified cheese and rancid butter', which are held in the stores nearby. The ship's steward, a man with 'a pale meagre countenance, sitting behind a kind of desk, having spectacles on his nose and a pen in his hand', is responsible for the distribution of provisions. Meat (salt pork and salt beef) together with dried fish, is available only four days a week, while on other days, known as 'banyan days', a meagre meal typically consisting of 'boiled pease … enriched with a lump of salt butter … and a handful of onions shorn, with some pounded pepper' is provided.[27] A daily allowance of hard biscuit, butter and cheese supplements this monotonous and unhealthy diet.

Roderick is disconcerted by his first experience of sleeping in a hammock and it takes some time 'before I could prevail upon myself to trust my carcase at such a distance from the ground, in a narrow bag, out of which, I imagined I should be apt, on the least motion on my sleep, to tumble down at the hazard of breaking my bones'. His sleep is disturbed by an early morning call for the larboard (port) watch, but he does not wake until 'eight o'clock, when rising, and breakfasting with my comrades, on biscuit and brandy, the sick were visited and assisted'.[28]

Roderick is shocked when he first visits the sick bay, leading him to conclude that he 'was much less surprised that people should die on board, than that any sick person should recover'. The sick bay accommodates fifty 'miserable distempered wretches, suspended in rows, so huddled one upon another, that not more than fourteen inches space was allotted for each with his bed and bedding, and deprived of the light of the day, as well as of fresh air'.[29] The restricted space makes it difficult for the surgeon's mates to attend to their patients and Roderick finds that by 'pushing my head with great force between two hammocks towards the middle … I made an opening indeed, but not understanding the knack of dextrously turning my shoulder to maintain my advantage, had the mortification to find myself stuck up as it were in a pillory, and the weight of three or four people bearing on each side my neck, so I was in danger of strangulation'.[30]

Roderick demonstrates his medical knowledge and discharges his duties satisfactorily and, within six weeks, is appointed as third mate. Surgeon's mates 'were a very inferior class of warrant officers, but might, nevertheless, be gentleman of some education'.[31] Roderick, who is part of this gentleman class, is fortunate that, despite his enforced entry to the service, he has been promoted to a level that almost matches his qualifications. As a surgeon's mate, he is expected to treat men wounded in action as well as dealing with fever, tetanus, insanity and other illnesses. He is kept busy as there are high sickness rates on board and a death is recorded virtually every day. When the surgeon transfers to another ship, Roderick describes his replacement (Dr Mackshane) as 'grossly ignorant and intolerably assuming, false, vindictive, and unforgiving; a merciless tyrant to his inferiors, an abject sycophant to those above him'.[32] But Roderick is fortunate in having virtually no contact with the lieutenants or with the captain, who is too much of a gentleman to know a surgeon's mate, even by sight.

When the captain receives his orders to sail, he announces that there will be 'no sick in this ship while I have the command of her'.[33] He orders all sixty-one occupants of the sick bay to be brought on deck for review. Many are 'brought up in the height of fevers, and rendered delirious by the injuries they suffered in the way', and in consequence 'some gave up the ghost in the presence of their inspectors; and others, who were ordered to their duty, languished a few days at work … and then departed without any ceremony'.[34] As a result of the captain's action, the number of sick is reduced to less than a dozen.

Roderick expresses his fear of being transported to a 'distant and unhealthy climate' under the 'dominion of an arbitrary tyrant, whose command was almost intolerable'. Soon after departure, a severe storm threatens the ship and Roderick's vivid description clearly derives from Smollett's own experiences: 'the sea swelled into billows mountain-high, on the top of which our ship sometimes hung as if it were about to be precipitated to the abyss below! Sometimes we sunk between two waves that rose on each side higher than our topmast head, and threatened by dashing together, to overwhelm us in a moment!'[35] During the storm, Jack Rattlin's leg is broken and Mackshane orders an amputation, but Roderick prevents him from carrying it out. Although it is the standard treatment for shattered limbs, it is unnecessary in this case and Rattlin makes a full recovery.

As *Thunder* enters 'warm latitudes ... the weather became intolerable, and the crew very sickly'. Tensions on board increase and Roderick's relationship with the surgeon deteriorates rapidly. Mackshane accuses him of being a spy and of conspiring against the captain's life; together with Morgan, he is arrested and pinioned to the deck, remaining there for twelve days, 'exposed to the scorching heat of the sun by day, and to the unwholesome damps by night'.[36] During his captivity, the crew exchanges fire with a French squadron, but he remains helpless as cannonballs fly overhead. A man next to him has his head shot off and Roderick is splattered with his brains. It is only as the ship nears Jamaica that the case is resolved. Oakum tries the two men but a witness exposes the false evidence on which the proceedings are based, and they are released, thus avoiding a court martial in Jamaica, where they could have cleared themselves.

On its arrival at Cartagena, the English fleet, the largest ever to be despatched to the Caribbean, lies off the coast for another ten days, with Roderick ascribing the delays 'to the generosity of our chiefs, who scorned to take any advantage that fortune might give them, even over an enemy'.[37] When the action begins, marines are landed and *Thunder* is ordered to batter the castle of San Luis de Bocachica. But instead of 'dropping anchor close under shore ... we had exposed ourselves to the whole fire of the enemy from their shipping and Fort St Joseph, as well as from the castle we intended to cannonade'. The ship is

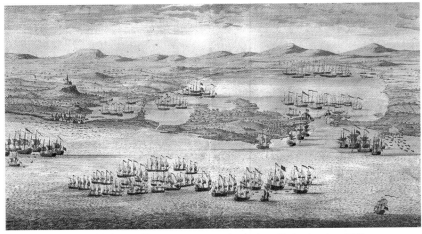

The British fleet at Cartagena, an engraving by Isaac Basire, London 1741.
(Biblioteca Nacional de Colombia)

anchored at too great a distance from the castle to damage its walls but, in any case, 'three parts in four of our shot did not take place; for there was scarce any body on board who understood the pointing of a gun'.[38]

Although casualties quickly mount, the surgeon Mackshane does not get up until the first mate threatens to report him to the admiral. He has recourse 'more than once to a case-bottle of rum' as he goes to work 'and arms and legs were hewed down without mercy'. At the height of the battle, Crampley orders Roderick to dress the captain's splinter wound on the quarter-deck, where he

Admiral Edward 'Old Grog' Vernon (1684–1757), commander of British forces at Cartagena, by Thomas Gainsborough. (National Portrait Gallery)

witnesses 'a most infernal scene of slaughter, fire, smoak, and uproar!'. Roderick has previously fought a boxing match with Crampley and believes that his reason 'for honouring me … with this piece of service, being that in case I should be killed or disabled by the way, my death or mutilation would be of less consequence to the ship's company, than that of the doctor or his first mate'.[39]

The two forts eventually fall to superior English forces, who now control the outer harbour. Roderick points to the availability of fresh water as the greatest benefit of this victory, particularly after 'we had languished five weeks on the allowance of a purser's quart *per diem* for each man, in the Torrid Zone, where the sun was vertical, and the expence of bodily fluid so great, that a gallon of liquor could scarcely supply the waste of twenty-four hours'.[40] In the tropics, beer is replaced by grog (brandy or rum diluted with water), the drink named after Admiral Vernon, whose nickname was 'Old Grog', from the grogram coat he always wore.

The crew's provisions, which include 'putrid salt beef, to which the sailors gave the name of Irish horse', deteriorate in the heat and are devoid of the 'fresh stock, turtle, fruit, and other refreshments' that are readily available in Jamaica.[41] Roderick acknowledges that they could save 'a great many valuable lives', recognising the benefits of citrus fruits, which James Lind, a pioneer of naval hygiene, was to explain in his 1753 *Treatise on the scurvy*. Lind shared Roderick's criticisms of the naval diet, which he described as 'extremely gross, viscid, and hard of digestion', and of the terrible conditions under which the sick and wounded were treated.[42]

Entering the inner harbour, a second landing is made near Cartagena with the aim of taking San Lázaro castle, which, as mentioned above, commanded the city. But, as Roderick reports, the operation is doomed to failure because it depends on soldiers armed only with muskets. He criticises Vernon for failing to organise a diversionary attack, with the result that the enemy gives the attackers 'such a hearty reception, that the greatest part of the detachment took up their everlasting residence on the spot'. The survivors rapidly withdraw and the number fit for service shrinks to 1,500 men.[43]

Smollett's portrayal of the treatment of the sick and wounded in *Roderick Random* is similar to the description in his factual *Account*. According to Roderick, the large number of wounded are 'squeezed into certain vessels, which thence obtained the name of hospital-ships, though … they scarce deserved such a creditable title, seeing few of them could boast of their surgeon, nurse, or cook; and the space between decks was so confined that the miserable patients had not room to sit upright in their beds'. Their wounds being neglected, they 'contracted filth and putrefaction, and millions of maggots were hatched amidst the corruption of the sores'.[44] Roderick points out that every great ship in the fleet could have spared at least one surgeon for this service, but no action is taken. Morale is further damaged 'by the objects that daily and hourly entertained our eyes', including the practice of throwing the dead overboard rather than interring them.

Although no further attempts are made to take Cartagena, the fleet faces a major new risk with the onset of yellow fever, which kills 75 per cent of those affected. Patrick Murray, Lord Elibank, who served with a marine regiment, confirmed the impact of the disease, as described in *Roderick Random*: 'We lost above a 3d of our People as well officers as Soldiers, in 3 weeks that we remained in Carthagena Harbour. Everyone was taken alike; they call the distemper a Bilious Fever; it kills in 5 days; if the Patient lives longer 'tis only to Dye in greater Agonies of what they then call the Black Vomit.'[45] As the fleet leaves Cartagena, Roderick experiences the symptoms of the disease: 'the face and eyes turned yellow, the bile in the vomit was mixed with blood, red patches appeared on the body, and the victim haemorrhaged'.[46] Roderick knows that if he remains in the cockpit he will die and, although his old enemy Crampley tries to keep him there, he moves to the middle-deck and, against the odds, survives.

In Jamaica, Roderick transfers to the sloop *Lizzard* and soon leaves for

Roderick Random and Midshipman Crampley settle their differences in a boxing match, an etching by Thomas Rowlandson, 1793. (Lewis Walpole Library)

Britain. When the captain dies, he is succeeded by Crampley, with Roderick predicting that 'the tyranny of our new commander would now be as unlimited as his power'. Roderick's naval career is brought to a dramatic conclusion when *Lizzard* hits a sandbank off the English coast and the crew abandons ship. As he attempts to join the ship's boat Roderick is 'baulked by the captain, who was so eager in excluding me', but drawing his pistol he forces his way on board. When they reach the shore, Roderick fights Crampley, gaining the advantage before being knocked out from behind. When he regains consciousness, he finds himself alone in a 'desolate place, stript of my cloaths, money, watch [and] buckles'.[47] This story is inspired by the fate of *Wager*, a warship that was wrecked on the coast of what is now Chile in 1741 during Anson's circumnavigation of the globe.[48]

An early biographer of Tobias Smollett expressed the view that *Roderick Random* provides an 'ample account of what he saw, suffered, and did in the Cartagena expedition; and though it is a startling and painful picture, there is no reason to believe that it is an exaggerated one'.[49] The historian and essayist Thomas Carlyle also argued that Smollett's mission was 'to take Portraiture of English Seamanhood, with the due grimness, due fidelity; and convey the same to remote generations before it vanish'.[50] But Smollett's satirical novel does not provide a narrative account of the Cartagena expedition, using instead relatively brief descriptions of historical incidents as a vehicle for Roderick's imaginary adventures, which dominate the chapters describing his naval service. Nor is it directly based on the author's own experiences, as Smollett explained in a letter to Richard Smith in 1763: 'The only similitude between the Circumstances of my own Fortune and those I have attributed to Roderick Random consists in my being born of a reputable Family in Scotland, in my being bred a Surgeon and having served as a surgeon's mate on board a man of war during the Expedition to Carthagene. The low Situations in which I have exhibited Roderick I never experienced in my own Person.'[51]

The journals (1740–41) kept by Lieutenant Watkins, who also served on HMS *Chichester* during the Cartagena expedition, confirm the accuracy of many – but by no means all – of Smollett's historical references.[52] They also suggest that the fictitious *Thunder* was given some of the characteristics of *Chichester*.[53] For example, the weather conditions she faced on the voyage to the Caribbean, including the severe storms she encountered, accurately reflect Smollett's experience on *Chichester*.[54] On the other hand, some incidents are significantly modified in the novel, including the account of the fight with French warships in which *Thunder* participated but *Chichester* did not. Smollett places *Thunder* in the midst of the fighting off Cartagena while *Chichester* did not participate in the operation.

Roderick's account of his abortive attempt to join the navy and of his subsequent impressment 'achieves a functional realism', with his treatment providing a model for other novelists to follow.[55] His descriptions of his role as surgeon's mate, life in the cockpit and the poor quality of shipboard food and drink seem closely to reflect the reality of life at sea. Nor was his description of conditions below deck, which could only delay the recovery of the sick, much exaggerated. Sir John Pringle, a leading military physician, writing some twenty years after the publication of *Roderick Random*, witnessed scenes similar to those described in the novel, reporting that 'even at this late period few measures had been taken to preserve the health of seamen, more than had been known to our uninstructed ancestors'.[56]

There is, however, much less certainty as to whether Roderick's descriptions of discipline on board *Thunder*, where conflict is endemic and brutal officers make excessive use of the lash, accurately reflect the reality of life in the eighteenth-century navy. Roderick's indictment is supported by some contemporary evidence, with Admiral Vernon, for example, describing the service as being manned by 'violence and maintained by cruelty',[57] but recent research suggests that the 'image of a strictly ordered, hierarchical society repressing all deviance' is far from accurate, with brutal captains being the exception rather than the rule. Discipline at sea was relaxed, officers' authority was weak and 'ships functioned ... on an implicit basis of co-operation and consent which sprang from the experience of seamen bred from boyhood to the necessity of teamwork for survival'.[58]

Roderick's fictional account of the 'incompetence, oppression and tragedy'[59] he experienced during his naval service proved to be a significant influence on the public image of the navy and on later eighteenth-century novelists. Among early naval historians, Smollett's novel was regarded as a thinly disguised autobiographical account, with some authors uncritically adopting his portrayal of the Royal Navy as a 'haven of cruelty and corruption'.[60] More recently, historians have cautioned against taking Smollett's words too literally and substantially revised his bleak picture of life in the Royal Navy, particularly as it relates to naval officers. As a result, Smollett has now 'lost his historical authority',[61] with N. A. M. Rodger arguing that *Roderick Random* 'is a poor, or rather an over-rich, substitute for documentary evidence'.[62] The novel remains a compelling read, enlivened by a cast of noteworthy, often comical, characters and dramatic scenes, but its ill-defined mixture of fact and fiction presents a distorted image of eighteenth-century naval life.

Tobias Smollett, see colour plate 4

Beyond Lady Barbara:
Women as Portrayed in British Naval Fiction

Linda Collison

'Women ain't no good on board, Jack, that's sartain.'[1]

Frederick Marryat, author of numerous novels including *Frank Mildmay*, *Mr Midshipman Easy*, and *Poor Jack*, published in 1840, from which the quote is taken, is generally recognised as the father of British naval fiction. 'Unlike Smollett,[2] who gives us real ships but very little sense of an ocean surrounding them, Marryat provides both real ships and a real sea,' the great Polish–British novelist Joseph Conrad observed.[3] A Royal Navy officer himself, Marryat wove the influence of his experiences into his novels. It is noteworthy that he frequently mentions women in his stories – women as mothers, nurses, aunts, servants, captain's wives, steward's wives, sweethearts, lovers. And, despite the sailor's insouciant tone that Marryat adopts throughout his work, ever present in the background is an 'awkward emphasis on the body, violence, cruelty and random death'.[4]

A century later, C. S. Forester further developed the British naval novel with his eleven-book series recounting the adventures of Horatio Hornblower as he rises from midshipman to admiral during the Revolutionary and Napoleonic Wars. Forester, and other writers following in his wake, wove historical people, events, and nautical detail into the fabric of their fiction in such a way as to seemingly recreate an era – a mythos of naval culture featuring the individualised hero in command of a ship.

Forester's Hornblower is a conflicted protagonist – reserved, almost secretive in nature – who deeply resents the upper class. He struggles for self-confidence, fighting seasickness as well as the enemy; he is a believable, fallible, hero. Serialised in magazines, adapted to film and television, Hornblower inspired a literary cult, complete with a fictional biography, *The Life and Times of Horatio Hornblower* by C. Northcote Parkinson. 'I loved how after researching Horatio Hornblower for my son's literature class that a Canadian historian went to the Nautical Museum in England looking for the Display on Horatio Hornblower, thinking that he was truly a real historical person,' writes one Amazon reviewer of Parkinson's faux biography.[5] The power of fiction to influence popular perceptions of history cannot be overlooked.

And what of the women in Forester's fiction? By and large they are shown only in relationship to the main character – as wives or lovers. Maria, Horatio's middle-class shore wife, is sketched with a few words – *short, tubby, stout, gauche, apple cheeks*. This is not a marriage that can provide our ambitious officer with any social advantages or interest.[6] Enter Lady Barbara Wellesley, requesting passage back to Britain. Forester idealises her as an attractive, well-born woman 'completely at ease, conversing with a fearless self-confidence that nevertheless (as Hornblower grudgingly admitted to himself) seemed to owe nothing to her great position'. Quite the opposite of his dowdy shore wife: 'His own Maria would have been too gauche ever to have pulled that party together.'[7] Lady Barbara is perfect – she is everything he could desire in a wife. Horatio is a humanised hero.

Amazon reviewer Mary Ann, a professed 'Hornblower geek,' writes, 'My only complaint was that I thought more attention should have been devoted to Maria, his first wife … The ironical thing is that I have always found her – meant to be less interesting than Lady Barbara – far more of a rounded and sympathetic character.'

Other authors imagined their own naval protagonists; Dudley Pope[8] created the Lord Nicholas Ramage series; Douglas Reeman,[9] as Alexander Kent, wrote the Bolitho novels. Soon the literary seas were filled with fictional frigates and officers of 'Nelson's Navy', rising through their mettle and merit, outwitting, out-sailing, and out-shooting the enemy, occasionally rescuing well-born women and wealthy countesses. Most include many mentions and cameo appearances of historical figures, and some insinuate their fictional officers into historical naval engagements. David Donachie[10] gives us John Pearce, the marine Markham, as well as fictional biographies of Admiral Nelson and Lady Hamilton in his *Nelson and Emma Trilogy*. Julian Stockwin[11] invents Thomas Kydd, a young man pressed into service, who makes his way 'up through the hawsehole' to obtain his commission.

Richard Woodman,[12] a decorated professional mariner, has written three naval fiction series; Nathaniel Drinkwater's set squarely in the Nelson era. Several female novelists write Nelson-era fiction; among them are M. C. Muir',[13] who wrote the Oliver Quintrell series, and V. E. Ulett,[14] who wrote *Blackwell's Adventures*. Altogether, there are hundreds of Georgian-era naval novels, and more being published every year. Many are highly praised for their historical accuracy and their perceived realism.

And what of the Georgian females? How do novelists portray them?

Alan Lewrie, the bawdy protagonist conceived by Dewey Lambdin,[15] writes about women in a parody of John Cleland's[16] ribaldry: 'And she cried out like a virgin on her wedding night, though she writhed and clung to him like a limpet, matching his every moment ... Why, dear Lord, is every woman I meet and hop into bed with as feeble in the brains as cold, boiled mutton?'[17]

Some readers don't want to read about sexual exploits in naval novels. A male fan of Richard Woodman's *Nathaniel Drinkwater* series writes in an Amazon review, 'The characters are all believable and very human and although there are the inevitable encounters with the opposite sex, they are believable without the Mills and Boon explicit rubbish that seem [sic] to dominate books from the lower order of authors in this genre these days.'

Just as in real life, fictional women can be more than persons in need of rescuing, bedding, or marrying. Julian Stockwin,[18] in *Tenacious*, gives us Isabella, a 'Minorquin' who helps protagonist Thomas Kydd conceive of and carry out a plan against the Spanish. 'She was practical and intelligent, and if anything was to be rescued of the mission it would have to be through her.'[19]

Admirals alone cannot win a war. Without the seamen and the specialised warrants, without the craftsmen ashore, without the shipwrights, the pursers and the provisioners, ships don't sail and guns don't fire. Without women, it can be hard to keep a crew on board for very long. There was a surfeit of post-captains but never enough able seamen, or even landsmen, in Nelson's navy. Whereas most authors focus on one officer as he makes his way from midshipman to admiral, Alaric Bond[20] takes a different approach in his *Fighting Sail* series. Instead of limiting us to the quarterdeck, Bond shows us the whole ship from the viewpoints of multiple characters; from captain to quartermaster, from purser to able seaman, from first lieutenant to the ship surgeon's wife, he immerses the reader in the world of the ship.

Antoine Vanner[21] has ventured beyond Nelson's Navy to Victoria's – a time of transition from sail to steam. The *Dawlish Chronicle*s feature Royal Navy officer Nicholas Dawlish aboard gunboats in far corners of the world, protecting Britain's empire. Mrs Dawlish is a motivated woman of humble origins; one who drives the action in *Britannia's Amazon*, an onshore Victorian detective story paralleling her husband's adventures at sea.

Returning to C. S. Forester's women: Aboard *Lydia*, Hornblower is concerned about the comfort of Lady Barbara when action with *Natividad* becomes imminent. 'The orlop meant that Lady Barbara would be next to the wounded, separated from them only by a canvas screen – no place for a woman. But for that matter neither was the cable tier. The obvious truth was that there was no place for a woman in a frigate about to fight a battle.'[22] Forester then shows us just how useful a woman could be on the orlop deck after a battle. 'Insensibly he came to shift some of his responsibility onto Lady Barbara's shoulders; she was so obviously capable and so unintimidated that she was the person most fitted in all the ship to be given the supervision of the wounded.'[23]

In real life, the orlop *was* the place for women in a frigate about to fight a battle, as primary sources tell us. Betsey Wynne Fremantle, nineteen and newly wedded, lived aboard the fifth-rate HMS *Inconstant* (36) with her husband, Captain Thomas Fremantle.[24] Betsey writes on 8 August 1796, 'Sir John Jervis got us all in a terrible scrape in the evening. He went exceedingly near shore it fell calm all at once and we were all within gun shot without a possibility of getting away. The French fired from all their Batteries, the *Goliath* being nearest they only aimed at her luckily for us, for we were equally near and some of the shots came so near to us that C. Foley was almost tempted to send us ladies in the Cockpit.' Betsey continues, describing how they at last got away from the shore with the help of the crew towing the ships away with the ships' boats. Apparently, Captain Foley (*Goliath*) was somewhat of a bother:

> If C.F. [Captain Fremantle] had no intention to marry me I dare say the old Gentleman has some idea of it himself. It makes me quite miserable. I hide this from Papa for he has a great partiality for C. Foley, he certainly would give him the preference. For my part as I do not think riches alone can make me happy my choice is in favour of the absent friend.[25]

Betsey married her absent friend and sailed aboard *Inconstant* with him for some months.[26] Any young woman, aboard or ashore, had to deal with the hazards of childbirth. Betsey hints of her own pregnancy in the same paragraph as she relates the naval activities of the day:

> Friday, July 21st Captain Miller came on board with 350 of the *Theseus'* men they are all to land in the night but in order to keep out of sight it was late when the three frigates got in shore and day light by the time the troops were landing, they therefore returned without doing anything, I was unwell as usual, slept below, had a woman with me, the sailmaker's wife.[27]

Few fictional captains bring their wives aboard to set up housekeeping, but the young Mrs Fremantle wasn't the only woman in real life to accompany her naval captain husband on his assignment and write about her experience. In 1791 Mary Ann Parker accompanied her husband, captain of a naval supply ship, the former fifth-rate frigate HMS *Gorgon* (44), on a delivery to New South Wales. She writes of finding an American schooner anchored near an uninhabited island. 'The master, his wife, and four or five men were aboard without a grain of tea or scarcely any provisions.' The men of the *Gorgon* helped the Americans hunt turtles ashore to provision their schooner. One of the children from the naval ship was buried on this same island.[28]

Transport ships regularly carried the wives and children of soldiers who were married 'on the strength', and many of these females were present in some of the major fleet actions of this period.[29] These women are seldom seen in historical naval fiction, even as part of the background. We tend to forget they were ever there.

Although every naval author has his loyal fans, Patrick O'Brian is arguably the most acclaimed. His writing, his ability to recreate naval society, has been

Hester Maria Elphinstone, Viscountess Keith, born Hester Maria Thrale (1762–1857) appears as 'Queenie', Viscountess Keith, a supporting character in Patrick O'Brian's Aubrey/Maturin series. A learned woman, Queenie is Jack Aubrey's friend and former tutor; she helps to advance his career. The historical Hester was nicknamed 'Queeney' by her mother's friend, Dr Johnson. Painting by Sir Joshua Reynolds, (Public domain, courtesy of Wikipedia.org).

compared to that of Jane Austen. 'The detail of the world of the ship is wonderful. It's a complete and distinct society … It's Jane Austen at sea,' says Lucy Eyre of the *Guardian*.[30] Austen too, wrote of the navy, given that two of her brothers were naval officers. In *Persuasion* we are introduced to Sophia, Captain Wentworth's sister and Admiral Croft's wife. Sophia Croft was a supportive wife who felt entirely at home on a naval warship. Historian Sheila Kindred[31] proposes that the character was drawn from Jane Austen's real-life sister-in-law, Fanny Palmer Austen, who often accompanied her husband Charles aboard the sixth-rate HMS *Cleopatra* (32). Kindred details some of the naval social life in Bermuda and Halifax, pointing to the importance of the support naval wives might give to their husbands' careers. Later, Captain Austen and his family lived aboard *Namur*, then a receiving vessel in home waters, where Fanny gave birth to her fourth child, and died, aboard ship.[32]

Patrick O'Brian shows us the greatest variety of women and girls – some as minor characters, some as colourful details sketched into the setting. Besides the expected wives and lovers, he gives us the spy, Louisa Wogan, the orphaned Indian girl, Dil, the convict, Clarissa Oakes, and many others. Queenie, Jack Aubrey's childhood friend, is the historical Hester Maria Elphinstone, Viscountess Keith, born Hester Maria Thrale, a friend of Samuel Johnson.

In O'Brian's fiction the intellectual Queenie once tutored Jack in mathematics. An odd pair: handsome creatures both, but they might have been of the same sex or neither. Nor was it a brother and sister connection, with all the possibilities of jealousy and competition so often found therein, but a steady uncomplicated friendship and a pleasure in one another's company.[33]

Such sketches of female characters who are neither lovers nor wives add both interest and authenticity to historical fiction. Chris Durbin[34] gives us a peek at an influential woman of business; a shipyard owner at Deptford Wharf during the Seven Years' War. Durbin says Mrs Winter is a historic character who makes a minor cameo appearance in *Perilous Shore*, the sixth book in his Carlisle and Holbrooke Naval Adventures series. The writer discovered her while researching Navy Board minutes regarding the building of flat-bottomed boats for the raids on France in 1758.[35] This micro-historical detail illuminates a woman who played a role, however minor, in Britain's naval success.

O'Brian gives us glimpses of the women of the lower deck – Mrs James, the Marine sergeant's wife, aboard HMS *Surprise* in *The Far Side of the World*. She plays no part in the story, but O'Brian acknowledges her existence and in doing so adds texture to his setting. In *The Hundred Days* he introduces Poll Skeeping, who had been at sea, off and on, for twenty years. Poll is a loblolly (an assistant to a ship's surgeon) who had trained at Haslar. 'She is up to anything in the way of blood and horrors,' Aubrey says to Maturin, whom he frequently enlightens, along with the modern reader, about the ways of the ship. Says Poll, in answer to the doctor's question as to how women like her came to be aboard:

> Why, sir, in the first place a good many warrant-officers – like the gunner, of course – take their wives to sea, and some captains allow the good petty-officers to do the same. Then there are wives that take a relation along – my particular friend Maggie Cheal is the bosun's wife's sister … and so it went, relations in ships – I had a sister married to the sailmaker's mate in *Ajax* – friends in ships, with a spell or two in naval hospitals – and here I am, loblolly-boy in *Surprise*, I hope, sir, if I give satisfaction.[36]

As for shore wives, Aubrey's dependable Sofie is developed throughout the series, as is her volatile cousin Diana Villiers. O'Brian contrasts their opposite temperaments to good effect. Villiers is an often-adversarial character who breaks Maturin's heart in various ways throughout the twenty-volume series. Independent-minded and impetuous, hers is the plight of most Georgian women who, by necessity, must depend on a man to survive. In Villiers, O'Brian has created a complex character who is not idealised, nor is she quite demonised.

Few other authors include warrant wives in their crew. Alaric Bond, in his

A woman searching for her husband among the casualties below deck. (W. N. Glascock. *Naval Sketch Book*, Vol. I, London: 1835, frontispiece). (Print courtesy of Roy and Lesley Adkins).

Fighting Sail series, gives us a very believable one in Kate Black Manning, a merchantman's daughter who becomes the ship surgeon's assistant, marries him, and lives aboard for a time, continuing as his assistant. Bond also includes a subplot involving Kate's maid, who like many women of the era, turns to prostitution in hard times.

'There was only one woman on board, the Boatswain's wife.'[37] This, from Pope's *The Black Ship*, a revealing account of the *Hermione* mutiny. Pope, an acclaimed naval historian, chooses not to reveal any warrant wives in his fictional series.

According to primary sources, the wives of warrants and petty officers frequently lived on board; although not on the muster rolls. Their husband's ship was their home. N. A. M. Rodger suggests there were many practical ways in which they might have made themselves useful, even earning an income aboard, by washing, sewing, or looking after children.[38] Admiral Jervis accused them of wasting water on washing, yet the women are known to have assisted the surgeon and the gun crews during action. In any case, women were sometimes aboard. Though they have largely been ignored by the novelists,

A woman with her child tending the wounded. (*The Log Book; or, Nautical Miscellany*, London: 1830, p33). (Print courtesy of Roy and Lesley Adkins).

they were part of the ships' company and, as such, part of the ship's success or its failure.

What a novelist chooses to include or ignore affects our perception of history. The art and craft of writing requires making choices, but those choices colour our collective memory of historical events. Who was important enough to include in the telling? Who was important enough to give voice to? Are some classes of people so insignificant or so repulsive as to be left out of the telling altogether?

'It was very strange that the Admiral – a religious and good man – could not bear the sight of a female,' gunner William Richardson comments, referring to Admiral Sir William Wallace, in his memoir *A Mariner of England 1780–1817*. Speaking for the seamen, Richardson considered the Portsmouth working girls important enough to include in his story. He describes the incident aboard the fourth-rate frigate HMS *Minerva* (48) having just returned to Britain from Bombay after a passage of three months and seventeen days:

> As the Admiral was dressing to go on shore, he saw out of the cabin windows two wherries pulling up to the ship full of girls; he came out much agitated, and sending for Captain Whitby, desired him not to allow any such creatures to come near the ship, so they were hailed to keep off; but as soon as the Admiral got on shore they were permitted to come on board, and the ship was soon full of them.

Captain Whitby merely waited until the admiral was ashore before allowing the women to come aboard.[39]

Richardson also describes the day in 1806 when Her Royal Highness Princess Caroline, consort to the Prince of Wales, visited the third-rate HMS *Caesar* (80), Sir Richard Strachan's flagship. 'All the girls (some hundreds) on board were ordered to keep below on the orlop deck, out of sight until the visit was over.' But her Royal Highness had a keen eye and spied some of the girls trying to get a glimpse of her from the hatchway. 'Sir Richard,' the Princess says, 'You told me there were no women aboard the ship, but I am convinced there are, as I have seen them peeping up from that place, and am inclined to think they are put down there on my account. I therefore request that it may no longer be permitted.' The princess and her retinue were escorted back to the quarterdeck again, and the girls were set free. 'Up they came like a flock of sheep, and the booms and gangways were soon covered with them, staring at the princess as if she had been a being just dropped from the clouds,' Richardson relates.[40]

Others found the practice shocking:

It is well known that immediately on the arrival of a ship of war in port, crowds of boats flock off with cargoes of prostitute ... The whole of the shocking, disgraceful transactions of the lower deck it is impossible to describe ... Let those who have never seen a ship of war picture to themselves a very large low room (hardly capable of holding the men) with 500 men and probably 300 or 400 women of the vilest description shut up in it, and giving way to every excess of debauchery that the grossest passions of human nature can lead them to; and they see the deck of a 74-gun ship the night of her arrival in port.[41]

"'That no women be ever permitted to be on board, but such as are really the wives of the men they come to, and the ship not to be too much pestered even by them. But this indulgence is only to be tolerated while the ship is in port, and not under sailing orders," Admiralty Regulations and Instructions, 1790.' This regulation, Rowbotham says, was universally disregarded.[42]

There was not always a clear distinction between a sailor's wife and a prostitute, historians Roy Adkins and Lesley Adkins point out. Sometimes sailors married prostitutes but often sailors' wives were forced to turn to prostitution to survive. A seaman's wife was not told when her husband's ship would return or to what port, and mail delivery was not always reliable. Accompanying their husbands on board might have presented a better alternative for some who had no other means of support.[43]

The typical ship, says N. A. M. Rodger, spent less than half her time in commission at sea, but the men were still needed aboard while in port or off-shore at anchor.[44] Novelists sometimes refer to the women aboard in port as Bond does in *True Colours*. 'The only exception was a prolonged period in his second ship, a third rate that had lain three months at anchor with the Wedding Garland hoisted, and all manner of women running riot throughout the crowded decks.'[45]

Robert Hay, in his memoirs *Landsman Hay*, describes the market-like atmosphere aboard *Salvador de Mundo*, a three-deck guard ship, permanently anchored in Plymouth Harbour:

On the lower deck, appropriated to the ship's crew, almost every berth was converted into a shop or warehouse where commodities of every description might be procured: groceries, haberdashery goods, hardware, stationery, everything, in fact, that could be named as the necessities or luxuries of life. Even spirituous liquors, though strictly prohibited, were to be had in abundance, the temptations of the enormous profits arising from their sale overcoming any fear of punishment … As those who were of the regular ship's crew were but few in number, and chiefly employed manning officers' boats, it might be thought this lower deck a desirable berth, but as the greater number kept their wives and families on board, it was pretty much crowded day and night.[46]

The gunner Richardson writes of his wife, Sarah, daughter of a master stonemason of Portsea, who accompanied him on his second assignment to the West Indies, aboard the former Dutch frigate, the fourth-rate HMS *Tromp* (60). The wives of the captain, the shipmaster, the purser, and the boatswain were also aboard for this assignment, as was the wife of the sergeant of marines and 'six other men's wives had leave to go'. On 2 August 1800, he tells us, the captain's wife was delivered of a fine boy.[47]

In Fort Royal, Martinique, yellow fever overtook the ship. The shipmaster and his pregnant wife died, and the boatswain died, leaving his wife and daughter on board. When Sarah got sick, Richardson took her ashore and put her in the care of a French physician and an African nurse, Madame Janet, at his own expense. Sarah lived and William brought her back home, aboard ship.

Another memoirist clearly has an eye for the ladies; he notices them wherever he goes. At anchor in the West Indies, John Nicol describes 'the female slaves, who brought us fruit and remained on board all Sunday until Monday morning – poor things! And all to obtain a bellyful of victuals.'[48] Later, aboard a transport ship bound for New South Wales, 'Every man on board took a wife from among the convicts.' His was Sarah Whitlam, whom he 'courted for a week and upwards, and would have married her on the spot had there been a clergyman on board'. Sarah had been transported for stealing – her sentence was seven years. 'I knocked the rivet out of her irons upon my anvil, and as firmly resolved to bring her back to England when her time was out, my lawful wife, as ever I did intend anything in my life. She bore me a son in our voyage out.'[49]

A cooper like his father before him, Nicol then served aboard the second-rate HMS *Goliath* (80) under Captain Foley in the Battle of Aboukir Bay. He mentions the gunner's wife as being of good comfort during the battle, bringing them both a drink of wine to fortify them. Several of the ship's women were wounded in the action and one, from Leith, died as a result of her wounds. 'One woman bore a son during the heat of action.'[50] Even when a woman died at sea, the death was seldom recorded. Their names were not listed in ships' muster books, and since only those people who were mustered had any official existence, the lower-deck women are largely invisible to us. Although the naval writers know their dates and admirals, although they pepper their accounts with historical people and convincing nautical and tactical detail, for the most part they ignore the great numbers of prostitutes who entertained, comforted and satisfied the desires of the men of the lower decks, shared their hammocks and their meals. Although they weren't officially sanctioned, they were there.

Roy Adkins writes:

> During the Battle of Trafalgar, women were probably working as powder monkeys on board many of the ships, but their names are unknown because their presence was not officially recognised. The only female powder monkey of the Napoleonic Wars about which any amount of reliable information has survived is Ann Hopping, who later remarried to become Ann Perriam (also known as Nancy Perriam). She was the wife of a gunner's mate and, although not at Trafalgar, she took part in several other major battles.[51]

Adkins quotes an article published in 1863:

> Upon Sir James Saumarez's subsequent removal to the *Orion*, Hopping and his wife followed him. Mrs. Perriam served on board the latter ship five years, and during that time witnessed and bore her part in, besides many minor engagements, the following great naval battles: at L'Orient, on the 23rd of June, 1795; off Cape St. Vincent, on the 14th of February, 1797; and at the glorious battle of the Nile, won by Nelson on the 1st of August, 1798. Mrs. Perriam's occupation while in action lay with the gunners and magazine men, among whom she worked preparing flannel cartridges for the great guns.[52]

British naval fiction set in the Georgian age is alive and well, some two centuries after the Battle of Trafalgar, and continues to shape popular perceptions of history. A new generation of readers is discovering the genre, even as authors continue to invent new commanders, new ships, and new ways to thwart Bonaparte. Readers take part in online forums and in social media groups devoted to their favourite authors. Facebook, Reddit, Goodreads, and HistoricNavalFiction.net have many thousands of active members among them. Within the genre there are some well-drawn female characters, though admittedly, they are few. In general, women tend to be conceived as love interests for the protagonist. The scarcity of authentic women in historical naval fiction affects how we 'remember' our history. Ashore and aboard, females of all classes were witnesses and participants, helping or hindering the war effort, affecting the outcome. Wives, widows, servants, shipowners, merchants, princesses, prostitutes – they all played their part.

'God bless,' called Queenie, 'and Liberate Chile, and come home as soon as ever you can'… while the children screeched out very shrill, fluttering handkerchiefs. And at the very end of the mole, when the frigate turned westward along the Strait with a following breeze, stood an elegant young woman with a maidservant, and she too waving, waving, waving …[53]

Prostitutes coming aboard ship, see colour plate 5

The Rise of the Fouled Anchor:
The Visual Codification of the Royal Navy during the 1700s

Lily Style

The Royal Navy at the start of the Georgian era in 1714 looked nothing like its glamorous Nelson-era counterpart at the century's end. Lacking designated uniforms, officers were viewed as 'base, coarse and unrefined'.[1] However, less than a century later, Royal Navy officers were resplendent in blue and white uniforms emblazoned with gilt buttons sporting the fouled (rope-strewn) anchor motif, which is still in use today. What caused the navy to change from ill-reputed mufti to uniformed respectability, and from whence, out of the blue, did the iconic fouled anchor arise?

Naval use of the anchor motif, albeit unfouled, can be traced back to the Lord Admirals of Scotland in 1515. The first record of its use by the English Admiralty comes forty-three years later in the reign of Queen Mary. The fouled version first appears in the seal of the Earl of Nottingham, Lord High Admiral, in 1601. In 1619, Nottingham's successor Buckingham, was granted 'an Ensigne with ye Ld Admiralls Badge & Motto'. This appears to have been the fouled anchor because he adopted it as his emblem.[2] The fouled anchor, according to the *Oxford Companion to Ships and the Sea*, is 'an abomination to seamen when it occurs in practice, as the seal of the highest office of maritime administration is purely on the grounds of its decorative effect, the rope cable around the shank of the anchor giving a pleasing finish to the stark design of an anchor on its own'.[3]

The first English language naval dictionary, entitled *A Naval Expositor*, was produced circa 1732 by Thomas Blanckley, Clerk of the Survey for Portsmouth Dock. His dictionary, 'SHEWING all the Words and Terms of Art belonging to the Parts, Qualities, Proportions of Building, Rigging, Furnishing and Fitting a Ship for Sea', includes meticulously hand-drawn illustrations, the first of which is of an anchor. Blanckley's definitions gift the modern reader with a fascinating window to the inner workings of the early Georgian navy, and bear traces of his intellectual struggle to codify naval hardware into concise, accurate phrases. His definition of 'board' is three-plied:

Elm: Is used for several Services about the Yard, on board ships, & repairing Boats &c

Firr: For sheathing ships bottoms, flooring their cabbins, & masking moulds &c

Wainscot: For building Barges, Pinnaces, & Wherrys & other uses relating to the Joyner

A humiliating Royal Navy defeat to the French and Spanish at Toulon in 1744 was offset by the heroic return of Commodore George Anson. He, and the 188 men who returned with him, had survived marooning in the Pacific to capture a Spanish Manila galleon carrying a fortune in cargo. Anson earned £91,000 prize money from the haul, and a pathway into the Board of Admiralty. One of the Board's senior officers, Vice-Admiral Edward Vernon, was actively determined to reform the sluggish, ineffective navy.

Anson, later elevated to the peerage as Lord Anson, and Admiral of the Fleet, Vice-admiral of Great Britain, and First Lord Commissioner of the Admiralty[4], was equally keen to reform the navy, and joined forces with Vernon. Of these, one reform, instigated in 1748, was the ruling that all commissioned officers must wear a uniform. This would serve to unite officers as a proud brotherhood clearly distinguished from the coarse hoi polloi of non-commissioned crew.[5] Confusingly, however, no pattern was at first decreed.[6] The introduction of naval uniform mirrored the impact of Thomas Blanckley's illustrated dictionary as a revolutionary step in visually codifying the navy.

Anson's biographer Sir John Barrow wrote in 1839 that blue and white was chosen for the Royal Navy's uniform on the whim of George II, who had been impressed by the appearance of the Duke of Bedford's wife riding in those colours. However, the author concedes, the story may be nothing more than colourful rumour.[7]

Thomas Blanckley died in Portsmouth on the morning of 29 December 1747 aged sixty-nine. His eldest son, Thomas Riley, who had already taken his position of Clerk of the Survey, inherited his *Naval Expositor* manuscript. Quick off the mark, he commissioned an esteemed London-based Huguenot printmaker, Paul Fourdriniers, to produce copperplate engravings of his father's illustrations, and recruited subscribers to finance mass printing. He was evidently supported by Anson, as the subscribers' list is headed by 'RIGHT Honourable the Lords of the Admiralty (as a board)'. Also named is the Duke of Bedford (whose wife's attire was rumoured to have inspired the uniform's colours) and Joseph Allin: Surveyor of His Majesty's Navy (and, by the way, his father-in-law). The printed version of the *Naval Expositor*, released in 1750, comprises an elaborate frontispiece surmounted by a fouled anchor. This appears to be the first instance of the motif being used to represent the navy, rather than the Admiralty only. Beneath the fouled anchor, the words 'by Thomas Riley Blanckley' are prominently emblazoned. It is unclear, however, whether he deliberately set out to fool posterity into believing he created the *Naval Expositor*, because he acknowledges the true authorship in his will (proved 23 May 1753):

> Also I give and bequeath all the manuscripts of my late father ... Also I give and bequeath the copper plates and blank books of the Naval Expositor composed by my late father and lately by me published ...

In the latter part of the decade, in 1758 (the birth year of Horatio Nelson), buttons bearing the fouled anchor were produced for officers' uniforms. This, however, pre-dated their formal introduction by sixteen years.[8] The fouled anchor was now, for the first time, associated with Royal Navy officers.

News in 1772 – the year after Horatio Nelson joined the navy – that

The frontispiece for the *Naval Expositor* published in 1790.

the fouled anchor was being formally added to Royal Navy buttons was lamented as a downslide into the capricious following of fashion; and that the anchor motif was fit only for servants, not the great heroes of the British navy. The anchor, it was argued, had, since Old Testament times, symbolised hope, and should not therefore be purloined. If given choice over the design of their personal buttons, as huntsmen did, officers could signal their personal disposition, knowledge and taste by choosing 'a Variety of marginal engravings, full as entertaining and as useful as those which illustrate Blankley's *Naval Expositor*'.[9] Nonetheless, anchor buttons were introduced two years later. *The Hampshire Chronicle* reported on 13 June 1774:

> We are informed that the Captains uniform of the navy is going to be

altered, and that Sir Richard Bickerton will appear in the new dresses at the sea-ports when Lord Sandwich is there, for the approbation of the corps, the old coat is to have the addition of a row of lace round the pockets and sleeves, with anchor buttons; and the undress frock is to be lapelled with blue, with button-hole, worked with gold thread, anchor buttons, plain white waistcoat and breeches. After the approbation of the corps is obtained, it will be shewn to his Majesty for his concurrence.[10]

Royal Navy button with fouled anchor, introduced 1772.

The introduction of uniforms was so successful that it extended to include midshipmen and standing warrant officers in 1787.[11] This ongoing process of visual codification enabled people to picture the navy in their minds' eyes. Like modern day football clubs, the navy now had its own colours and an emblem (the fouled anchor) to cheer on. Thus branded, a pictorial snowballing effect ensued as artists and cartoonists translated all things naval into mass-produced prints,[12] graphically imprinting team Royal Navy into public consciousness. The momentum of this visual snowballing effect was so great, and its glamour so strong that Louis XVI of France decreed the use of blue and white with anchor buttons for his own navy. An unspecified English gentleman in Paris wrote in the summer of 1786:

> I was highly pleased to see, in consequence of the new Order from the King for regulating the Marine uniform, that it is entirely formed upon that worn by the British naval Commanders. Even the *Anchor* upon the Button has been introduced in preference for the *Fleur de Lys.* In short, English Fashions now prevail here as much as French did with us formerly.[13]

However, the anglicisation of the French navy was abruptly curtailed by the revolution, which began in May 1789. No longer aspiring to mimic, the French now sought to impose their republican government on Britain. So began the revolutionary wars, from which the aspiring young naval captain Horatio Nelson stepped forth into glory. Having cut his teeth defeating Napoleon's forces at Capo Noli in 1795, his resounding victory at the Nile on 1 August 1798 cast him as the superhero protector of all who resisted the encroaching republican yoke. Women in Britain wore 'gold anchors that celebrated their hero',[14] and, in Naples, Emma, Lady Hamilton, who was at this time the fashion-setter of Europe, as well as bosom friend of Queen Maria Carolina (sister of the ill-fated Marie Antoinette), wrote to him adoringly on 3 September:

> My dress from head to foot is alla Nelson ... Even my shawl is in blue with gold anchors all over. My earrings are Nelson's anchors; in short, we are be-Nelsoned all over.[15]

The naval use of the fouled anchor rose so rapidly through the latter half of the eighteenth century, that it had evidently transmogrified to symbolise not just the Royal Navy, but its new, international hero: Horatio Nelson. In dashing blue and white, festooned with gold fouled anchors and medals of valour, Nelson epitomised the rebranded navy. Exultant and adoring, the Hamiltons commissioned a lavish dinner service sporting enormous, gilt fouled anchors for his fortieth birthday on 29 September 1798.[16]

Use of the motif as the ubiquitous symbol for the navy through its emblazonment on uniform buttons continued to rise. Surgeons were issued their own uniform in the fateful year of 1805; masters and pursers two years after this, although common seamen had to wait until 1857.[17]

The fouled anchor motif can, therefore, be charted to have first been used by Scottish admirals in the 1500s and by the English a century later. It came to symbolise the British navy as a whole during the latter years of the 1700s, and went on to represent the pre-revolutionary French navy. Throughout much of

The dinner service celebrating Nelson's fortieth birthday, 29 September 1798. It is of English manufacture, probably Coalport, and decorated in Naples.

91

Master Chief Petty Officer collar button, US Navy.

Right: Grave marker in the Old Cemetery in Cobh, Ireland, shows an example of the fouled anchor. The marker pays tribute to the eleven men who died in a gun battery accident on HMS *Mars* in 1902 when the ship was off the west coast of Ireland.

the world it became a ubiquitous symbol of the traditions, adventures, and perils of life at sea.

The US navy followed suit in 1905 by issuing fouled anchor insignia to chief petty officers.[18] The letters U, S, and N were added to the symbol not, as is commonly assumed, to signify 'United States Navy', but for Unity', 'Service', and 'Navigation'.[19] Back in Britain, the fouled anchor has remained a symbol of the Lord High Admiral, who is currently Prince Philip.[20]

Detail showing buttons with fouled anchor, see colour plate 6

Spain and American Independence:
The Best-Kept Secret of the Georgian Age

Chipp Reid

There was nothing about the French frigate *Aigrette* that marked her as particularly special. She carried thirty guns, was 123ft long, and had the shallow draft and easy handling that made her a workhorse of the fleet, a perfect scout and an even better messenger ship. On 16 August 1781, she was in Havana harbour, part of a large French fleet under the command of François Joseph Paul, Comte de Grasse, Marquis de Grasse-Tilly. Small as she was, as nondescript as she was, the *Aigrette* would play a pivotal role in one of the signal events of the Georgian Era – the independence of the United States. The little French frigate would make the victory at Yorktown possible and do so without firing a shot. As she left Havana, the *Aigrette* carried the money the

Battle of the Virginia Capes, 5 September 1781 by V. Zveg. The French fleet, left, under Vice Admiral the Comte de Grasse, held off a British squadron under Rear Admiral Sir Thomas Graves off the mouth of Chesapeake Bay. Although a French naval victory, it was all due to Spain, which paid the French squadron and freed up needed warships from patrol duty to serve with de Grasse. (Courtesy of the U.S. Navy Art Collection, Washington, DC, US Naval History and Heritage Command)

Franco-American army desperately needed to pay its soldiers and purchase supplies, and she carried an agreement that allowed de Grasse to concentrate his fleet and carry a second French division to Virginia.

The story of the *Aigrette* and her larger-than-life place in American and world history is one that is almost impossible to find. Her name never comes up in documentaries about the American War of Independence. She never features in movies or books about the conflict. There are no heroic depictions of the little frigate executing her mission even though it led directly to the creation of a new nation and changed the balance of power in Europe and throughout the Western world for the remainder of the century. The primary reason for this is a still-powerful prejudice historians have dubbed the 'Black Legend', a form of anti-Hispanism that colours much of how film, television, and art depict Spaniards specifically and Latinos in general.

The history of the Black Legend dates to the mid-sixteenth century, when Spain began to carve out her empire in the New World. Britain, France, and Holland all watched in envy as gold, silver, and other riches flowed across the Atlantic. The break between Britain, Holland, and Spain over religion exacerbated their animosities. Spain, for both Britain and Holland, became the great Catholic oppressor, where Inquisitors tortured and burned anyone who dared to question the Roman church. From roughly 1566 right up until the present day, the depiction of Spaniards, and more recently Latin Americans has remained consistent with this prejudice.[1] In terms of the Georgian period, English (and American) literature, history books, movies, and/or television shows portray Spain, especially the Armada Española (the Spanish Navy) as either completely incompetent and little more than an annoyance to Britain's fabled Royal Navy, or, more usually, it is rarely if ever mentioned. Outside of British bombast over the victory of Admiral John Jervis at the Battle of Cape St Vincent, the Armada receives extremely little notice. Even Trafalgar, the signal victory of the age for the Royal Navy, receives this treatment as many historians regard it as a battle between the French and English, with the silly Spaniards getting in the way of both.[2]

This depiction of Spain and the Armada Española defies both logic and the historical record. British and American naval historians especially ridicule José Cordoba y Ramos, the luckless Spanish admiral at Cape St Vincent, and Federico Gravina, the doomed Spanish admiral at Trafalgar. They completely ignore, however, Spanish naval officers such as Alejandro Malaspina, who spent five years on a circumnavigation that charted more islands, identified more species, and produced more scientific samples than James Cook's cruises; Don Cosme Damián Churruca, who died in action at Trafalgar and remains a hero in the Spanish Navy; José de Mazzaredo, who battled valiantly against Carlos

IV and his favourite, Manuel de Godoy, to reform and modernise the navy; and Blas de Lezo, the heroic defender of Cartagena in 1741 and a man who epitomised 'swashbuckling'.[3]

Arguably the most famous Spaniards in film were Zorro, who, despite being Latino, was a 'hero' as he fought against the despotism of the Spanish monarchy, and Inigo Montoya, the revenge-driven though lovable character of the film *The Princess Bride*. The depths to which the Black Legend has shaped the perception of Spaniards was plain in one 'exchange' in *The Princess Bride* in which the hero and Inigo were about to fight a duel. Inigo offers to give the hero his 'word as a Spaniard' about a truce, to which the hero replies, 'No good, I have known too many Spaniards.'

More recently, Latinos have replaced Peninsula-born Spaniards as the villains of film, novels, and television. When Hollywood needs a 'bad guy', Latinos are invariably at the top of the list. Whether it is the wildly popular pay-to-view Netflix series *Narcos*, the still-popular, conspiratorial television series *24*, or any of a number of crime shows, film and television invariably depict South and Central Americans, especially Colombians and Mexicans, as drug-dealing cutthroats whose greed is only surpassed by their willingness to murder anyone in their way. While there is no denying the violence and criminality of South and Central American drug cartels, the same programmes that seem to revel in detailing the violence of their members do nothing to show they are hugely in the minority of their respective populations.

When the everyday people do make the screen, they normally fall into a category of 'the bandit, male buffoon, female clown, Latin lover, dark lady, and the harlot'.[4] This depiction is completely in line with the depiction of Spaniards before and during the Georgian period, during which English, French, and Dutch writers used a common theme. 'When the Spaniard has the upper hand, his cruelty and hauteur are unsupportable. When reduced to his proper stature by some unimpeachable Nordic hero, he is cringing and mean-spirited, a coward whose love of plots and treacheries is exceeded only by his incompetence in carrying them out.'[5]

In the 1990s, Hollywood released a pair of films ostensibly about Christopher Columbus. Both subscribed to a rigidly anti-Spanish, revisionist viewpoint that portrayed Columbus as a gold-crazed madman whose quest to find a route to China fell to the wayside when he found he could enslave the native peoples who inhabited the Caribbean and reap a fortune in the slave trade. This dovetails with the late twentieth- and twenty-first-century efforts to decry Columbus' voyages and turn him into the quintessential Spanish villain.[6] And, it is not just Hollywood that has succumbed to this historically inaccurate though politically correct view of Spain. Textbooks in use across the United States excoriate the

Spanish conquest as well as the South American leaders of the early nineteenth-century wars of independence in Venezuela, Colombia, Argentina, Mexico and elsewhere. One such text, which historians have called 'influential', is Howard Zinn's *A People's History of the United States*.[7]

Zinn follows the stereotypes of the Black Legend almost to a letter. In his telling, the natives of North, South, and Central America and the Caribbean were peaceful, happy, and had no wants. 'These Arawaks of the Bahamas Islands were much like the Indians on the mainland, who were remarkable (European observers were to say again and again) for their hospitality, their belief in sharing. These traits did not stand out in the Europe of the Renaissance, dominated as it was by the religion of popes, the frenzy for money that marked Western civilisation and its first messenger to the Americas, Christopher Columbus.'[8] He claims Columbus, on meeting the Caribbean natives, questioned them on just one topic. 'The information Columbus wanted most was: Where was the gold?'[9] He makes this assertion despite the fact Columbus had no knowledge of the golden empires of South America, which Spain had yet to encounter.[10] Zinn's depiction of Spain also serves to further anti-Hispanism. He describes Spain in stark terms:

> Its population, mostly poor peasants, worked for the nobility, who were 2 per cent of the population and owned 95 per cent of the land. Spain had tied itself to the Catholic Church, expelled all the Jews, driven out the Moors. Like other states of the modern world, Spain sought gold, which was becoming the new mark of wealth, more useful than land because it could buy anything.[11]

It is of little wonder, then, that the treatment of Spain, whether in the time of Columbus or Trafalgar, often comes in the harshest possible terms and at the expense of historical fact. Whether it is the stridently xenophobic, anti-Latino rhetoric of many contemporary US politicians,[12] or the continuing portrayal of Latinos as drug-dealers or buffoons, the 'Black Legend' continues to poison the Anglo-American (and Dutch) opinion of all things Spanish. It accounts for why the story of the *Aigrette* and how instrumental Spain was to American independence remains largely unknown, ignored, or even suppressed. As Frank Verona, editor of the journal *Hispanic Presence in the United States: Historical Beginning*, points out in his essay, 'Spain and Hispanic America: Forgotten Allies of the American Revolution':

> There are many possible explanations for these glaring historical omissions. One reason may be that American historians have inherited

the traditional British dislike of Spain. It may stem from the fact that Spain declared war on Great Britain in June 1779 as an ally of France but not of America. The United States invasion of Florida, the Texas conflict, and the war against Mexico and Spain during the 19th century may account for the biased reporting. One wonders if the 'Black Legend' propagated by Great Britain to discredit Spain at the peak of its glory in the 16th century, persists to the present. Or it may just be a case of simple historical neglect. Regardless of the reason, this historical injustice must be corrected.[13]

The French army that landed outside of Newport, Rhode Island, on 10 July 1780 had two missions – one public and one private. Publicly, the nearly 4,000-man expeditionary force had orders from King Louis XVI to conduct a campaign against the British forces in North America in concert with and under the command of General George Washington. Privately, however, French Lieutenant General Jean-Baptiste Donatien de Vimeur, Comte de Rochambeau, commander of the French land troops, had specific orders to cooperate with the Spanish governor-general of Louisiana, Bernardo de Galvez, in a planned combined Ibero-French assault on the British stronghold of Jamaica.[14]

De Galvez was the key to the Jamaica plan, although there is no evidence Rochambeau even knew about the Spanish governor when the Frenchman landed in Rhode Island. Just thirty-five years old, de Galvez led the 1780–81 campaign that culminated in Spain retaking Pensacola and ousting the British from the Mississippi River Valley. He was also instrumental in developing the Spanish pipeline – lifeline might be a better descriptor – to Washington and the Continental Congress that provided money, weapons, and

Conde Don Bernando de Gálvez, the Spanish governor of Louisiana and Commander-in-Chief of Spanish Forces in the Caribbean. De Galvez authorised the financing of the French and Americans in the Yorktown campaign. (Courtesy of the Museo Nacional del Prado, Madrid)

supplies to the colonial cause, while providing one of the few protected trade routes for American exports.[15] New Orleans was the hub of this aid, with de Galvez working closely with American merchant and commercial agent Oliver Pollock. Starting in 1777, de Galvez threw the weight of Spain's North, Central and South American holdings behind the American cause. The artillery Horatio Gates used to defeat British General John Burgoyne at Saratoga came from the arsenals in Havana, Cuba, and Cartagena, Colombia. Many of the uniforms Gates' troops wore arrived from Veracruz, Mexico, while Gates paid his men in Spanish dollars minted in Lima, Peru.[16] That money moved from Lima to Cartagena to Havana to New Orleans before making its way up the Mississippi River. Pollock created a supply line that moved Spanish money, weapons, and war materiel up the Mississippi to the Ohio River, where it floated on to Pittsburgh, then went overland to Philadelphia. Unlike France, which made cash loans – and expected the Americans to repay them in cash – Spain allowed the colonials to secure their credit with agriculture. American rice, wheat, and corn flowed into New Orleans and then into Havana, where Spanish merchants took full advantage of new Spanish trade policies to ship it to French and Dutch colonies in the Caribbean or to Europe.[17]

The Spanish-money-for-American-grain network was the real beginning of what would culminate in the Yorktown campaign, even though at the time not even the remarkable de Galvez could know. The arrival of French Army regiments to form a combined Franco-American siege of New York changed the equation for de Galvez and for Spain. King Carlos III formally declared war on Britain on 16 June 1779. The clandestine Spanish support was now out in the open and although Spain did not recognise the independence of the United States, at first, it agreed to support the budding new nation in its struggle against Great Britain. This decision is likely one of the main reasons why American historians overlook, minimise or simply ignore Spain's contribution to US independence. Carlos III wanted revenge on Britain for the defeats his nation suffered at the hands of the British starting in 1741 when the monarch was the ruler of Spanish-controlled Naples.[18] The English capture and looting of Havana in 1761 only added to that desire. Carlos, however, was not ready to recognise the legitimacy of colonies rebelling against their mother country as he feared the message it would send to Spain's extensive and economically vital colonies in South and Central America and the Caribbean.[19]

Those fears, however, did not prevent Carlos from not only supporting and encouraging the American revolt, but in using it to Spain's favour. Carlos had three stated goals – the recapture of Menorca, the capture of Gibraltar, and the protection of Spain's holdings in the New World. He sent the bulk of the Spanish Army to Gibraltar while the Armada Española was the main instrument in the campaigns against Menorca and in North America, and it was a powerful instrument. After he ascended to the Spanish throne in 1763, Carlos embarked on a massive naval construction campaign. It is a fact few English naval historians even acknowledge. By the outbreak of the American War for Independence, Spain was already in a position to challenge Britain for supremacy of the Caribbean, if not the entire Atlantic.[20] British naval historian Herbert Wilson asserted:

> In our fight for life 1798–1808, the Battle of St. Vincent serves to illustrate once more the hopeless feebleness of the Spanish Navy. Nelson and our great captains looked upon the 'Don' with undisguised contempt. 'A Spanish ship chased is a Spanish ship taken,' was a saying of those days, which seems still to hold true. Of all things, national character changes most slowly, and what Spaniards were in the last century they still remain.[21]

It was, and is, a typically English view of the Spanish, one that refuses to even contemplate the idea that Spain could somehow best Britain at sea. It was this same attitude that, 200 years later, the British transplanted onto Argentina during the Falklands War in 1982. This explains why the success of the Argentinians, with their Exocet air-to-surface missiles, flown on Argentine Navy Super Etendard aircraft, came as a bitter surprise and shock to the British public.[22] It also explains why both British and American naval histories rarely, if ever, mention the two largest defeats the Royal Navy suffered prior to the Yorktown campaign, both of which came against the Spanish. In August 1780, Spanish Admiral Luis Cordóba y Cordóba led a combined Ibero-French fleet into the English Channel, where it intercepted the vaunted Jamaica Convoy, taking fifty-five ships. Nine months later, Cordóba y Cordóba repeated his feat, capturing another twenty-four ships in the Channel in the midst of a nasty gale.[23]

Spain's increasing power and ability at sea, along with a new sense of confidence in action against Great Britain, would bear fruit on 19 October 1781, as the Spanish would make it possible for the French to not only remain in North America alongside Washington's army but, more important, allow Admiral François Joseph Paul, Comte de Grasse, to concentrate his entire fleet and seal the fate of General Charles Cornwallis. It was due in large part to de Galvez, Cuban Governor-General Diego José Navarro Garcia de Valladares, and the unsung hero, Francisco Saavedra de Sagronis, who made Yorktown possible by ensuring the finances for the campaign. The financing was the key element, and where the *Aigrette* played her huge yet all-but-forgotten role.

Rochambeau arrived in North America with little more than great expectations.

The French division that landed in Rhode Island lacked heavy siege guns, transport, or enough food for more than a few weeks. Rochambeau expected his heavy equipment to come from France while his American allies provided food, ammunition and other supplies.[24] The problem was that the French arrived at the absolute low point in the American cause. Washington, who was perpetually broke, literally did not have the money to feed or pay his own troops, and could do nothing to aid Rochambeau. In addition, morale was low. The Continentals had suffered their single-worst defeat on 12 April 1780 with the surrender of Charleston. Cornwallis was rampaging through the Carolinas. Plus, the alliance with France had yet to really bear any tangible results.

Rochambeau spent a year idle in Rhode Island, ostensibly to support the squadron of Jacques-Melchoir Saint-Laurent, Comte de Barras, which remained in Newport under blockade by a British squadron. Even before Rochambeau landed, French reports to Paris revealed just how destitute Washington's treasury was and the effect it had on the French land forces. 'There is great poverty and want in reigning in North America, and a great lack of everything in the state of war upon which we are engaged. Even the simple wants of daily life are lacking,' wrote Gérard de Reyneval, the first French diplomat to the United States. 'It is necessary therefore to provide abundantly all the needs of the expeditionary forces and to convert into merchandise, that is, into necessary articles, some of the funds placed at the disposal of the division.'[25]

With Rochambeau waiting in Rhode Island, idle, as the French Navy never appeared off North America in strength, the Royal Navy received a large reinforcement at the start of 1781. The bulk of the American army was either arrayed in lines to the north of New York City or was in the Carolinas, now under the command of Nathaniel Greene, trying to blunt the campaign of Charles Cornwallis. The long year had almost completely depleted Rochambeau's war chest, while Washington was almost in despair over the state of his army. In a letter to New Hampshire General Assembly President Mesheck Ware, Washington admitted:

> The aggravated calamities and distresses that have resulted to the soldiers from the total want of pay for nearly twelve months, the want of clothing in a severe season, and not infrequently, want of provisions, are beyond description ... unless some immediate and Spirited measures are adopted to furnish at least three months' pay, in money which will be of value to them, and at the same time ways and means are devised to clothe and feed them better (more regularly I mean) than they have been, the worst that can befall us can be expected.[26]

Not even the long-awaited junction between Washington and Rochambeau in June 1781 alleviated the situation. Rochambeau expected the Americans to supply his force as it marched from Newport through Connecticut toward Westchester County, New York. The French quickly discovered, however, their American hosts would part with agricultural goods only for hard currency, a commodity that was in extremely short supply for both Rochambeau's division and for Washington. The American general petitioned Congress for help, and its response was to issue more paper currency, making the Continental scrip all but worthless.[27]

Washington and Rochambeau met in Wethersfield, Connecticut, on 22 May 1781 to map out their campaign. Washington wanted to strike at New York, and the anticipated arrival of the fleet under de Grasse would make that possible. Rochambeau, knowing that his small division was inadequate for any assault on the fortified British-held city, and that his days in North America were finite with plans moving forward for operations in the Caribbean, pushed Washington to move south to Virginia, where Cornwallis was then operating.[28] Washington, however, remained adamant that he wanted to strike Sir Henry Clinton in New York. The French marched south to the Hudson, taking up positions in June, with still no definite plan of operations.[29] At the same time, de Grasse, with twenty-seven ships of the line, set sail from Brest for North America.

Although Washington expected the French fleet to sail directly to New York,[30] de Grasse (with Rochambeau's knowledge[31]) instead set a course for Santo Domingo, present-day Haiti. He arrived at Cap François (modern-day Cap-Haitien) on 18 July. Waiting there for him was a thirty-four-year-old Spanish army officer, intelligence agent, and diplomat – Francisco Saavedra de Sagronis. A native of Seville, Saavedra served in the Regimento del Rey (The King's Own) in the 1775 Spanish campaign against Algiers, where he suffered a leg wound. He met and became friends with Bernardo de Galvez, as well as his uncle José, who was the Secretary de Indias – the minister in charge of Spain's colonies in Central and South America, and his father Matias, who was the viceroy of New Spain (Mexico). Thanks to these connections, Saavedra had secured a special post as Spain's commissioner in Havana, where he was responsible for coordinating Ibero-French actions against the British while also safeguarding Spanish interests in the war with Britain.[32]

Saavedra and de Grasse met on board the first-rate *Ville de Paris* (110) on 20 July 1781. The news from de Grasse was grim. The French fleet sailed from Brest in the expectation that a frigate carrying the payroll for Rochambeau and hard currency to pay for expenses of both the French land and sea forces would precede him. That frigate, however, never arrived, neither in North America nor at Cap-Haitien. The ship had suffered massive damage in a gale and limped back into Brest.[33] Neither was there any currency in Santo Domingo – the French governor told de Grasse he was all but bankrupt as the Royal Navy had blockaded the island. For Rochambeau, his financial problems were acute, although he was careful to never fully reveal to Washington just how little money he had. Instead, the general wrote de Grasse of his needs, telling the admiral in a 1 June 1781 letter, 'God grant us safety in our convoy, soldiers and money.'[34] The need for more men, Rochambeau told de Grasse, was nearly as great as the need for funds. 'The four thousand men I have with me is really nothing,' he wrote. 'You do not have to be very tenacious in holding your ground to lose one-third of your force in an infantry action. I repeat and repeat that I need at least 12 battalions, six thousand men at least, and a detachment of cavalry.'[35] Two weeks later Rochambeau was even more pointed, telling de Grasse, 'We are in a dire position. We are in urgent need of more troops, supplies and most of all money. The Continental paper [money] is completely worthless.'[36]

Saavedra listened intently as the French admiral, 'described the stringent circumstances he was in, telling me that the lack of money was making it impossible for him to launch the expedition to the north and that consequently his fleet would remain idle in port, thus losing the opportune juncture for executing an operation apt to hasten an advantageous peace'.[37] The Spaniard never noted in his journal his initial reaction to the news. However, immediately after narrating the admiral's admonition, his journal makes it appear Saavedra made a rapid decision. Although he 'had absolutely no authority'; to fund his expedition, Saavedra suggested de Grasse 'send a frigate to Havana to solicit what money they could'.[38] It was a fateful offer, one the French admiral accepted the following day. In effect, Saavedra had just made the Spanish crown responsible for funding the final step of American independence.

His offer also placed Spain in an awkward position. Poor weather had delayed the usual shipment of silver from Veracruz and gold from Peru via Cartagena in Nueva Granada (Colombia). The Spanish governor of Cuba expected to receive more than one million silver Spanish pesos ($75 million in 2018 dollars), money that was supposed to not only pay the expenses for Puerto Rico and Spanish holdings on Santo Domingo but also to pay, in part, for the attack on Jamaica. Saavedra agreed to lend the French 100,000 pesos of the 500,000 earmarked for Puerto Rico. However, that money would only cover French expenses for the months of July and August – and July was already in arrears. The Spaniard knew he had to do more and noted in his journal that Havana could be the source of more funds.[39]

He also took it upon himself to solve the other French problem – manpower. De Grasse told Saavedra he only planned to take nineteen of his warships north because of the need to defend French Caribbean possessions from the Royal Navy. He also would leave a small division of 3,000 soldiers earmarked for an attack on the Bahamas in the region. De Grasse asked Saavedra whether Spain could lend him four ships of the line to join in the American campaign. Spain, however, had yet to recognise the independence of the United States and Carlos III feared what would happen if he openly supported colonies breaking from their mother country. Instead, Saavedra told de Grasse that Spanish ships would patrol French possessions, provided the admiral took his entire force north. In addition, Spain would release the division of French troops from the Caribbean, nearly doubling the number of men Rochambeau would have in the field. De Grasse agreed to all of the proposals.[40]

Saavedra left for Havana on 2 August, arriving at the city on 15 August 1781. That day he met with the city treasurer, who told him there was no ready cash available in Havana as the ship from Veracruz carrying the silver consignment had yet to arrive. Saavedra, however, knew he had to raise the money somehow. 'A decision urgently had to be made, because without money the Comte de Grasse could do nothing, and to allow him to wait off Mantanzas [a city and bay ninety kilometers north of Havana] for a long time would be to expose his fleet to great danger. It seemed that the best thing to do was to turn once again to the citizenry, making known the urgency of the case, so that each man would give what he could.'[41]

The appeal went out that morning. Within six hours of the appeal, the merchants of Havana had contributed 500,000 silver pesos – $34 million in 2018 US dollars – Saavedra gave the news to de Galvez, who had arrived in Havana only that afternoon. 'He was told of the promptitude with which the 500,000 pesos needed by the Comte de Grasse had been collected and he was delighted.'[42] The fund-raising campaign for American independence became one of the significant events in the history of Spanish Havana. In Cuban folklore, the merchants became like women who donated their jewels to the hallowed cause of freedom.[43] The myth continues to hold sway in Spain and Latin America, even though the actual list of donors still resides today in the Archivos General de Indias in Seville, Spain.[44]

The frigate *Aigrette* arrived the same day the merchants contributed the money. Saavedra presented the specie to the French captain, who accepted it gratefully.[45] The *Aigrette* returned to the French fleet, and on 4 September, de Grasse arrived off the mouth of the Chesapeake. The 3,000 men he brought landed and joined forces with a division of troops in Virginia then under the command of the Marquis de Lafayette. The Franco-American army was then in Philadelphia. Although Admiral Sir Thomas Graves attacked de Grasse on 5 September, the Royal Navy could not save Cornwallis. In six weeks, the

British general surrendered, all but guaranteeing the emergence of the United States as a new nation.[46] And, it was due to Spain and a forgotten hero, Francisco Saavedra de Sagronis.

Just how much the Black Legend plays a part in the lack of knowledge of Spain's contribution to American independence is a matter of debate. Spain, under Carlos III, never publicised its role for fear of what impact it would have on its already restive South American colonies. The role of the *Aigrette* and her delivery of much-needed funds, as well as that of Spain in assuming responsibility for French colonies to allow de Grasse to gain local supremacy of the Chesapeake, faded into obscurity, buried in a revived anti-Hispanism that now includes not just Spaniards, but anyone of Latin blood. It is the best-kept secret of the Georgian Era, one that remains secret today not because of a lack of knowledge, but because of a sixteenth-century prejudice that holds sway in the twenty-first century.

Vice Admiral Francois Joseph Paul, the Comte de Grasse, who commanded the French fleet at Yorktown. De Grasse and Spanish diplomat Francisco Saavedra worked together to finance the campaign that sealed American independence. Oil on canvas by Jean Baptiste Mauzisse. (Courtesy of the National Museum of the Castles of Versailles and Trianon)

Don Francisco Saavedra y Sagronis, see colour plate 7

Sir Andrew Pellet Green:
Vice Admiral Sir Thomas Fremantle's Protégé

Charles A. Fremantle

Andrew Pellet Green was born on 8 September 1777 on his family estate near Bedford, the second son of eight children. He was educated at Butterworth's Naval Academy, Chelsea, until he joined the Royal Navy aged sixteen on 14 April 1793, and went to sea with Captain Thomas Lenox Frederick, who commanded the third-rate HMS *Illustrious* (74). Frederick was a friend of his father, and had achieved fame serving in the West Indies in the American War of Independence. Frederick was later to take part in the Battle of Cape St Vincent in 1797 when he commanded the second-rate HMS *Blenheim* (90), second in the line of battle with

Andrew Pellet Green as a young officer, artist unknown. (Green family collection)

Nelson's third-rate HMS *Captain* (70) thirteenth, but he died in 1799 leaving Green without an influential sponsor. Frederick had married Lucy Boscawen from Lord Falmouth's naval family with connections to the Fremantles.

Illustrious joined Lord Hood's Mediterranean Fleet, and Green's first taste of action was in July 1793 with two French frigates off Toulon. They escaped in the dark, leaving his ship with its sailing master, Stacey, dead and two men wounded. The following day, they captured a French corvette bound for Marseilles from Tunis. They landed their prisoners at Gibraltar, had a short refit, and then joined Hood's fleet at Toulon. Anglo-Spanish forces had occupied the town, but were forced to abandon it on 20 December 1793 after coming under bombardment from Revolutionary French, controlled partly by the young Napoleon Bonaparte. Thomas Fremantle, then a post-captain, in command of the sixth-rate frigate,

HMS *Tartar* (28), was employed in helping to destroy French ships and stores, by which his name might have become known to Green.[1]

Illustrious was next sent to blockade Tunis for a wearisome four months before joining the third-rate HMS *Agamemnon* (64), commanded by Nelson who, with the help of Fremantle and ships' landing parties, was besieging French forces in Bastia, Corsica. The town surrendered on the 22 May 1794. Nelson lost the vision of his eye in a similar operation at Calvi, Corsica, while ashore directing the fire of ships' guns that had been landed to attack fortifications. Fremantle described the Bastia attack in a letter to his brother William.[2]

Illustrious continued with the routines of blockade and convoy escort duties, while Lord Hood was replaced by Vice Admiral Hotham as commander of the Mediterranean Fleet. The French were determined to recapture Corsica, and sent Rear Admiral Pierre Martin with a fleet to probe Hotham's defences. Fremantle had taken command of HMS *Inconstant* (36) in January 1795 and with Nelson's *Agamemnon* formed part of Hotham's fleet when it sailed to defend Corsica. Green and *Illustrious* were also with this fleet.

The French captured the third-rate HMS *Berwick* (64) on 8 March.[3] She had been badly damaged by gales, and was on her own, sailing to Leghorn to affect repairs. She was completely outnumbered and surrendered after her captain was beheaded by a cannonball.

The fleets met on 14 March 1795 with initial action by Fremantle and Nelson resulting in the capture of two French ships of the line, *Ca Ira* (80) and the *Censeur (74),* both of which surrendered to *Illustrious* and the third-rate HMS *Courageux* (74). During the action, *Illustrious* was sandwiched between the French ships and received heavy damage with British casualties of thirty-five dead and ninety-three wounded. The French had fought this battle with their admiral embarked in a frigate as ordered by their government.[4] They had 400 casualties, but the damage to *Illustrious* caused her to founder two days later. Her anchor cables broke in a fierce gale, and she ended up on the rocks of Valence Bay near La Spezia (The Republic of Genoa). Hotham's frigates rescued her crew, including Green. *Courageux,* which had been captured from the French in 1761, also came to a sad end in December 1796, when a gale off Gibraltar blew her onto the rocks off Morocco with the loss of 464 officers and men.

Green became very ill with a fever and had to be hospitalised for four months in Bastia. He then joined the former Frenchman, HMS *Censeur* (74), under the command of Sir John Gore. *Censeur* and Green missed Admiral Hotham's next action off Hyeres, France, on 13 July when English gunnery proved superior to that of the French, who had been instructed to fire red-hot shot and a type of explosive shell projectile, and were thus eight times slower in reloading![5]

Censeur had been jury rigged and was undermanned with both men and armaments, but was given the task of helping to escort the valuable Levant convoy to Britain. Unfortunately *Censeur* and thirty of the merchant ships of the convoy had the misfortune to meet six French ships of the line on 7 October 1795 off Cape St Vincent under Rear Admiral Joseph Richery. The ship was recaptured after a four-hour battle, which used up all her powder, and taken into neutral Cadiz, Spain. Green, now aged seventeen, became a prisoner in the French Ship *Resolution*, where he was treated abominably, but after landing on parole, he returned to Britain and home in December 1795.[6] The captured ships were blockaded in Cadiz by Rear Admiral Mann until August 1796, when Richery's ships sortied from Cadiz and resumed the task of attacking British commerce in the West Indies and Canadian waters. Richery returned to Brest in triumph having captured or destroyed one hundred British merchant vessels!

Green joined the third-rate HMS *Thunderer* (74), under command of Captain Benn, in March 1796. Departing Britain in April, *Thunderer* carried the flag of Sir Hugh Christian, who commanded the escorts to the convoy carrying General Abercrombie's force of 16,000 soldiers. Their orders were to capture the islands of St Lucia, St Vincent, and Grenada in the West Indies. They arrived in Barbados, where orders had been left for them to proceed to St Lucia and land the embarked soldiers and for Christian to assist Abercrombie in the attack. Green participated in the subsequent actions to take the island.

Subsequently, *Thunderer* and Green spent the hurricane season in Port Royal, Jamaica, under the command of Sir Henry Hervey and operated from there for the next four years with Green participating in plenty of boat actions. Spain had joined the war against Britain in October 1796 and thus the French and Spanish colonies in the West Indies and the Americas provided ample work for the Royal Navy. *Thunderer* took part in the Battle of Jean-Rabel on 17 March 1797, when the French frigate *Harmonie* (40) was forced ashore and burnt by her crew.[7] The British captured the corvette *Eveille* (18) on 15 October 1799, and the schooner *Pegasus,* which was flying false United States colours and carrying sixty-eight slaves from Martinique.

Green's boat's actions may have come to the attention of Fremantle's great friend, Admiral Sir Hyde Parker, Commander-in-Chief, Jamaica, whose forces took no fewer than forty-seven armed vessels and 225 merchant ships in a space of eight months during 1799![8] Green's ship lost 800 men and officers, through sickness, which helped to give him rapid promotion to acting lieutenant. He returned to Britain in the third-rate HMS *Brunswick* (74) in 1799 after hearing of the death of his father.

Fremantle took command of the third-rate HMS *Ganges* (74) in August 1800 and requested the appointment of Green as one of his officers. Green joined in

September and endured more blockade work off Brest with the Channel Fleet until February, when the ship was detached to form part of a North Sea Squadron under Hyde Parker, with orders to counter the Armed Neutrality by attacking the Danish Fleet at Copenhagen. *Ganges* was next to Nelson's *Elephant* in the battle but was relatively unscathed. Green would have seen his captain in close consultation with Nelson as they secured peace with the Danes.[9]

Nelson then sent *Ganges* to Russia to negotiate the release of 200 merchant ships impounded at St Petersburg. Green would have found this experience very useful for his later work with the Russians when they became allies against the French.

Ganges was next sent to the West Indies, when the war against France resumed after the Peace of Amiens in 1803. Green was delighted to have Fremantle, his 'excellent and gallant friend', as his commanding officer. He dined ashore with Fremantle and his wife Betsey on 16 August, but was soon moved on to the sixth-rate frigate, HMS *Eurydice* (24), where he came under the command of William Hoste, one of Nelson's favourite officers, and one of the great frigate captains of the Napoleonic wars.

Green was the lieutenant in charge of the frigate's boats in the recapture of the *Lord Elson* in November 1804, and the Prussian ship *Edward* in June 1805. Green was mentioned in Nelson's letter to the Admiralty, which forwarded a report by Hoste of the capture on 6 October 1805 of the Spanish privateer *Muesto La Solidad* (6) with a convoy stating:

> Great praise is due to Lieutenant Green and the officers and men under him, for their exertions, and the gallant manner in which they attacked, whilst under fire from the Spanish ship, taking four of the convoy before *Eurydice* closed with them and captured the Spanish ship.[10]

In his last letter to the Admiralty dated 12 October 1805, Nelson stated that he authorised Green to join the second-rate HMS *Neptune* (98) at Fremantle's and his own request just before the Battle of Trafalgar. Under Fremantle's command, *Neptune* formed part of the weather column, third ship in line behind Nelson's *Victory* (98). With Green aboard, Fremantle steered *Neptune* in support of the flagship, engaging the French flagship *Bucentaure* and the massive Spanish flagship, *Santisima Trinidad*.

He served as third lieutenant and 'Signals Lieutenant' in the battle and thanks to him we have a record of the battle published by Fremantle's grandson Admiral Sir Edmund in 1921.[11] After the battle, Green was in charge of removing 450 prisoners with many wounded from the *Santissima Trinidad* (130), which had surrendered to *Neptune*. His assistant, Lieutenant John Edwards, wrote:

HMS *Neptune* engaged, Trafalgar, 1805 by John Francis Sartorius. In this image, *Neptune*, seen in bow profile, exchanges broadsides with the Spanish *Santisima Trinidad*. In the background to the right, HMS *Conqueror* fires into the dismasted French flagship *Bucentaure*. (Public Domain)

What a sight when we came to remove the wounded, we had to tie the poor mangled wretches round their waists, or where we could, and lower them into the tumbling boats, some without arms, others no legs, and lacerated all over in the most dreadful manner. At about 10 o'clock we had got all out to about 33, which I believe it was impossible to remove without instant death.

For his participation in the battle, Green was awarded the General Service Medal with Trafalgar Clasp.

Collingwood ordered *Neptune* to tow the *Victory* to Gibraltar with Nelson's body. Fremantle took a lock of Nelson's hair and his

Example of General Service Medal with Trafalgar Clasp.

best spying glass, the latter of which was lost when his great grandson Admiral Sir Sydney's flagship HMS *Russell* was mined off Malta during the First World War.

Neptune returned to Britain in November 1806 after a year of blockading duties in the fleet commanded by Collingwood. Green left the ship in 1807, with a spell in charge of a press gang before an assignment to join the staff of Lord Hutchinson, the Minister Plenipotentiary to the Russian Court, as a sort of naval attaché. He missed the Battle of Eylan fought in the snow on 7 February 1807 (when Napoleon was almost defeated), but was to assist the Russian army in Poland with command of the cutter HMS *Favourite*. He and his companion, Lieutenant Hanchett, were taken up the River Eider, and then across country to Copenhagen to collect their ships, with Hanchett getting the *British Fair* instead of another cutter, which had to be repaired. Green was employed assisting the Russian General Karminski in the defence of Danzig. Soult's army took the town, with Green escaping by the skin of his teeth as he left for Pillau in Prussia. He helped to defend this town, and claimed that it was thanks to him that it was the only fortress in Prussia that had not surrendered to the French at the Peace of Tilsit in 1807. Green re-joined Lord Hutchinson at Riga, and travelled with him to Reval, St Petersburg, and Stockholm.

With Russia declaring war against Britain in November 1807, Green took command of HMS *Gleaner* (10) a 153-ton ketch, taken over by the Royal Navy on 12 July 1808. He captured the Danish sloop *Emanuel* on 10 January 1809. Subsequently, he was employed by the Admiralty in carrying confidential dispatches to and from the British forces on the Iberian Peninsula; his duties included taking on board an aide to the French General Junot in order to carry news of the Convention of Cintra to La Rochelle, and thence to Bonaparte. During this mission, *Gleaner* sprang a leak in the Bay of Biscay, and was towed into Santander.

At Santander, Green witnessed the arrival of the Marquis de Romano's Army, which had been transported in British ships from Denmark to assist in the rebellion against French rule in Spain. Green took part in the battle and helped to evacuate English troops after the defeat of the British commander, General Sir John Moore, at Corunna. Green saw Moore five minutes after his death, and carried the dispatches about the battle to Britain. Further voyages with dispatches included news of Wellington's Victory of Bussaco; the dispatches were carried home by Wellington's aide-de-camp, Captain Ulysses Burgh, a friend and colleague of another of Wellington's aides-de-camp, John Fremantle. Fremantle was the nephew of Thomas Fremantle; the son of his elder brother Stephen who died after helping to take Martinique.

Green was promoted to Commander on 1 February 1812 and took command of the new brig HMS *Shamrock* (10) in November. Initially based in the Downs, but then tasked in April 1813 to work with British forces under Captain McKerlie based in Heligoland (an archipelago in the North Sea), they were to assist the Russians, under Colonel Alexander Radlinger, who were besieging Cuxhaven (on the lower Saxony coast, facing the North Sea, at the mouth of the Elbe).[12] Green took command of a squadron consisting of HMS *Hearty, Blazer, Piercer,* and *Redbreast* and nine gunboats. On 28 November, Captain Farquhar arrived in HMS *Desiree* (24) to take command of the squadron. He sent a report to the Admiralty stating:

> I arrived and found Captain Green had collected the squadron to cooperate with the Russian troops ... I ordered the gunboats to take position and to cannonade the enemy battery and to land 10 guns, six 18 pounders, two 32 pounders, and two 6 pounders within 400 yards of the French batteries. When the enemy saw our guns they surrendered. The expedition with which Captains Green and Banks, who had the direction of forming and completing the seamen's battery, performed that *service*, I trust will speak for itself.

The French surrendered 300 officers and men and all their forts, and for his service, Green was made a Knight of the Royal Hanoverian Guelphic Order, and of the Swedish Order of the Sword. Green stayed on as a volunteer with Captain Farquhar, who took his force up the River Elbe to support the Swedes who were fighting the Danes at Gluckstadt, which surrendered on 5 January 1814.[13]

The closing year of the Napoleonic Wars saw Green achieving post rank and the command of the sixth-rate HMS *Wye* (24) on 16 May 1815, carrying the flag of his friend, Rear Admiral Sir Thomas Fremantle as Commander-in-Chief Channel Islands. They launched an invasion with the support of French Royalists under the Duc d'Aumont, landing at Arromanches, Normandy, but by that time Napoleon had been defeated at Waterloo. Fremantle was appointed Commander-in-Chief Mediterranean in 1818 with Green as his flag captain in the second-rate HMS *Rochfort* (80). Green was entrusted with Adolphus Fitzclarence, illegitimate son of the Duke of Clarence, as a midshipman, who followed a naval career like his father (later William IV). One of their cruises near to Mount Etna in eruption is described in Betsey's diary.[14]

Fremantle was promoted to vice admiral in August 1819 and became Sir Thomas Fremantle, Knight Grand Cross of the Bath. He died suddenly in post on 19 December 1819, which left Green with the duty of arranging his funeral and consoling his grieving widow and his eight surviving children, two of whom, Charles[15] and Henry, were serving in the Mediterranean Fleet. The burial was in the Protestant cemetery in Naples, now a school playground.

Green erected a memorial in the Upper Baracca Gardens in Valletta, Malta, which stands to this day. The inscription reads as follows:

> SACRED TO THE MEMORY of Sir Thomas Francis Fremantle, Knight Grand Cross of the Bath, Guelph, Saint Ferdinand and Merit, Saint Michael and Saint George. Knight Commander of Maria Theresa, Baron of the Austrian Empire and Vice Admiral of the Blue, who died at Naples in the Chief Command of His Majesty's Naval Forces in the Mediterranean on 19 December 1819 in the 54th year of his age. This Monument is erected by Captain A P Green and the Officers of His Majesty's Ship Rochfort in which he had his Flag as a testimony of their respect for his character and talents.

Green retired on half pay in May 1820 and married Harriet Cutting. They had five boys and one girl, with the three eldest becoming senior officers in the Army. He joined Colonel John Fremantle[16] as an aide-de-camp to Queen Victoria, and received a knighthood in 1832. He became a rear admiral in 1849, and a vice admiral in 1856 two years before he died at home at the age of eighty-one on 26 December 1858.

The memorial to Vice Admiral Sir Thomas Fremantle in Barrakka Gardens, Valletta, Malta. Admiral Fremantle was the author's great, great grandfather.

HMS *Rochfort* during the internment of Sir Thomas Fremantle, 22 December 1819 at Baia Bay, Naples. (National Maritime Museum, Greenwich, London, and Creative Commons CC-BY-NC-SA-3.0 license, Public Domain)

Andrew Pellet Green as a vice admiral, artist unknown. (Green family collection)

In 2005, Greens and Fremantles came together to celebrate the 200th anniversary of Trafalgar. HRH Princess Anne dedicated the Northmoor Heritage Neptune Wood in Oxfordshire, where more trees were planted to make this one of the thirty-three woods commemorating the battle. The families have kept in touch ever since, with the author of this article being given access to the Green family memorabilia by Keith and Andrew, great, great grandsons of Andrew Pellet Green.

Commander Sir James Pearl

Sean M Heuvel

One of the more notable Canadians who served in the Royal Navy during the Great War with France was Commander Sir James Pearl of Yarmouth, Nova Scotia. A distinguished veteran of the Battle of Trafalgar, where he served as a midshipman in HMS *Neptune* (98) under Captain Thomas Fremantle, Pearl was among a select group of Canadians to receive the honour of knighthood as well as other accolades from the British Crown. However, despite these achievements, promotion in rank was slow in coming for the ambitious Pearl, who made his grievances known to the highest levels within the Royal Navy. Nevertheless, he spent much of his later life as a heroic icon to residents in his native Yarmouth. Overall, Pearl's story is a fascinating portrait of an ambitious Royal Navy hero who was caught up in the military politics of the Royal Navy's late Napoleonic era.

While Pearl is closely associated today with his native Nova Scotia, his family was not originally from that region. Pearl's great-grandfather, John Pearl, left Yorkshire for America in 1670 and later ran a mill in Massachusetts.[1] Pearl's father, David Pearl, was a ship's carpenter who had grown up in Windham, Connecticut. However, as one of fifteen children, David saw little chance for inheritance or opportunity in New England, and therefore departed the region for better prospects in Yarmouth, Nova Scotia, in 1764.[2] While in Yarmouth, David married Eunice Allen, daughter of a distinguished Seven Years' War veteran, in 1769 and subsequently had six children, all born between 1771 and 1784.[3] After several years in the area, David and his family moved sometime after 1784 to New York City, where they began to show up in city records in 1796.[4] His youngest son James was born around 1790, making it difficult to determine whether his birthplace was Yarmouth, or New York, or even somewhere else.[5]

Despite the uncertainty over his place of birth, existing evidence suggests that David and his wife Eunice were minimally involved in their youngest son's life.[6] Instead, James Pearl was raised primarily by his oldest sister, Eunice. Interestingly, the paternal role in young Pearl's life was ultimately played by a young Royal Navy officer named George W. Blamey, who was later elevated to post-captain.[7] Blamey married Eunice in July 1792 and thereafter functioned as a surrogate father, mentor, and close friend to Pearl.[8] Pearl grew up on then-

Lieutenant Blamey's stories of the sea and they likely played a major role in fuelling Pearl's desire to serve in the Royal Navy.

In May 1799 he was entered in the ship's books as a volunteer first class aboard HM sloop *Pheasant* (18) under Blamey's tutelage.[9] Over the next several years, Blamey and Pearl served together aboard several ships (whenever young Pearl had the opportunity to go to sea) as they each advanced steadily in rank, including the sloop *Hawke* (16), the fourth-rate HMS *Assistance* (50), and the third-rate HMS *Leviathan* (74).[10] During this period, the pair served primarily on the Halifax and West Indies stations and Pearl eventually advanced in rank to master's mate and even acting lieutenant.[11] However, it is known that Pearl, having somehow crossed the Atlantic, joined *Neptune* at Portsmouth on 29 October 1802 where, aged twelve, he was immediately rated master's mate, and he served in her, with a short break in the autumn and winter of 1803–04, for the next several years.

The highlight of Pearl's naval service was the Battle of Trafalgar, where under the command of Captain Thomas Fremantle,[12] he was on the poop deck in charge of the signal flags.[13] In that capacity, he would have received Lord Nelson's famous signal, 'England expects that every man will do his duty.'[14] During the battle, *Neptune* was second behind *Victory,* and as she followed the flagship through the Franco-Spanish line of battle, she took on the French flagship *Bucentaure* (80) and later pulled alongside the Spanish four-decker *Santísima Trinidad* (112) – at the time the largest ship in the world – to engage in a fierce combat.[15] From Pearl's exposed position as signal-midshipman, he would have undoubtedly seen intense action, as *Neptune* fought various French and Spanish ships of the line. *Neptune*'s crew were successful, despite suffering considerable material damage,[16] and the loss of forty men.[17] However, fifteen-year-old Pearl was fortunate to come out of the battle completely unscathed.[18] Following Trafalgar, Pearl and the rest of *Neptune*'s crew had the distinction of towing the battle-scarred *Victory*, bearing Lord Nelson's body, to Gibraltar.[19]

A few years after Trafalgar, Lieutenant Pearl served heroically during another ferocious battle on 11 April 1809 along the French coast at Basque Roads (known to the French as Île-d'Aix).[20] At the time, the Channel Fleet under Admiral Lord James Gambier had arrived off the coast of Basque Roads to find a fleet of fourteen heavily protected French ships at anchor.[21] Seizing the opportunity, the admiral ordered Captain Lord Cochrane to lead a daring assault on the French fleet that included eight fire ships.[22] Pearl served aboard one of those fire ships, the former fifth-rate HMS *Mediator* (32), under Captain James Wooldridge.[23] During the operation, he successfully helped guide the ship into the French fleet despite heavy fire.[24] Pearl and his colleagues were then blown out of *Mediator*, with Pearl receiving severe wounds to his head.[25] The operation was a major success, causing significant damage to the French fleet and acute embarrassment to Napoleon, who had proclaimed that such a feat would have been tactically impossible for the British to achieve.[26] However, Pearl was deeply upset following the battle when he learned that, since he did not have sufficient seniority in his existing rank, he would not receive promotion.[27] Although he did receive a £50 sword from the Patriotic Fund, this apparent snub left Pearl deeply embittered.[28]

Pearl's final combat action took place later in 1809, when a disastrous major British expeditionary force attempted to attack the French-held port city of Flushing on Walcheren Island, Holland.[29] During that operation, Pearl served with his old mentor, George Blamey, aboard HM sloop *Harpy* (18) and engaged in heavy fighting with a French flotilla.[30] While the overall British operation was a failure, *Harpy* was successful in her mission and Blamey was awarded with a promotion to post-captain.[31] However, for reasons that are unclear, Pearl was again passed over for promotion despite his heroism in battle.[32] This further fuelled his resentment toward the Royal Navy and prompted him to consider other career opportunities.[33]

From roughly 1810 to 1814, Blamey and Pearl served together once again in *Harpy* and later in HM sloop *Comet* (18) on the Newfoundland Station.[34] Both men were quite taken by St John's and its surrounding areas and Blamey retired there as a post-captain in 1815.[35] Meanwhile, the ambitious Pearl was eager to find opportunities for advancement within the Royal Navy. However, with the Great War drawing to a close, opportunities for command assignments as well as promotion were sparse. Therefore, Pearl began to pursue opportunities for service as a merchant trader. This was a common practice in the peacetime Royal Navy, where officers languishing on half-pay would request a leave of absence to seek their fortunes in the merchant fleet.[36] In Pearl's case, he was approved for leave and spent the next decade in the Orient commanding trading ships. Most notably, he commanded the merchant ship *Indiana*, which traded primarily in the Indo-China seas.[37] Pearl made a fortune there selling textiles, spices, and even opium.[38]

A highlight of Pearl's tenure with *Indiana* occurred on 7 February 1822, when he and his crew saved 190 survivors of a Chinese junk (*Tek Sing*) that had struck a reef and sunk in the Gaspar Strait off the coast of Dutch-controlled Indonesia.[39] For his heroism during this operation, Pearl was later awarded a gold medal by King William I of the Netherlands.[40]

Sadly, this period was also marked by personal heartbreak for Pearl. He had fallen in love and become engaged to a young woman named Lucy Eleanor Kerehappuch Crook, who had died unexpectedly aged twenty-eight on 16 July 1822.[41] Pearl later paid for a small monument to be erected in her honour in

King William I of the Netherlands by Joseph Paelinck c1819.
(Found at https://royal.myorigins.org/p/King_William_I_of_the_Netherlands)

Wiltshire.[42] Following this loss, Pearl participated in the last military engagement of his storied career. In 1824, he volunteered to serve with the British Army during the First Anglo-Burmese War, which broke out after the Burmese seized an island belonging to the East India Company.[43] During that conflict, Pearl served under Brigadier General Joseph W. Morrison and commanded thirty transport ships and 300 boats during the Battle of Arakan in 1825.[44] Pearl later received the repeated thanks of the Government of Bengal for his great services during that campaign.[45]

Following his years of service in the Orient, Pearl returned to Britain in 1826 to plan his next career move. While Pearl had held the position of captain in the merchant fleet and later even owned his own ship, promotion in the Royal Navy continued to elude him.[46] In May 1827, he tried to address this by writing a personal letter to the Duke of Clarence, the 'Sailor King'.[47] The memorial summarised Pearl's career at length and noted his failure to be promoted despite numerous examples of competency and heroism in battle. For instance, reflecting on his aforementioned service at Basque Roads in 1809, among his other achievements, Pearl wrote:

> That your memorialist has never received the slightest reward or consideration from the Admiralty, or His Majesty's government for his services on that memorable occasion … In verification of all of the foregoing statements your Memorialist begs most humbly to refer Your Royal Highness to the official documents hereto annexed. Trusting your Royal Highness will on consideration of his case extend to him your most gracious patronage and protection. And your Memorialist as in duty bound, will ever pray.[48]

In response, the Admiralty promoted Pearl to the rank of commander in September 1827 and, following a short stint as commanding officer of the schooner HMS *Starling* (14), he retired from active service altogether.[49] Despite Pearl's long naval service, his advancement prospects were limited by various technicalities and the challenges inherent in earning promotion in the peacetime Royal Navy.

With his naval service behind him, Pearl sailed for Nova Scotia in summer 1828, where he endeavoured to try his luck with farming.[50] He returned to London in spring 1829 to marry Anne Hawkins, before permanently settling in St John's, Newfoundland, in November of that year.[51] In St John's, the Pearls enjoyed life among its upper crust of society, and travelled in social circles that included the governor, Captain Sir Thomas John Cochrane (with whom he had served with at the attack on the Basque Roads).[52] During this period, Pearl

King William IV as Lord High Admiral: 1827 print by William James Ward after Abraham Wivell's painting. (Wikipedia Commons)

continued to nurse his resentment toward the Admiralty for his lack of promotion and believed that the 1,000 acres of land[53] granted to him were small compensation for his limited advancement in rank.[54] As such, during a November 1830 visit to Britain, Pearl began to lobby for a knighthood among his network of contacts who worked for the Crown.[55] While this endeavour raised the eyebrows of several of Newfoundland's leading citizens, it may have laid the groundwork for his appointment to the Royal Guelphic Order (in the rank of knight) by Clarence, who had become King William IV, in 1836.[56]

Two years later, Pearl was also invested as a knight bachelor by Queen Victoria.[57] At some point during this period, Pearl was also invested as a knight in the Order of St John of Jerusalem.[58] Oddly, news of these accolades never reached the Newfoundland newspapers or *The Times* in London, which routinely reported such knightings.[59] This is even more intriguing considering that Pearl would have been the only knighted person in Newfoundland at the time, and that the Pearl family's other social activities were routinely reported by local newspapers at the time.[60]

During his twilight years, Pearl was actively involved in raising and educating his nieces and nephew – he never had children of his own – and spent most of his time on his estate, known as Mount Pearl. [61] He died on 13 January 1840 following a short illness and was buried with full military honours.[62] Pearl's wife, Lady Anne, remained in Canada for only a few more years, returning to London in 1844, where she passed away a decade later.[63] Pearl's estate was ultimately destroyed in a fire, but the modern-day city of Mount Pearl later developed around the original property. It serves as a fitting tribute to this most fascinating Royal Navy officer.

While Pearl did not achieve the full recognition that he felt he deserved, he led a remarkable seafaring life that is most worthy of further study. He will continue to serve as one of the more compelling examples of Canadians who served in the Royal Navy during the Great War 1792–1815.

Captain John Houlton Marshall

Lisa L. Heuvel and John Rodgaard

John Houlton Marshall (1768–1837) served in twenty-one ships including the first-rate HMS *Britannia* (100) at the Battle of Trafalgar.[1] He was born on 9 October 1768 in Halifax, Nova Scotia, a port that had gained prominence beginning in the Seven Years' War (French and Indian War, 1756–63) as the Navy's North American base. The son of Mary and Elias Marshall, he had an early connection to ships: his father rose from carpenter's apprentice in 1752 to carpenter's mate and carpenter, achieving the position of Master Shipwright of HM Careening[2] Yard, Halifax, in 1793.

When Marshall was aged ten, his name was placed on the muster books of the sloop-of-war HMS *Albany* (16), while she was stationed in Halifax in 1778.[3] *Albany*, formerly an American vessel named *Rittenhouse,* was captured in 1776 during the American War of Independence.[4] Most likely, Marshall continued on the ship's muster until the ship was broken up in 1780.[5] His appointment was, in all probability, an arrangement between his father as a shipwright in the

The Commissioner's House in Halifax Naval Yard.

dockyard and the ship's captain. It does not appear that Marshall had a prominent patron during this period in his naval service.

His name appears again, as one of her midshipmen, in January 1782, on the books of the sixth-rate frigate HMS *Hussar* (26), another former American, *Protector*, which had been captured by the fifth-rate frigate HMS *Roebuck* (44) in May 1780.[6] The family record shows that the fourteen-year-old Marshall left the ship in June that year and remained at Halifax until he was entered in the books of the transport *Assistance* as an able seaman in July 1784. He continued aboard *Assistance* until transferring to the sixth-rate frigate HMS *Ariadne* (20) and once more as a midshipman.[7]

In June 1787, he transferred to the fourth-rate HMS *Leander* (52) and remained in this ship on the American Station through July 1788, when he transferred to the sloop-of-war HMS *Brisk* (16). There he remained under the command of Captain Edward Buller for the next seventeen months, until, in February 1790, he was transferred to the fourth-rate HMS *Adamant* (50), flagship of Vice Admiral Sir Richard Hughes. It was Hughes, as commander of the West Indies station in 1783, who was criticised by one of his captains, Horatio Nelson, for suspending the Navigation Acts to allow trade with the United States. Captain Nelson told his admiral that he did not have the legal power to do so, and was critical of Hughes for not living in 'the style of a British admiral … he does not give himself that weight that I think an English admiral ought to do'.[8]

Marshall's sojourn in the flagship continued until he was transferred to the fifth-rate frigate, HMS *Alligator* (28) when she arrived in Halifax in September 1791.[9] Under the command of Captain Isaac Coffin, Marshall was the frigate's sailing master for just one month, and in December 1791 he was appointed to the recently rebuilt fifth-rate frigate HMS *Winchelsea* (32) as a master's mate on the American and West Indies stations until August 1793.[10] Marshall left this familiar part of the world later that year for the Mediterranean.

Sailing in the store ship and former fifth-rate frigate HMS *Gorgon* (44) as a supernumerary, he joined Admiral Hood's flagship, *Victory*, at Toulon. Hood's fleet and British, Spanish, Neapolitan and Sardinian soldiers had occupied the home of the French Mediterranean fleet and were under siege by Republican French forces. Marshall probably participated in the withdrawal of allied forces and the evacuation of the city in December of 1793, and was transferred to the sixth-rate frigate HMS *Ariadne* (24) on 30 June 1794. While on board *Ariadne*, he was promoted to lieutenant on 13 July 1794.

Marshall returned to the West Indies Station in *Ariadne* where, in December 1795, he was appointed to the third-rate HMS *Scipio* (64) as her first lieutenant. Early in 1796, Marshall received his new commanding officer, fellow North American, Captain Francis Laforey. Aboard *Scipio*, both North Americans sailed under the command of Laforey's father, Admiral Sir John Laforey, commander of the Leeward Islands Station. During his time as *Scipio*'s first lieutenant, Marshall saw action in Admiral Laforey's campaign, resulting in the capture of the Dutch South American colonies of Demerara, Essequibo, and Berbice.[11] With the success of the campaign, Marshall sailed *Scipio* back to Britain, where she was paid off in 1796.[12]

With *Scipio* paid off, Marshall was appointed to the third-rate HMS *America* (64), operating on the North Sea. In January 1798, he then joined the fifth-rate frigate HMS *Naiad* (38), under the command of Captain William Pierrepoint, which was fitting out at Limehouse on the Thames prior to her commissioning on 27 February 1798.[13] Pierrepoint would prove to be a very successful frigate captain in *Naiad,* taking numerous prizes between April and September 1799. As *Naiad*'s first lieutenant, Marshall benefited from considerable prize money, and more was to come. Under Pierrepoint's command, Marshall first distinguished himself when *Naiad,* together with three fifth-rates, *Ethalion* (38), *Triton* (32) and *Alcmene* (32), was cruising in loose company off Cape Finisterre in October 1799. *Naiad* spotted two frigates and, after a chase, the Spanish *Santa Brigida* and *Thetis* were captured, together with millions of pounds worth of cargo and Spanish reales.[14]

When captured, *Santa Brigida* alone yielded a rich cargo of indigo, sugar, annatto,[15] various drugs, and close to 1.5 million Spanish reales, while *Thetis*' cargo consisted of cocoa, sugar, cochineal and 1.3 million Spanish reales. The prize money was paid to officers and seamen on 14 January 1800 with Marshall's share coming to just over £5,000.[16] In his after-action report, Pierrepoint specifically mentioned Marshall: 'I profited by the able assistance of J. H. Marshall, my First Lieutenant, to whom I have given charge of the prize.'[17] Marshall sailed *Santa Brigida* to Britain. He continued to distinguish himself aboard *Naiad*. In a dispatch written by *Naiad*'s new commanding officer, Captain W. H. Ricketts on 17 May 1801, to Admiral William Cornwallis, he briefly described a cutting-out expedition led by Marshall:

> Sir,—The boats belonging to the *Naiad* and *Phaeton*, manned by volunteer officers, seamen, and marines, under the direction of Lieutenant Marshall, highly distinguished themselves on the night of the 16th instant, by the capture of *l'Alcudia*, and destruction of *El Raposo*, armed Spanish packets, in the port of Marin, near Pontevedra, under the protection of a five-gun battery, 24-pounders, prepared to receive them. *L'Alcudia*, the largest, commanded by a very old lieutenant in His Catholic Majesty's service, was moored stem and stern close to the fort, and her sails had been sent on shore the

preceding day. This service was undertaken from information that she was a corvette of 22 guns. I am happy to state, that four men only, belonging to the two ships, were wounded.[18]

Marshall left *Naiad* on 19 October 1799, and did not receive another ship until 4 July 1803, when he reported aboard the third-rate HMS *Magnificent* (74) as first lieutenant.[19] He was in *Magnificent* when the 74 was operating with the blockading squadron off Brest, France. Marshall survived the sinking of *Magnificent* when she was wrecked off of Brest on 25 March 1804. The Scottish marine artist John Christian Schetky captured the sinking in his painting *Loss of The Magnificent, 25 March 1804*.[20]

On 13 July 1804, Marshall was assigned to *Britannia,* later to serve as her second lieutenant at Trafalgar.[21] As the oldest ship in Nelson's fleet, *Britannia*'s nickname was 'Old Ironsides'.[22] She was the flagship of Rear Admiral William Carnegie, Earl of Northesk, third in command of the British fleet. At Trafalgar, when *Britannia* took up her position in Nelson's weather column, Marshall's position in the ship would have given him an excellent view of how the battle developed and evolved. Northesk wrote of *Britannia's* battle:

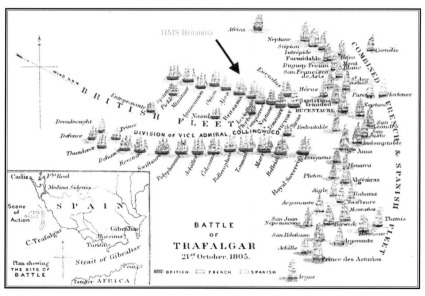

The Battle of Trafalgar showing the positions of the British Fleet and the combined French and Spanish Fleet. The annotation on the position of HMS *Britannia* was added by the authors. This map was originally published by William Blackwood and Sons, Edinburgh and London, 1848.

On passing through the line [the French/Spanish line], and hauling up, she was the fourth ship of the van division in action, (*Victory*, *Temeraire*, and *Neptune,* alone preceding her), and, in a short space of time, completely dismasted a French ship of 80 guns ... She afterwards singly engaged, and kept at bay, three of the enemy's van ships, that were attempting to double upon Lord Nelson's flagship ...[23]

Marshall gave a fuller account of the battle and its aftermath:[24]

Britannia, Gibraltar Bay, November 29, 1805
My Dear Father,

As I am aware that a variety of reports may be in circulation, I take the first conveyance since our Arrival at this Port, to inform you The Almighty has blessed his Majesty's Fleet with a Glorious Victory – over the Combined Force of France and Spain. On the 21 October we attacked the Enemy in two Divisions. The Larboard led by Vice Admiral Collingwood, Commenced this glorious Battle – the sight was Animating to every Seaman to see with what determined Bravery he forced their Line.

It appears from the French Admiral's (Villeneuve) statement, that at the time they put to Sea, he had no Idea our force were more than 21 Sail of the Line, as he well knew we had a Squadron off Carthagena, at least Six sail – therefore flattered himself, that with 33 of the Line, he might venture to give us Battle with some prospect of success. But he has had the modesty to say from the Specimen we gave him, he is now satisfied – that allowed we had been, but 21, the event would [have] been the same, as it was impossible to resist the Attack.

We have certain information that an Admiral arrived at Cadiz the morning after they sailed, to supersede Villeneuve. It is likely he was aware of this and had determined to try the event of a Battle. After the Action we had a continued Gale from the South-West, therefore were obliged to destroy most of the Captured Ships, some Burnt, others Sunk, and many Wrecked. Thus, has terminated the exertions of this Once daring Force – who had threatened to Annihilate us, if we continued the blockade of Cadiz. How the pride of those French Rascals must be humbled, to see our Ships at Anchor Triumphant off their Harbour.

The Spaniards I sincerely Pity – they are an Honorable Enemy. The conduct of the Governor at Cadiz, is truly Noble. When a Truce was established for the purpose of sending the wounded prisoners on shore, he wrote to the Admiral, saying – as he knew the Accommodation for wounded at Gibraltar was by no means adequate to receive the number we must have, requested the Admiral to send any number of English to Cadiz he thought proper, that every attention should be given and when recovered, they should be sent back to the Fleet. We have four Seamen in Cadiz Hospital at this moment, wounded on board one of the Captured ships when wrecked near that Port. The officer with the party has said the greatest attention is paid to their Comforts.

The loss of our ever to be lamented Chief [Lord Nelson], has been severely felt by all the Fleet, and as a mark of their high esteem, propose to erect a Monument to his Memory near some Naval Arsenal. The subscription to be confined to the Officers and Men serving lately under his Orders. I enclosed you a Copy of the public Letter of Thanks together with a list of the Captured Ships, which I believe [corrected] Our loss on Board Britannia, 10 Killed and 41 Wounded, among the former is Lieutenant [Francis] Roskruge, Navy. I wrote you very fully immediately after the Action, enclosed to Mr. Page, which letters I hope will go by the December Mail from Falmouth.

My Affectionate Love to my Dear Mother, Sisters, & Brothers,

Believe me, truly your Son.
J. H. Marshall
P.S. The Enemy's ships, in general, were totally dismasted. After the Action we endeavoured to get them in Tow, but the Gale increasing, it was with much difficulty (I assure you) we could take the prisoners out and Destroy them [the ships]. Many of our Boats and Crews were lost in this service. Divine providence protected our Fleet. At one time inevitable destruction appeared our fate, but our crippled ships Anchored and were fortunate in riding out the Gale, many, not four Miles from the shore. Our ship was under reefed Courses for two days – Main Yard shot through the slings, and three shot in the Bowsprit, two within the rigging. However, we fished the latter and got safe to Gibraltar, where we are now refitting and Hope soon to go to England.

Marshall was one of thirty men and boys who fought at Trafalgar, serving from what is now considered Atlantic Canada.[25] As recognition of his service at Trafalgar, Marshall received £65 11s 5d prize money and an additional £161 as a Parliamentary Award.[26] Returning to Britain, Marshall left *Britannia* in 1806, but, unlike Northesk who was never employed at sea again, he obtained a berth

Saint Lucia 2005 commemorative postage stamp featuring
HMS *Britannia* in action against *Bucentaure*.

in the third-rate HMS *Atlas* (74) on 25 August the same year.[27] Back in the Mediterranean, *Atlas* became the flagship of Rear Admiral Purvis and Marshall would remain with her until she returned to Britain early in 1807.

Marshall's next appointment, on 11 February, was to the North Sea and the Baltic as the first lieutenant in HMS *Majestic* (74), a third-rate veteran of the Battle of the Nile. He continued with her through the end of 1809, when he then transferred to the second-rate HMS *St George* (98) in March 1810. The *St George* was the flagship of Rear Admiral Robert Carthew Reynolds, who became second in command of the Baltic Fleet under the command of Vice Admiral James Saumarez. Marshall had an excellent opportunity to observe the operations of the Baltic Fleet in its attempt to protect British trade and in operating successive blockades of German ports that were under French control. However, his tenure as the *St George*'s first lieutenant was a short one. He left in July.

Marshall returned to Britain and was originally slated to be without orders for the rest of the year. An exception was made, however, for this Trafalgar veteran, when he became the first lieutenant of another Trafalgar veteran, the third-rate HMS *Africa* (64). It appears this appointment was made specifically so that Marshall could be promoted to commander on 21 October, the fifth anniversary of the Battle of Trafalgar.[28]

Marshall finally received a command of his own with the Cruizer-class brig-sloop HMS *Halcyon* (18), which he commissioned on 13 July 1813. *Halcyon* escorted convoys to the West Indies during the War of 1812. Unfortunately, while procuring supplies in Annotto Bay, Jamaica, *Halcyon* was wrecked on a reef on 22 June 1814. Fortunately, all officers and crew were saved.[29] Marshall returned to Britain in 1814. *Halcyon* was Marshall's last at-sea appointment, as his own Memorandum of Service shows. This must have been a disheartening episode for such an experienced sea officer, who spent so many years at sea. He later took up residence in Britain and apparently never returned to Halifax. Marshall was finally promoted to captain on the retired list. He died at his home on Charlotte Street, London, on 2 May 1837 and was buried in Catacomb 29 at Kensal Green Cemetery. His wife, Mary Helen Marshall, died on 12 July 1850 and is buried with him in the same tomb.

Portrait of Commander John Houlton Marshall (artist unknown), on display at Province House, in Halifax, the meeting place of the Nova Scotia House of Assembly since 1819.

In a small way, Marshall's legacy is very much alive for naval historians. He wrote at least two letters to his father after Trafalgar, in which he describes that battle and Nelson's death. These documents, along with Admiral Cuthbert Collingwood's official account, represent significant first-person reports of the Battle of Trafalgar.[30] Today, Marshall's known letters can be found in the Nova Scotia Archives; his portrait is located at Province House, Nova Scotia, a gift to the Nova Scotia Historical Society.[31]

Loss of the Magnificent, see colour plate 8

Plate 1. *Nelson in conflict with a Spanish launch, 3 July 1797*, Richard Westall, 1806.
(National Maritime Museum)

Plate 2: *Apotheosis of Nelson*, Scott Pierre Legrand, *c*1805–18.
(National Maritime Museum)

Plate 3. *Immortality of Nelson,* oil on canvas by Benjamin West, 1807. Nelson's lifeless body is elevated, in both a physical and metaphorical sense. (National Maritime Museum)

Plate 4. *Tobias Smollett,* 1721–71, at the age of about forty-three, by Nathaniel Dance-Holland, 1764. (Yale Center for British Art)

Plate 5. Prostitutes coming aboard ship. Thomas Rowlandson (British, 1756–1827) 'Cattle Not Insurable,' published 1809. (Rosenwald Collection, Open Access) https://www.nga.gov/collection/art-object-page.31821.html accessed 2/8/2020.

Price One Shilling Coloured

Plate 6. *Rear Admiral Horatio Nelson* by Lemuel Francis Abbott, 1799, detail showing buttons with fouled anchor.

Plate 7. Don Francisco Saavedra y Sagronis, Spanish soldier, diplomat and intelligence agent, who made the victory at Yorktown possible. Saavedra ensured the financing for both the French and American forces that trapped the British at Yorktown, and made reinforcements available to Vice Admiral the Comte de Grasse and Lieutenant General the Comte de Rochambeau.
(Courtesy of the Museo Nacional del Prado, Madrid)

Plate 8. *Loss of the Magnificent*
by John Christian Schetky, 1839.
(Royal Museums Greenwich)

Plate 9. Portrait of Sir Home
Popham in lieutenant's uniform
by unknown artist.
(Wikipedia Commons)

Plate 8. Portrait of Mrs M.A.T. Whitby, principal beneficiary of Cornwallis' will (two versions). (Courtesy of Mrs Alice Loftie)

Plate 9. Memorial window at All Saints Church, Milford, dedicated on 5 July 2019 to Cornwallis and Captain John Whitby; also to Admiral Robert Man and Rear Admiral John Peyton. (Photograph courtesy of Paul French, Southpoint Films Ltd (two versions))

Admiral
Sir William Cornwallis
1744 1819

Admiral
Robert Man
1745-1813

Rear Admiral
John Peyton
1752 1809

With fame and honour and respect well blest
'Midst Milford's lichen'd graves they now may rest'

Captain
John Whitby
1774-1806

Captain Ralph Willett Miller

Gerald Holland

Born in 1762, Ralph Willett Miller was a native of New York City, descending from a family who had been part of English colonial society since 1629 when his great-grandfather, Thomas Willett, arrived in Plymouth Colony. Over the next twenty-five years, Thomas Willett established himself as a trusted agent working for the Plymouth trading post in the land now known as the state of Maine. He married Mary Brown and relocated to the area of Narragansett Bay, where he continued his rise in society as a merchant and Plymouth Colony's chief military officer. Conducting extensive trading with New Amsterdam, in September 1664 he helped contribute to the surrender of New Amsterdam to the English through his fluency in Dutch and his established trade relationship with New Amsterdam.[1] A year later, in June 1665, upon the naming of New York, Thomas Willett was appointed the city's first mayor, serving two terms (1665–66 and 1667–68). By the time of the War of American Independence, Ralph Willett Miller's immediate family, who remained loyal to the Crown, was forced from New York. His parents, along with his brother and two sisters, fled to Britain, where Miller was sent to study at the Royal Navy Academy.

Entering the Royal Navy at the age of sixteen in 1778, Miller sailed aboard the fourth-rate HMS *Ardent* (64), the flagship of Rear Admiral James Gambier. Seeing action in several engagements against the American and French navies, including the battle at Fort Royal in Martinique in April 1781, he was wounded three times.[2] After the battle, he was rapidly promoted to lieutenant by Admiral George Rodney. As a lieutenant, Miller served aboard the third-rate HMS *Terrible* (74) that fought against the French fleet under the command of Rear Admiral the Comte de Grasse at the Battle of the Capes on 5 September 1781. During that battle, the *Terrible* was so badly damaged that she was scuttled on 11 September. With the end of the 'American War' came a lull in Miller's service. Placed on half pay, he would not return to active sea service until 1793, when he would join the second-rate HMS *Windsor Castle* (98), the flagship of Vice-Admiral Phipps Cosby in the Mediterranean.

During the summer of 1793, French royalist forces had driven out the revolutionaries from the Mediterranean port of Toulon. The royalists requested support from Britain, Spain and two monarchies; the Kingdom of the Two Sicilies and that of Piedmont sent elements of their respective armies to what become known as the Siege of Toulon. On 28 August 1793, an Anglo-Spanish naval force, carrying a multinational ground force, entered the port. *Windsor Castle* was one of the British ships of the line comprising Admiral Sir Samuel Hood's squadron. French revolutionary forces laid siege to the port and by December, the royalist occupation was on the verge of collapsing. By this time Miller was assigned to Commodore Sir Sydney Smith. On 16 December, French revolutionary forces launched an assault that took the forts overlooking the port. With the French controlling the high ground, the allies began a general evacuation.

Admiral Hood ordered Commodore Smith to destroy the naval arsenal and French fleet to keep these assets out of French Revolutionary possession. Ever the one to volunteer for hazardous duty, Miller single-handedly boarded a French warship and set it afire. As he attempted to escape the inferno, he lost his footing and narrowly escaped drowning. Eagerly awaiting a promotion for his feats, Miller wrote to his father that, 'At all events I shall enjoy the noble reward of knowing that I have done essential good to my country, which I have served with all my heart and all my soul.'[3] The following summer of 1794, Miller found himself assigned to HMS *Victory* (104).

By 1796, Miller had been promoted to post-captain, and was selected to serve directly under Lord Nelson as his flag-captain aboard the warship of the same moniker, the third-rate HMS *Captain* (74). His first action serving under Lord Nelson came at the Battle of Cape St Vincent against the Spanish fleet on 4 February 1797. During this battle, Nelson's flag ship lost its foremast and had her wheel shot away.[4] Miller's expert seamanship was on full display when he was ordered by Nelson to wear out of the line in order to cut off the Spanish fleet. When the *Captain* was in position, Nelson ordered Miller to send over his crew and after an intense hand-to-hand fight, the Spanish surrendered. At one point during the melee, Nelson was forced to direct Miller to remain on board the *Captain*, as he was attempting to join the boarding crew.

Summer of 1797 found Nelson and Miller aboard the third-rate HMS *Theseus* (74). Their first action came with the assault on Cadiz, Spain, in an attempt to force Spanish Admiral José Mazarredo to depart the harbour for safety. Defending themselves with gunboats and smaller ships, the Spanish forced Nelson's fleet to abandon the siege. Following the failed siege of Cadiz, Nelson and his squadron shifted to Santa Cruz. Through the course of the attack against Santa Cruz, which included an amphibious assault, Miller led 'a forced march or rather scramble up a tremendous hill without a path and full of rocks and loose stones'. Despite the effort by his men, Miller was forced to withdraw due to 'hunger, thirst, fatigue, and sickness'.[5] The following evening, Nelson personally led the assault against the city, leading to his being wounded and resulting in the amputation of his right arm. Of the failed assault, Miller wrote in an angered tone that he was 'not surprised' that 'men unassisted by the high sense of honour, and that rational courage which causes officers to prefer death to shame, should have as a body behaved indifferently through the night' but that there were those who conducted themselves with 'great dignity'.[6]

With Nelson returning to Britain for recuperation, Miller assumed command of the *Theseus*. Returning in April 1798, Nelson resumed command with orders to find and destroy the French fleet. The result was the battle at Aboukir Bay (the Battle of the Nile) on 1 and 2 August 1798. During the battle, *Theseus* sustained considerable damage as eight large shot had found their mark against her hull and Miller was wounded in the face. In a letter home to his wife regarding the battle, Miller stated that the *Theseus* was 'in the most perfect order'.[7] With the victory in hand, Nelson directed Miller to sail the captured French prizes for Britain. However, at Gibraltar, Miller was turned back for Levant. He was needed to help thwart the continued threat levelled by Napoleon Bonaparte and his army.

Portrait of Ralph Willett Miller from the series of fifteen cameo portraits in Victors of the Nile, engraving by John Landseer, Robert Bowyer, Robert Smirke and William Bromley.
(Royal Museums Greenwich, Public Domain)

Upon his return, to Levant, Miller was assigned to Sir Sidney Smith once again, where he was tasked with collecting unexploded French ordnance to be refurbished for use by the British. Smith, in a letter to Lord St Vincent, wrote that Miller had 'been in the practice of collecting such of the enemy's shells as fell on the town without bursting, and of sending them back to the enemy better prepared and with the evident effect'.[8] On 14 May 1799, with a stockpile of French ordnance aboard *Theseus*, Miller was preparing the shells for use when an explosion occurred. The result was the killing or wounding of nearly eighty men, including Miller.

Sir Sidney Smith received word of the explosion from Lieutenant England, who described the incident in a letter the day after Miller's death:

> It is with extreme concern I have to acquaint you, that yesterday morning, at half-past nine o'clock, twenty 36-howitzer shells, and fifty 18-pounder shells, had been got up and prepared ready for service by Captain Miller's order, the ship then close off Caesarea, when in an instant, owing to an accident that we have not been able to discover, the whole was on fire, and a dreadful explosion took place. The ship was immediately in flames: in the main rigging and mizzen-top, in the cock-pit, in the tiers, in several places about the main deck, and in various other parts of the ship. Our loss from the explosion I here lament, has been very great; and Captain Miller, I am sorry to add, is of the number killed.[9]

Learning of the explosion and death of his shipmate, Nelson wrote, 'he is not only a most excellent and gallant officer, but the only truly virtuous man that I ever saw'.[10] At the suggestion of Captain Berry, Nelson proposed a monument to his fallen brother. In his plea, he wrote, 'I much doubt if all the admirals and captains will subscribe to poor dear Miller's monument; but I have told Davison, that whatever is wanted to make up the sum, I shall pay.'[11] Through the pleas of Nelson and others, a monument was erected to Miller's memory at St Paul's Cathedral. Miller's widow received a pension of £100 for the remainder of her life and his two daughters £25 per year until the day they married.[12]

The Popham Code Controversy

Chris Coelho

In early October 1805, en route to his invasions of Cape Town and Buenos Aires, Captain Sir Home Riggs Popham anchored his fleet in Funchal Roads, Portugal. Once onshore, his men drank 'madeira and water by the bucket, and devoured grapes by the bushel'. During the respite, Captain Fletcher Wilkie of the 38th (1st Staffordshire) Regiment of Foot took time to critique Popham, 'I should certainly say that he was not what is called one of Nelson's sailors.' Neither was he 'a soldier on board ship'. During his career, Sir Home never fought a battle at sea – he avoided them religiously – but he was famous, as Wilkie noted, for having made 'considerable improvements and given greater scope to the code of telegraphic signals'.[1] Nelson himself was about to use the Popham code to send his legendary pre-battle signal at Trafalgar: 'England expects that every man will do his duty.' The signal went down in history, but the bitter political fight that centred on the use of the new flag code at Trafalgar has been forgotten.

Popham's Background

Popham was a gambler, a 'dasher', a 'modern Pizarro', an argonaut, a fiddler, a filibuster, a raider, a buccaneer and a freebooter. Contemporaries referred to his 'money-getting spirit'. While Horatio Nelson sailed for glory, Home Popham swept for gold. For Sir Home, no scheme was too petty nor too great. Buenos Aires was to be his greatest adventure, as he captured nearly 30 tons of silver in prize money. And thanks to friends in high places, Popham's signal code was to be another lucrative project. The Navy Board eventually paid him £2,000 for his efforts (relative value today of about £120,000).[2]

Popham was a master of the art of patronage. His most powerful protectors were King George III's youngest son, the Duke of York, and Henry Dundas, 1st Viscount Melville. It was Prime Minister William Pitt who sent him to Cape Town. Popham's connections were invaluable in his rise in the Royal Navy. Involved in scandals throughout his career, Popham was ultimately able to defend himself from a position of strength, as a member of the House of Commons.

By way of an introduction to Popham's flag code: fifteen years before Trafalgar, the Royal Navy adopted Lord Richard Howe's *Signal Book for the*

Ships at War. Howe had originally developed his book during the War of American Independence. It simplified previous systems developed by other British admirals, by assigning a flag to each of the numerals 0 to 9. The Admiralty issued an official edition in 1799.

But the range of available signals was limited to those in the official book. As Captain of the fourth-rate HMS *Romney* (50) in the North Sea fleet, Sir Home Popham took it upon himself to test an adaptable signal code, which he printed in 1800.[3] In 1803 he published a more sophisticated second edition, entitled *Telegraphic Signals or Marine Vocabulary*. He wrote that his *Vocabulary* was '... by no means intended to interfere with the established signals'. He explained, 'It frequently however happens that officers wish to make communications of very essential moment far beyond the capacity of the established signals, and it is presumed that this Vocabulary will afford such convenience.'[4]

Using the existing flags and Popham's new system, naval officers could now send any message they chose and answer freely. The crew hoisted one to four flags that signalled a number from 1 to 3,000. Each number corresponded to a letter of the alphabet, a word, or a pre-set sentence, as listed in the guide. The sequence of lifts, however many needed, revealed the communication. In 1805, both the *Signal Book* and Popham's *Vocabulary* were in use. (Regarding the actual flags, the Admiralty had been forced to rearrange them following the capture of an unauthorised copy of the *Signal Book* by the enemy. In January 1804, Lord Nelson sent his officers 'a painted copy of the flags as now altered' to be pasted on page fourteen of their signal books.)

At Trafalgar, the flag officer on the *Victory* used the old *Signal Book* to send Nelson's final message, *Engage the Enemy More Closely* (Made with a single hoist of Flag No. 1: a blue cross on a white field, over No. 6: horizontal blue, white and red stripes.) For Nelson's pre-battle message, the flag officer used the Popham code. The Admiral had wanted to say, 'England confides that every man will do his duty'. But this sentence would have required *nineteen* separate hoists since 'confides' and 'duty' were not in Popham's book and had to be spelled out. By suggesting 'expects' in place of 'confides', Nelson's flag officer reduced the number of lifts. But the naval historian William G. Perrin later complained, 'The sentiment of the signal had been sufficiently spoilt by the substitution of "expects" for "confides".'[5] Checking the signal book, we see that Popham did include the word 'trusts'. Why the flag officer did not suggest 'trusts' is a mystery. (Perhaps he was less confident in the fleet than Nelson.) The last word in the message had to be spelled out either way.

The fact that Popham failed to include the word 'duty' in a naval code is characteristic of the man. Home Popham was born in Gibraltar in 1762. His mother died a few hours after his birth. His father was the British general consul

Nelson's signal at Trafalgar (Almay Stock Photo)

in Tétouan, Morocco, on the other side of the strait. Part of his father's job was to recover people and property lost to pirates and shipwrecks. The emperor expected valuable gifts in return for releasing enslaved seamen, and with his inadequate stipend, Joseph Popham fell into debt. He was recalled in disgrace when his son was seven and died five years later.[6] As his father had been badly mistreated by government, Home never felt a sense of duty to country.

Home Popham joined the service during the American War of Independence and in 1780 was present at the Battle of Cape St Vincent. He was a midshipman on HMS *Hyaena* (24), one of the smallest frigates in the victorious British squadron. But positioned behind eighteen ships of the line, it was said the *Hyaena* never fired her guns.

Ten years after joining the navy, on half-pay and with an empty purse, Lieutenant Home Popham took leave to join a trading syndicate based in Belgium. English merchants operating out of Ostend sent ships flying the imperial flag of Austria to the East India Company's exclusive territory. For illegal traders, Ostend offered the singular commercial advantage of duty-free inward and outward traffic. In March 1787, in requesting furlough, Popham promised the Admiralty he would not stop at any Company settlements in India. He claimed his destination was the Dutch colony of Fredericknagore [Serampore], upriver from Calcutta. Located near the seat of British government in Bengal, this place was said to swarm with 'adventurers of every nation [and] jacobins of every description … it is the asylum of all our public defaulters and debtors'.[7]

Popham later declared an accident on the voyage out – his 'ship struck on an unknown rock' near Mozambique – forced him to go to Bombay for repairs.[8] Popham had a good trip, both financially and romantically. He got married in Calcutta and, returning to Europe, set up his household in Ostend.

In planning a second trip to India, Popham did not bother to renew his leave and the Admiralty dropped him from the lieutenant's list. He was out of the navy. On this voyage he sailed under a Tuscan flag with 'false and fictitious papers' provided by a Leghorn (Livorno) firm for a fee. Included in the arrangement were the services of the necessary flag captain, a man named Francis Coppi.[9]

But in Calcutta in mid-July 1791, Coppi came up missing. Some thought he was about to inform on Popham following a dispute. One of Home's trading partners said he did not want to see the 'bare-faced Italian' unless the man was about to take 'his last swing from a ladder'. But this associate warned Popham, 'when we mean to punish a delinquent, we should be cautious not to involve ourselves in some degree of criminality, and thereby expose ourselves to censure'. When Coppi sent a letter pleading illness, Popham's contact said he expected to find him 'completely on his back'. Coppi met his death soon thereafter.

In November, Popham made a trip to Prince of Wales Island (modern-day Penang) for a cargo of rattan canes, sago, betel nuts, and black pepper. Back in Calcutta the next month, Popham sold his ship, the 500-ton *Etrusco,* and purchased a 950-ton American ship, *President Washington*. He renamed his new vessel *Etrusco*, without 'any scruple or remorse', to match his existing papers.[10]

In early 1793, Popham returned to Ostend and saw his wife for the first time in three years. He met his son, William. But in the harbour a British officer seized his ship as a prize of war, for carrying French property. This seizure triggered a long legal battle, and a large payment that was the subject of intense debate in the House of Commons for more than fifteen years. In this affair the unscrupulous Popham was accused of illegal trading, smuggling directly into Britain, bribery, and treason.

Regarding the charge of illegal trading, the British legislature had enacted strong provisions against subjects who traded in the East Indies without the license of the East India Company. In 1797 the Admiralty Court therefore condemned Popham's ship and cargo as prize to the king. Five years later, the Lords Commissioners of Appeals upheld this ruling.[11] But Popham defended himself, saying he had been received by the governor of Bengal, Lord

Cornwallis. Popham claimed this meeting as the unstated warrant of the Company. The nobleman's aide, Charles Stuart, protested: 'How acts of mere civility to him as a stranger are to be perverted into an apparent sanction of an illegal traffic!'[12] Popham seemed to win this argument by stating, 'It was the policy of the Company at that time, if not to encourage, certainly to countenance, the trade of English captains under foreign flags.'

The second accusation was that before arriving in Ostend, Popham had smuggled tea into Dungeness. His first mate testified this was done at twelve o'clock at night. Witnesses onshore said they saw five boats 'plying to and fro the whole night'. Popham admitted to having had 4,000 chests of tea on board.

As far as the allegation of bribery, Popham was accused of offering the *Etrusco*'s captor £40,000 to release his ship. When Popham denied this in the House of Commons he was warned by Stephen Lushington: 'Sir; Admiral Robinson is in town; I will call him to the bar of the house to prove the fact, and leave it to the house to judge, who is credit worthy.'

The fourth complaint was that of treason, 'the highest crime in the mind of the British public'. Forty cast-iron guns and some cases of small arms on Popham's bill of lading were never accounted for in India. In 1808, his accuser in Parliament stated: 'It has been said they were sold to the native powers, some of whom were at that period engaged in hostility with us.' Popham responded: 'Good God, sir! Is it possible that one of [Parliament's] members could have been guilty of carrying arms and ammunition to the enemies of his country? Such a person surely ought to be tied to a stake in Palace-yard.'[13]

In 1808, William Windham summed up the whole affair saying, 'Sir, this transaction began in fraud, continued in deceit, and ended in a gross imposition upon the government.' The latter was a reference to a large settlement paid to Popham by the Treasury in 1805. Popham had asked Henry Dundas, then Secretary of War, for help recovering his money. The charlatan had pleaded: 'I can bear the idea of having lost my all without repining but hate Charnock [his Ostend partner] to suffer.'[14] Prime Minister William Pitt soon granted the lawbreaker £18,000 (about £1,900,000 in present value). In 1808, Samuel Whitbread said, 'This money distributed to him was imprudently, improperly, and corruptly applied.' Lushington said, 'I am inclined to attribute corrupt motives to it but Mr. Pitt, who must be considered as chiefly responsible, is no more.'

Returning to Britain in August 1793, with the *Etrusco* scandal under way, Popham wanted back in the navy. He wrote to a secretary of the Admiralty: 'I hope you will nevertheless bear me in mind with Lord Chatham should you see him, as my friend Sir Harry Martin intends to make a particular intercession on my behalf with his Lordship on Friday ...'[15] Perhaps Popham's reference to the Comptroller of the Navy (Martin) helped convince the First Lord of the

Admiralty (John Pitt, the second Lord Chatham) to reinstate him. Popham was admitted back into the navy and in September named Agent of Transport to the British army at Flanders.

Popham's performance in the disastrous first British campaign of the French Revolutionary War earned him the admiration of the Army's commander, King George III's youngest son, the Duke of York. With the Duke's patronage, Popham 'outstripped the ordinary course of professional advancement'.[16] The following autumn, Popham's aide informed him: 'I have the pleasure to acquaint you, that the last mail brought a Letter from Lord Chatham, expressing, in very handsome terms, his readiness to obey His Royal Highness's commands, and adding, that you should immediately be appointed Master and Commander.'[17] Only five months later Popham was promoted again, this time to post-captain. And so, despite having not served at sea in over eight years and with no notable record as a lieutenant – let alone master and commander – Home Popham was made a captain in the Royal Navy. This explains why Popham was 'anathema to all orthodox naval officers, especially to those senior to him. Everything about him was irregular.'[18] Popham was promoted for his service on land by the King's second son. He was later knighted by the Tsar of Russia. 'He was intimate with politicians but loathed by Admirals.'[19]

Home Popham was in and out of the Navy, and later Parliament, as suited his interests. His priority was making his fortune. In his naval signal book Popham did not fail to include several pre-set sentences based on the word *laden*. As in 2876: she is laden with treasure; 2153: she is laden with cochineal; 2166: she is laden with cotton; 2325: she is laden with valuable goods; 2377: she is laden with indigo; 2517: she is laden with naval stores; and 2860: she is laden with timber. These were the prizes of his dreams.

The Popham Signal Code

Returning to the Trafalgar signal, we recall that 'duty' had to be spelled out with individual hoists. Was not a synonym available to speed things up? The historian Perrin thought the substitution of 'best' or 'utmost' for 'duty' would have 'hopelessly ruined' the message. The flag officer on the *Victory* wisely suggested neither of these nor 'obligation', which was also in Popham's book. It is worth noting that the sailor Jack Nasty-face claimed the actual signal was the more personal 'England expects *each* man will do his duty.'[20]

Here we arrive at the first controversy. The pre-battle signal was made using Popham's code. In the immediate aftermath of Trafalgar, Popham's supporters seized upon this fact to claim Nelson's victory as a triumph for *their* man. On the first day of funeral ceremonies for the legendary admiral, the *Courier* claimed:

VOCABULARY.   101

T 19

2853 Tell him
2854   them
2855   all
2856 Tetuan
2857 Texel
2859 Thursday
2860 Timber.   She is laden with timber
2861 Topmast.   Main topmast is sprung
2862   Fore topmast is sprung
2863   Can you spare a topmast?
2864   I have not got a topmast
2865   I have got a topmast
2866 Topsailyard.   Main topsailyard is sprung
2867   Fore topsailyard is sprung
2869   Can you spare a topsailyard
2870   I have not got a topsailyard
2871   I have got a topsailyard
2872 Torbay
2873 Toulon
2874 Town.   Set fire to the town
2875   Throw some shells into the town
2876 Treasure.   She is laden with treasure
2877 Transports.   Are transports
2879   Several are transports
2880 Tripoli
2881 Tuesday
2882 Tunis
2883
2884
2885
2886
2887
2889

o 2

T 2853 to 2904
V 2905 to 2934

U 2935 to 2957
W 2958 to 29
X 2978 to 2982
Y 2983 to 2992
Z 2993 to 2998

Page from Popham's naval signal book: Telegraphic signals; or marine vocabulary (C Roworth Printers, 1801). (National Maritime Museum, Greenwich).

It was by this new telegraph that Lord Nelson, at a distance, out of sight of Cadiz, was enabled to communicate with his cruizers close in with the port, and to know what the enemy was doing as accurately as if he had been on the spot; while he was so far away that the enemy did not believe him to be within reach. It was by this telegraph, too, that he said to his fleet as it was going into action, 'England expects every man to do his duty.' Sir Home Popham's telegraph was indeed of great use to Lord Nelson: and we hope this may be mentioned without offence to those gentlemen who, by their naval inquiries, and false accusations, had nearly ruined Sir Home.[21]

The *Courier* was correct in predicting a backlash. *Corbett's Political Register* immediately complained, 'Yet, 'ere the remains of the gallant, the public-spirited, the disinterested, the honest-hearted, the clean-handed hero have received the rites of the sepulchre, up start the partizans of Sir Home Popham, and advance for him a share of the honour won at Trafalgar!' This irate publisher claimed another newspaper had gone so far as to declare that, 'without the aid of Sir Home Popham's telegraph, the victory at Trafalgar, would, probably, have not been won!'[22]

The details of another Popham scandal will help us to better understand the political war going on behind this skirmish. Five years before Trafalgar, War Secretary Henry Dundas sent Popham on an expedition to the Red Sea. Popham was to transport a force contrived to support Sir Ralph Abercromby's Mediterranean expedition against the French Army left stranded in Egypt by Napoleon. The prior month, Popham had sent Dundas a long memorandum

The Battle of Trafalgar by J. M. W. Turner, 1822. (Wikipedia Commons)

regarding this pincer movement. Sir Home sailed in December 1800 with the *Romney*, three transports carrying 1,500 men, and the sloop *Victor*. While the troops arrived too late to participate in the British victory, Dundas, who was also President of the Board of Control of the East India Company, had assigned Popham other projects to be accomplished on his mission. Dundas had said: 'I am the more eager for obtaining the services of Popham for that purpose, for there is mixed with it so many considerations of a political nature, and where the naval officer will have to act with and conciliate the Sherif of Mecca, and others on both sides of the [Red Sea].'[23]

Regarding one of their schemes, Popham told the Governor-General of India, the Marquess Richard Wellesley, the Company could make a monopoly of a trade good 'which the luxury of the times has made a necessary article of existence in Northern Europe, particularly in France ... Mocha Coffee'.[24] The plan called for a new agent to contract with the planters at the great coffee fair at Bet il Fakeih in Yemen. The new man would replace the current banyan, the Hindu merchant who, as the company's representative, had amassed a fortune of 'twenty lacks of dollars' or two million Spanish dollars. Popham's coffee monopoly was to be maintained by force: he envisioned two ships built exclusively for the Red Sea service 'mounting twenty twenty-four pounders, battering guns, and one mortar', which, 'as commanding the destruction of the towns, would keep the whole country in a state of subjection'.

But Popham now lost his powerful minister. Henry Dundas left office when William Pitt resigned in March 1801. The change in government was bad news for Sir Home. The new first Lord of the Admiralty was John Jervis, Earl of St Vincent. St Vincent particularly disliked Popham's Red Sea expedition, which he considered as poaching on Rear Admiral John Blankett's preserve.[25] St Vincent and Blankett were the type of admirals who despised Sir Home Popham.

In the Addington government, St Vincent led a campaign to clean up shipyard corruption. One of the highest-profile profiteers he ensnared was Sir Home Popham. During this expedition to the Red Sea, Popham submitted extravagant bills for repairs to the *Romney* and another ship at Calcutta. The amount in question was given as £80,000 (about £6,232,000 today). St Vincent declared the captain responsible for the sum, saying he had 'unnecessarily subjected the public to this heavy expence'. St Vincent impressed Popham's pay and ordered a review. St Vincent said Popham had purposely gone to Bengal instead of Bombay for the so-called repairs. He reminded the public that Bombay 'is the depot of stores for the ships of his Majesty, and that the East India Company have a commodious arsenal and docks there, which are always open to the repair and equipment of the King's ships'. At Calcutta, on the other hand, 'everything of the kind is in the hands of Merchant-builders'.[26] Popham's friends complained the Admiralty Board was taking 'every step that could be devised to harass and injure him'.[27] The truth is that Popham was probably guilty. The acting naval officer at Calcutta, a merchant named Matthew Louis, enjoyed the patronage of Admiral Rainier. It was Rainier who recommended Louis to Popham. Louis made 5 per cent commission on all bills submitted and the shipyard made 20 per cent on all repairs. What is unknown is how much went to Popham in kickbacks.

When William Pitt returned to power in May 1804, St Vincent was out as First Lord of the Admiralty, replaced by Henry Dundas, Lord Melville. Popham entered Parliament as member for the rotten borough of Yarmouth, Isle of Wight. The seat was said to have cost him £4,000.[28] The *Romney* scandal continued for years in and out of Parliament, with endless pamphlets, newspaper productions, and reports.[29] One of these was Popham's:

> Concise Statement of Facts, relative to the treatment experienced by SIR HOME POPHAM, since his return from the Red Sea: to which is added the correspondence, naval, military and commercial, to his Excellency the Most Noble Marquis WELLESLEY, &c. from SIR HOME POPHAM, during his command in the Red Sea, and his subsequent embassy to the states of Arabia.

Lord Nelson said he wanted to read Popham's infamous pamphlet: 'I should like to see Sir H - - - P - - - -'s book. I cannot conceive how a man that is reported to have been so extravagant of Government's money, to say no worse, can make a good story.'[30] In the Trafalgar controversy, Popham's supporters seized upon the moment as an opportunity in a long political war in which their man was a central figure.

The next question pertains to the actual origin of Popham's *Telegraphic Signals*. The nautical inventor Richard Hall Gower said of Popham's signal system, 'This mode of communicating significations, and even a complete language, is the invention of the author [Gower], and was first published in the second edition of his Seamanship in 1796.' Gower told his story as follows:

> Having quitted the sea service since the year 1802, the author was not aware that a telegraph of the kind had been introduced into the navy, under the patronage of Government, until accidentally explaining his invention to a naval friend, and setting forth the advantage to be derived by secret communication, he was informed, to his astonishment, that the thing was already done, by the recent introduction of Sir Home Popham's telegraphic signals.[31]

Gower admitted he could not prove Popham had robbed him as 'the thoughts of Sir Home may have run, by chance, parallel with the thoughts of the author'. He did not think 'Sir Home Popham would take merit for the invention of another'. [32] The naval historian Perrin later wrote:

> It may be that in this matter, as in so many other inventions, the first to make some practical use of an idea got the idea at second hand. However this may be in Popham's case, it is clear that the labour of perfecting the invention and what is perhaps equally important, of persuading others that it was really worth a trial, was undertaken by Popham alone.[33]

While Popham probably appropriated Gower's idea, the relationships he nurtured in the ministry over a long period made it possible to get the new system adopted by the Royal Navy under his name.

Following up on his *Telegraphic Signals*, in 1812, Popham produced a new system using twenty-three flags, which he denoted by the numbers 1 to 9 and the letters A to O. With this innovation, more than 11,000 preset signals could be made using three flags in one hoist. Four-flag signals numbered in the hundreds of thousands. The historian Perrin lamented that if this new code had been invented seven years earlier, Nelson could have made his signal in precisely his own words. Popham now gave Nelson's 'confides' priority status: he gave the word a three-flag code, whereas 'expects' was relegated to four.

While the Admiralty formally adopted Popham's system in 1816, it was in widespread use from the beginning. Not everyone thought this a positive innovation. One naval writer later complained that from 1803 'an alarming loquacity has prevailed afloat'. He continued:

> The Johnsonian system – or rather be it called the Popham-code – was not unattended with evil; nay it was constantly abused. The 'general signals' were deserted for the Telegraph-book [...] which was made the medium of indiscriminate, and, too often, indiscreet communication. Private prattle and public orders were together seen flying in the face of the fleet and it was but natural a 'sharper look-out' should be kept on the one than the other, curiosity sometimes succeeded in defeating discipline and delaying duty.[34]

This writer thought it inappropriate for a 'bluff weather-beaten captain of a battleship' to have to repeat the signal of a 'fashionable fop from port'; 'The fascinating Mrs. F. lately eloped with Col G of the guards'. Captain Fletcher

Wilkie mentioned that in the River Plate, while waiting for reinforcements, Popham 'put in practice his powers of telegraph'. There, the men quickly revised their captain's famous code. 'Reef topsails', for example, became 'send us some fresh beef'. Popham himself enjoyed the flag-chat that made life at sea less monotonous. In demonstrating the power of his 1812 code he gave the following humorous example, which could now be signalled with ease:

– Have you an idea a change of ministers is about to take place?
– Certainly not ministers are gaining strength.
– Your sister married to a Lord of the Admiralty.

And so, we see in the early nineteenth century Sir Home Popham introduced flag-texting to the Royal Navy. For better or for worse.

Sir Home Popham was promoted to rear admiral in 1814 and appointed Knight Commander of the Order of the Bath in 1815. In 1817 he was given the Jamaica post by Lord Melville's son. But his enemies could not forget his past offences:

Sir Home lately accepted the command of the West India station. The appointment, in fact, is equal to a second acquittal in regard to the vast sums which he was accused of having embezzled, under charges for repairs and stores; that command having been generally bestowed for the purpose of repairing the indigence which enterprising Commanders might have incurred in the course of long services.[35]

As this insult makes clear, Sir Home never made his personal fortune. He did make lasting enemies. We have looked at examples of his less than exemplary dealings. To mention one more, earlier in his career he made a private arrangement with a Cape Town merchant named Michael Hogan to transport wine and brandy on naval transports to the Indian market. When Popham failed to make good on payments, Hogan pursued him aggressively, suggesting at one point the seizure of Lady Popham's furniture. To avoid this embarrassment, Hogan ordered his agent to 'have my demand made up with interest, presented to [Popham] the moment he lands in England, and if he refused to pay for one moment, that he will be lodged in gaol. It would be well to wait silently his arrival in London where spunging houses are at hand. [I trust] to your correctness and activity in punishing a man of his injustice and ingratitude.'[36]

When he received his West Indies appointment, Popham owed his prize agent and banker £6,000 (present value of approximately £415,000).[37] Popham lost two children in Jamaica to illness and disease. He returned to Britain in 1820, himself a sick man, and died shortly thereafter.[38]

Popham in Buenos Aires

But we cannot leave Sir Home on this sad note. Popham had enemies, but he also had friends. He was a very intelligent man whose career was highlighted by stunning feats, including his unauthorised invasion of Buenos Aires in 1806.

Regarding earlier talk of a South America project, Lord Nelson had said, 'I hope we shall have no buccaneering expeditions, such services fritter away our troops and ships, when they are so much wanted for more important occasions, and are of no use beyond enriching a few individuals.'[39] But in early 1806, in Cape Town, Sir Home received information from a co-conspirator, an American merchant based in the River Plate. Buenos Aires was undefended, said the informant, the rich Spanish treasure ready to be taken away. And so Popham set sail.

In June, when Popham landed General William Beresford's small army near the capital, the viceroy fled into the interior. Buenos Aires capitulated, Beresford moved into the palace, and Popham shipped his treasure home. While he had no authorisation for his invasion, he thrilled Britain with his haul of shining silver, paraded from Portsmouth to London. Even more dazzling was his crafty circular. Britain cheered Popham's exploits and the rich South American market he declared open for business. The ministry recalled Popham and sent Sir Samuel Auchmuty, and then John Whitelocke, to secure the Plata. An army of merchants followed.

Facing a certain court martial, Sir Home Popham was counting on popular opinion to carry him through. As his powerful benefactors were out of office, he counted on the support of the manufacturing towns, which coveted new markets like the Rio de la Plata. Popham was so confident of a political victory he was on top of the world. In just twelve months, he wrote to Sir John Sinclair that his small expedition 'had captured the capitals of two quarters of the globe, South Africa and South America'. The achievement, he claimed, was unparalleled in history. A single Highland regiment and a few British seamen, he crowed, had forced the viceroy, 'at the head of five thousand men', to beat the capital. 'Indeed, Sir John, we do not deserve to be scolded.'

A *Gazette Extraordinary* published late on a Saturday night in September 1806 contained the particulars of Popham's 'brilliant achievement, which the firing of the Park and Tower guns had previously announced to the public joy'.[40] Notice of the capture of Buenos Aires had arrived from the spot in the form of the trophy-laden HMS *Narcissus* (32). At Portsmouth, Captain Ross Donnelly set out a flashy display of flags, field pieces and treasure chests filled with silver and gold. The following Saturday people lined the road to cheer the Buenos Aires cavalcade. The words 'Treasure Chest' appeared on the front of eight wagons drawn by forty-eight horses and adorned with flags, pennants and blue ribbons. Leading the way were the merchant Alexander Davison's Loyal Britons and the Clapham Volunteers. A 'most excellent' band played God Save the King and 'every British heart rejoiced at the scene'.[41] Having entered London, the procession stopped at St James's Square, where Elizabeth Popham and Harriet Davison presented 'a pair of colours on which was written, in gold letters on blue silk within branches of laurel, Buenos Ayres, Popham, Beresford, Victory'. Spectators were thrilled to witness the triumph of Old England. The procession advanced up The Strand to the Bank of England, where Captain Donnelly deposited bags of gold and jewels and 27 tons of Spanish silver. The sailors then pulled the captured guns to the ordnance office in the Tower of London.

Popham faced his court martial in March 1807. Many reporters filled the courtroom. The warrant said the captain had left the Cape of Good Hope without orders to 'attack the Spanish settlements on the Rio de la Plata … for which he had no direction or authority whatsoever'.[42] The *Times of London* complained the officers who planned the expedition had made their private fortune while the troops were prisoners of war. The schemers had taken Buenos Aires, shipped off the dollars, and lost their army. Having been ejected from the capital, Popham had captured a small village in present-day Uruguay. If raised to the peerage, the paper laughed, Sir Home should be given the title Baron Maldonado.

While Popham's guilt was a foregone conclusion, he got off largely unpunished. The court pronounced that while his conduct was 'highly censurable', there were extenuating circumstances to be considered. The members ordered a severe reprimand, and 'he is hereby severely reprimanded accordingly'. Once the sentence was read, the provost marshal returned Popham's sword with a 'respectful salutation' and the court was dissolved.[43]

Among Popham's numerous defenders was Jane Austen. She, for one, did not appreciate the court's seemingly mild rebuke:

ON SIR HOME POPHAM'S SENTENCE, APRIL 1807.
Of a Ministry pitiful, angry, mean,
A gallant commander the victim is seen.
For promptitude, vigour, success, does he stand
Condemn'd to receive a severe reprimand!
To his foes I could wish a resemblance in fate:
That they, too, may suffer themselves, soon or late,
The injustice they warrant. But vain is my spite,
They cannot so suffer who never do right.

In January 1808, London staged a formal ceremony to boost Popham and a second acclaimed officer. 'Sir John Stuart and Sir Home Popham arrived at Guildhall for the purpose of receiving the swords voted by the City of London for their respective services; the former on the Plains of Maida, and the latter at the attack upon Buenos Ayres.' The Chamberlain addressed Sir Home Popham:

> I give you joy; and in the name of the Lord Mayor, Alderman and Commons of the City of London, in Common Council assembled, return you Thanks for your gallant conduct and important services in the capture of Buenos Ayres, at once opening a new source of commerce to the manufactures of Great Britain, and depriving her enemy of one of her richest and extensive colonies in her possession. – And by unanimous resolution of the said Court, I am to present you with this Sword, as a testimony of the high esteem which it entertains of your very meritorious conduct.

The Chamberlain said when the news arrived of Popham's achievement in South America, '… it was received by the nation with an extacy of joy'. The Corporation of London said he had carried into effect a plan suggested by 'that great Statesman' William Pitt with the 'prowess of yourself and your gallant associates in arms'. Great Britain 'will ever regard the capture of Buenos Ayres, both from the ability with which it was planned, and from the energy and intrepidity with which it was effected, as an action worthy of being recorded in the brightest page of her history'. After the ceremony, the assembly continued to an elegant dinner at the Mansion House provided by the Lord Mayor. The double-girded Sir Home Popham explained: 'This, meaning the old sword, was presented to me by the East India Company.'[44]

Sir Home Popham has a place in history thanks to his invasion of Buenos Aires and his *Telegraphic Signals*, famously used by Lord Nelson at Trafalgar. Popham's monument at St Michael and All Angels Churchyard in Sunninghill, Berkshire, is a conservation project of the 1805 Club.

Portrait of Sir Home Popham, see colour plate 9

Cornwallis, a Woman Named Cuba, and the Caribbean

Barry Jolly

My friends, we will not go again or ape an ancient rage,
Or stretch the folly of our youth to be the shame of age.
G. K. Chesterton

It is a matter of naval folklore that, in 1781, Horatio Nelson, then a junior captain serving in the West Indies, was nursed back to health from a life-threatening condition by a Jamaican nurse. He then returned home to Britain in the third-rate HMS *Lion* (64) captained by William Cornwallis, a captain many years his senior. Nelson himself was in no doubt as to where the credit lay, writing to Cornwallis many years later:

> I never, never shall forget that to you I probably owe my life,

going on to say:

> and I feel that I imbibed from you certain sentiments which have greatly assisted me in my naval career – that we could always beat a Frenchman if we fought him long enough; that the difficulty of getting at them was oftentimes more people's own fancy than from the difficulty of the undertaking; that people did not know what they could do until they tried; and that it was always to err on the right side to fight.[1]

Without question, Nelson's own extraordinary self-regard did not prevent him from having the highest personal and professional respect for Cornwallis.

Cornwallis himself remains a much under-appreciated admiral; his most significant contribution to Britain's security during a lifetime of distinguished service being his maintenance of the blockade of Brest through unusually ferocious winters in 1801 and from 1803 to 1806. The blockade may have lacked the cachet of victorious fleet actions, but it was undoubtedly equally notable.

Nonetheless, in July 2019, The 1805 Club and Milford-on-Sea Historical

Etching of Admiral Sir William Cornwallis.

Record Society took steps to restore his standing on the occasion of the bicentenary of his death. A memorial service in Milford-on-Sea,[2] an exhibition at St Barbe Museum and Art Gallery in Lymington, and an article in *Hampshire Studies* all contributed to an overdue reappraisal.[3]

The emergence of suggestions of less than decorous conduct on the part of Cornwallis is therefore worthy of consideration. This article analyses the claims that Admiral Sir William Cornwallis had a number of illegitimate children in Jamaica and establishes the true nature of his relationship with the supposed slave, Cuba.

Most military and naval memoirs are written by senior officers, detailing their successes or other exploits. Rather less usual, and even less so 200 years ago, are recollections of sailors from the lower deck. One such, however, was written by William Richardson, and his comments on Admiral William Cornwallis are striking.[4]

The image of Cornwallis in retirement, in happy domesticity with Mrs Whitby (the widow of his almost perennial Flag Captain, John Whitby), his horses and his parrots, has long been accepted. So too, his religious faith, devotion to duty and care for his men.[5] The idea that he could have been 'a wild fellow' sits uncomfortably with his reputation as a staid and sober admiral of renown. Yet that is how he was depicted by Richardson in his memoirs published many years after his death.

Richardson's experience coincided with the accepted image of moderation. He described how, on the day, 24 April 1794, when Cornwallis returned to Britain after nearly five years in India, the admiral espied two wherries carrying girls approaching. Becoming much agitated, he sent for Captain Whitby and 'desired him not to allow any such creatures to come near the ship'. Once he had gone ashore, Whitby – the son of a vicar – nonetheless allowed his crew the welcome company of the young ladies. Richardson went on to comment:

> It was very strange that the Admiral – a religious and good man – could not bear the sight of a female; and yet he had been very much among them in his youthful days, and was called a wild fellow. It was reported on board here as a fact that he once went on shore to dine with the Governor at Madras, and, as some ladies began to take their seats at the table while he was there, he arose, took up his hat, and left the company, to the astonishment of them all, and came on board![6]

In the absence of any supporting evidence, any exuberance or unbecoming conduct by a young Cornwallis has been overlooked by historians. However, in 2006, a book on the Cornwallis family by the Rev N. B. Cryer was published with detailed information suggesting that Cornwallis had indeed sown some wild oats in his younger days.[7] The evidence is limited to some names with dates over several decades relating to events in Jamaica. They raise some interesting questions about the way Cornwallis – spent his youth.

Cryer set out the following claims:

The Hon. William Cornwallis R.N. fathered the following children:
By Elizabeth Spencer (a free negress) born in 1745 buried 13/12/1808
- (a free mulatto) born 14/10/1761 bapt 1/1/1783 (James Cornwallis)
m. Elizabeth (free mulatto)
  – Marcella[8] Elizabeth Cornwallis baptised 5/1/1780;
  – Charlotte Goldson Cornwallis born 18/9/81 bapt 6/12/81 and bur 10/8/83;
  – Priscilla Elizabeth Cornwallis born 24/1/91 bapt 23/10/91 bur 1/11/1816.
By Anne Arnot (a free mulatto) bur 8/10/1777
- Harry born 17/10/64 bapt 17/2/65
- William born 25/12/65 bapt 14/3/66 bur 20/6/66
By Cuta (or Cuba) (a free negress)
- James Cornwallis (free man of colour) born 26/10/71 bapt 11/10/72
bur 16/5/1812 m. Jane (or Johannah) Smith (a free woman of colour)

Cryer's genealogical information is correct in terms of the various names, thereby confirming that Cornwallis did indeed father a number of children in Jamaica, but there are a number of inaccuracies in Cryer's account together with shallow analysis and unsupported conclusions. A more accurate account is set out here, albeit allowing for some uncertainties that cannot be resolved at this distance in time.

The methodology of checking the dates has involved the use of the *Family Search* website – Cryer appears to have used this through the International Genealogical Index – which is not necessary and, indeed, results in missed data – in three ways: (i) the search engine, although this does not appear to cover the data in full; (ii) the digitised text by scrutiny (always with the risk of data being overlooked); and (iii) use of the index to ensure any omissions from the digitised text are corrected. The text in question here is the Jamaica, Church of England Parish Register Transcripts 1664–1880 for Port Royal,[9] which were created from parish records from 1825 onwards following the establishment of the Diocese of Jamaica.[10] The index was part of the same process. The transcripts and index are the digitised handwritten originals. All genealogical data have been sourced from this except where otherwise noted.

The first of Cornwallis' children was James Cornwallis, whose mother was Elizabeth Spencer. Elizabeth appears to have used the Cornwallis name, being registered as Elizabeth Spencer Cornwallis when she was buried on 13 December 1808. Her age was given as sixty-three. The only record found is of the baptism of Elizabeth, her sister Mary and James, which took place on 1 January 1783. Elizabeth's date of birth is shown as 7 July 1746, a rough confirmation of her age at death. Mary's date of birth is shown as 28 October 1748, and that of James as 14 October 1761. The reasons for this family baptism, when James was apparently already seventeen, are obscure.

Nonetheless, at this point, alarm bells ring. Although to all appearances, all three were fully cognisant of their dates of birth several decades earlier, the question must be asked of Cornwallis' whereabouts. The date of birth recorded for James implies conception in about January 1761, but this does not look to be possible, as Cornwallis was not in the West Indies at all in that year.

Cornwallis' service record before being made post-captain is missing, but can be inferred from his letters.[11] Although he was in Canadian waters in 1758–59, he had returned to Britain by March 1759 when he joined the fourth-rate HMS *Dunkirk* (60). He was then engaged in the Battle of Quiberon Bay, moving on to the Mediterranean, thousands of miles from Jamaica, and serving in *Dunkirk,* the second-rate HMS *Neptune* (90), and the third-rate HMS *Thunderer* (74). He returned to Brirtain from the Mediterranean in April 1761.

Similarly, he was not in Jamaica for the baptism in January 1783. Had he been so he would probably have been able to correct James' date of birth. However, he had returned to Britain after the Battle of the Saintes (12 April 1782) in the third-rate HMS *Canada* (74), and the ship had been paid off on 28 October 1782. His next appointment was to the third-rate HMS *Ganges* (74) on 22 January 1783, well clear of the West Indies on the date of the baptism.

This is not to question Cornwallis' paternity of James, which appears to be established by his name in the parish register: 'Hon William Cornwallis' leaving little room for doubt, and supporting evidence of the relationships will appear below. However, the actual date cannot have been before his first voyage to the West Indies. This was in March 1763, when his mother, Countess Cornwallis, wrote to him expressing concern about the climate and disease.[12] On this basis, Elizabeth Spencer could not have borne James until January 1764 at the very earliest.

There is another complication with the date. James Cornwallis is recorded as being a father in September 1781. Had he been born in 1761, he would have been twenty, but the later his date of birth, the younger he would have achieved parenthood. For Cornwallis himself and Elizabeth, the reverse is true: Cornwallis was born in 1744 and so only seventeen in 1761; Elizabeth was even younger: just fifteen. At the more probable date for James' birth of 1764, Cornwallis and Elizabeth would have been a more respectable twenty and eighteen, although James would have been a father aged only seventeen. Whatever the truth about James' date of birth, all three became parents by the age of twenty.

The second of Cornwallis' relationships was with a woman called Ann Arnot. Her own circumstances are of interest, as too are those of her sister, Mary, to whom attention should first be turned.

Mary Arnot was the long-time mistress of Captain Frederick Lewis Maitland RN.[13] Maitland had been posted to Port Royal in January 1757, and remained there in various ships for several years. During this time he fathered three children with Mary, the last of these being born in 1767.[14]

The parish transcripts confirm the relationship between the two sisters and fill out the detail. Ann Arnot had a daughter, Mary, by an Edward Oneal, in 1760, in all likelihood named after her sister.[15] When Ann died, she was buried by Mary Arnot (her sister) on 8 October 1777. Mary Arnot in turn, abandoned by Maitland, followed on 27 November 1782, being buried by her niece, Mary Oneal. These relationships are too strong for any thought of coincidence.

What is particularly striking is that Cornwallis began his relationship with Ann Arnot in 1763, at very much the same time as his affair with Elizabeth Spencer. It is also to be noted that Ann Arnot was already a mother by the time she met Cornwallis. She was to have another child subsequently, by a third father, on 28 November 1769.[16]

Bearing in mind the temporary nature of naval postings to Port Royal, living with others in similar circumstances would appear to have made sense for Cornwallis. Maitland's domicile, based on his longer-term relationship with Mary Arnot, may well have provided Cornwallis with a temporary home; it certainly covered the briefer sojourn of Cornwallis when his two children by Ann Arnot were born in 1764 and 1765.

The first of these two children was Harry, who was born on 17 October 1764 and baptised on 17 February 1765. The second child, William, was born on 26 December 1765 and baptised on 14 March 1766, but died a few months later on 20 June 1766. Three children in two years to two different women is a prolific rate of reproduction, and it certainly ties in with Richardson's assertion that Cornwallis 'had been very much among them [women] in his youthful days'.

The choice of names is intriguing. William Cornwallis himself was the fourth son of the first Earl Cornwallis, whose four sons were Charles (the soldier and politician whose reputation is intertwined with major events in America, Ireland, and India), James (the somewhat eccentric Bishop of Lichfield), Henry (who died of a fever aged twenty returning from the battlefields of Europe to take up his seat in the House of Commons), and the admiral himself, William. Thus three of his four sons in Jamaica had been named after the latter three of these. Oddly enough, when a fourth hove into view, he was not named after the Earl (Charles), but was another James.

Maitland and Cornwallis were not alone among naval captains living ashore. Another was Nelson, but here we enter the uncertain realm of his relationship with a woman known variously as Coubah, Couba, Cooba or Cuba. This woman was the famed nurse who is supposed to have helped in restoring Nelson to health in 1780 before he took passage with Cornwallis to Britain.

Jo Stanley has recently questioned aspects of the Cuba Cornwallis legends, pointing out that they all stem from the Clarke and M'Arthur biography of Nelson in 1809 and were embellished by Hill in his *A Week in Port Royal* in 1855. Neither account gave sources, but Clarke and M'Arthur did refer to Cuba as having a lodging house.[17] Nelson himself wrote that, 'Captain Cornwallis and I live together. I hope I have made a friend of him, which I am sure from his character you will be glad to hear.'[18]

It seems quite possible that they were in Cuba's lodging house. Cuba is reputed to have been a slave freed by Cornwallis, but it is difficult to see how Cornwallis could have owned a slave in Jamaica or had any hand in freeing one, especially one who was already in possession of a lodging house. In fact, Cornwallis' relationship with Cuba was of an entirely different nature: according to the Jamaica transcripts, on 26 October 1771 Cuba had borne Cornwallis a son, a second James.

The register entry shows her name clearly as Cuba, thereby ending the uncertainty on that point.[19] Slaves often took, or were given, the surnames of their masters, but in this instance Cuba became Cuba Cornwallis not because she was a freed slave but because she bore the then captain a son. The romantic appeal of Cornwallis freeing a slave, however much in character this would have been, must give way to the more prosaic, and in this instance indecorous, matter of parenthood.

Once again, the dates need to be examined with care. The registration entry was for baptism – 11 October 1772 – with the date of birth (26 October 1771) added in. Cornwallis was still in Britain in January 1771, the probable date of conception, but arrived in Jamaica in April, remaining there until July.[20] The actual date of birth, therefore, is likely to have been between January and April 1772.

The evidence points strongly to confirmation of Cornwallis' parentage of four children in Jamaica, albeit on different dates from those claimed by Cryer. Cryer also claimed to have found evidence of grandchildren; as before, the broad direction of his claims is correct, but the detail and the relationships very much less so.

In all, Cryer identified three grandchildren – Charlotte, Priscilla and Mercella – all of whom are shown as being the children of James (the son of Elizabeth Spencer) and a woman named Elizabeth Cornwallis. He also claimed to have found a marriage by the second James (the son of Cuba) to a Jane (or Johannah) Smith. However, an examination of the parish register transcripts suggests that he conflated the identities of three women. The more probable situation is as follows.

The first of the three girls was Charlotte Goldson Cornwallis, born on 18 September 1781 and baptised on 2 October. The parents are shown in the register as James and Elizabeth Cornwallis. Clearly, this was too early for the father to be Cuba's son, and so it is more likely that the father was Elizabeth Spencer's son. It will be noted that neither James nor his mother had been baptised at this date; it is suggested, given later events, that the baptism may have been to seek divine assistance for a poorly child – her death is recorded as 10 August 1783 – or even at the request of William Cornwallis.

Charlotte Goldson Cornwallis's mother was recorded as Elizabeth, the same as James' own mother, but such a coincidence looks unlikely in this instance. Discounting an incestuous relationship, the more probable explanation is that James misinterpreted the vicar's question about mother's name, and supplied that of his own mother. Such circumstances are by no means unknown; bearing in mind that he had not been baptised at this stage and may well have been a stranger to the church and the vicar, this is quite plausible. The daughter was christened Charlotte Goldson Cornwallis, suggesting her mother's surname was Goldson rather than Spencer.

The registers do not bear out Cryer's record of a marriage between a James Cornwallis and a Jane (or Johannah) Smith, but they do show two girls born to a woman, or women, of those names: Priscilla, daughter of Jane Smith, and Mercella, daughter of Johannah Smith. The respective dates of baptism are well apart: Priscilla (born 21 April 1791), 23 October 1791, and Mercella, 5 January 1800.

Both girls had a second Christian name, Elizabeth. There does not seem to be any reason for a granddaughter of Cuba to be named this way, but good reason for Elizabeth Spencer's to be so, suggesting that both girls were the daughters of Elizabeth Spencer's son James rather than that of Cuba. The evidence is scant, but, irrespective of the identity of the mothers, the most likely explanation is that all three girls were the daughters of the first James.

Whether the mother was one and the same as Cryer claimed is a moot point, however. It is a reasonable possibility given a classically minded vicar, but other evidence may suggest otherwise. A Johanna (but without a final 'h') Smith was baptised on 20 October 1799,[21] only a few months before Mercella. If this was Mercella's mother, even allowing for the difference in spelling, the timing – ten years after the birth and baptism of Priscilla – is odd; it may well be that Jane and Johanna(h) were different people. The jury remains out on this particular matter.

The available evidence, for all its weaknesses and limitations and corrected to take account of Cryer's numerous aberrations, tends to suggest that Cornwallis had four children in Jamaica during the 1760s and 1770s. A corrected genealogy would be as follows:

Children and grandchildren of Admiral Sir William Cornwallis in Jamaica
By Elizabeth Spencer: born 7 July 1746; bapt Jan 1783; died 13 Dec 1808:
- James Cornwallis: born 14 October 1764(?); bapt 1 January 1783:
  - Charlotte Goldson Cornwallis: born 1 September 1781 bapt 6 December 1781; buried 10 August 1783.
  - Priscilla Elizabeth Cornwallis: born 21 April 1791; bapt 23 October 1791; bur 1 November 1816.
  - Mercella Elizabeth Cornwallis baptised 5 January 1800.
By Anne Arnot: bur 8 October 1777:
- Harry: born 17 October 1764; bapt 17 February 1765.
- William: born 26 December 1765; bapt 14 March 1766; bur 20 June 1766
By Cuba: died 1848:
- James Cornwallis: born January – April 1772(?); bapt 11 October 1772; bur 16 May 1812.

The Maitland family website states that there is no evidence of any provision being made by the Maitland family for the three children of Frederick Maitland. John, the youngest, prospered, but he would still have had to endure an impoverished childhood. Similarly, there is nothing to suggest that Cornwallis made any provision for any beneficiaries until his death on 5 July 1819, by which time most of those detailed above had died. Interestingly, however, when Cornwallis wrote his will in 1816 he made a bequest of £300 to Mary Spencer, sister of the late Elizabeth Spencer of Port Royal, Jamaica.[22]

This, too, raises questions: why was the sister of Elizabeth Spencer the sole beneficiary in Jamaica, especially as Cornwallis did not have any offspring in Britain or indeed elsewhere? Ann Arnot and Elizabeth Spencer were dead; so too were two of the four sons – William and Cuba's James. The grandchildren may have been rather more distant, but Charlotte and Priscilla had also passed away.

Lithograph of Newlands – Cornwallis' home in Milford by Grove (1832).

There are three children or grandchildren left unaccounted for. Detailed scrutiny of the Port Royal register transcripts has failed to discover any record of the deaths of the first James and of Mercella, although the absence of information may be a function of incomplete records or simply that they had moved away from Port Royal. What is very evident, however, is that Cornwallis was fully aware of the death of Elizabeth Spencer and that her sister Mary was probably still alive.

The other still living was Cuba, who lived to a very ripe old age, dying in 1848. Cuba was well established in Port Royal society and traded heavily on the Cornwallis name. Cornwallis would not have appreciated this, and the omission of Cuba from his will is therefore unsurprising.

William Cornwallis died a bachelor, but also a father and a grandfather. In his middle and later years he shunned the society of women apart from the widow and daughter of his long-term protégé and flag captain John Whitby, treating both as daughters in the same way that he had treated John Whitby as a son. Such was the relationship that they were to be the principal beneficiaries of his substantial estate.[23] He wrote his will forty-five years after the last of his three liaisons with Jamaican women, all of whom, as records attest, were negresses or mulattos. There was just one indirect beneficiary amongst them, but whether this was as a token gesture of redemption, a sense of duty, or a long-concealed residue of devotion will never be known.

Portrait of Mrs. M. A. T. Whitby, see colour plate 10
Memorial window at All Saints Church, Milford, see colour plate 11

A Second Naval War:
The Immediate Effects of the American War on Royal Navy Operations, June 1812–July 1813

S. A. Cavell

The American declaration of war against Great Britain on 18 June 1812 instantly created the need for a Royal Navy fleet more than four times the size of the one then on station in North America, if a strategy of blockade and commerce protection was to be implemented. It also demanded the creation of a centralised command structure to oversee the region and give cohesion to the various theatres now in play, from Newfoundland to the Leeward Islands. The Admiralty's response to these matters was, however, uneven. The redeployment of warships lagged far behind the creation of a central command structure. Some historians have attributed the lack of speed with which the navy responded to war as a show of ambivalence towards the American threat – one that the government took time to recognise as a serious challenge.[1] The principal reason, however, for the six- to twelve-month lag in the reassignment of warships was not incredulity, but a necessary delay brought about by developments in Napoleonic Europe and the British government's need to address local threats before turning to those an ocean away. The following is an examination of the naval events that immediately affected Britain's capacity and willingness to answer America's call to war.

In Whitehall, the month-old Liverpool government was aware of long-standing pressures that had been placed on the American government. The Order in Council of 1807 had announced Britain's intention to shut down all neutral trade with France in an effort to enforce its Continental blockade. American shipping suffered as a result and the frequent search and seizure of US merchant vessels escalated tensions. While Britain's focus remained fixed across the Channel, American collateral damage, and the resulting furore, forced a repeal of the Order. The change did little to alter America's path towards war. Hawks in Congress used the depredations, and the attendant issue of impressment, as pretence for a war that could further their territorial ambitions in Canada.

From the start, the burden of a new American theatre of operations fell almost entirely on the Royal Navy. At the Admiralty, Robert Dundas, Lord Melville, faced the unenviable task of finding warships to deploy to American waters and appointing men to command them. Melville had taken up the position of First Lord just three months earlier equipped with no previous experience in the management of naval matters or service at sea to help him navigate the issues. His skill as an administrator was, nonetheless, evident in his decision to retain the services of long-standing Admiralty secretaries John Croker and John Barrow, who smoothed his transition and laid the foundations for one of the most successful and long-lived Admiralty Boards of the era, which lasted until the fall of the Liverpool government in April 1827. In the summer of 1812, however, Melville faced a steep learning curve.

His appointment of Vice Admiral Sir John Borlase Warren as Commander-in-Chief of the North American Station represented a rapid response to the start of this second naval war. Warren, a long-serving, active, and independent officer, who bristled 'when subjected to control', was tasked with overseeing five previously independent stations; Newfoundland, Halifax, Bermuda, Jamaica, and the Leeward Islands, in order to facilitate an effective blockade of the American coastline, make war on US merchant shipping, and protect British trade.[2] Conceptually, the creation of a single, unified command seemed expedient, but the vast distances and massive scope of administering the various stations made Warren's job virtually impossible, even before problems of supply and logistics were considered.

Ultimately, the merging of the stations created more problems than it solved. Foremost among them was the tendency of the Admiralty to look at the combined total of the warships on nearby stations with little regard for the fact that ships could not be transferred to the coast of North America without injuring the effectiveness of the other squadrons. In early 1813, First Secretary Croker calculated Warren's force at ninety-seven ships when, in fact, less than half that number were available for service on the east coast of the United States.[3] The Admiralty's orders to Warren further complicated matters. A mandate to both 'blockade and negotiate' crippled his command and muddied the waters of Britain's naval objectives.[4]

Opposition MP George Canning famously complained that, 'Admiral Warren was busied with negotiating when he ought to have been sinking, burning, and destroying'; a position that Croker was obliged to defend.[5] Warren also faced a conundrum in that attacking American trade was likely to cause greatest harm to the British army, whose success on the Peninsula relied on regular shipments of American grain. For his first six months as commander-in-chief, Warren was forced to make do with pre-war allowances of ships and men in North America, which limited his operational effectiveness and saw a series of embarrassing defeats in one-on-one frigate actions. Melville's redeployment of warships took time. The clearest means of assessing the navy's response in terms of ship and manpower assignments is provided in the Admiralty List Book for 1812–13. The survey for July 1812 shows little change in the distribution of warships from January of that year, with only two additional brigs sent to support wartime needs in North America, bringing the total number of vessels on station to twenty-five. It should be noted that only one third rate, the decrepit, HMS *Africa* (64), was included in this number. The majority were sloops and gun brigs whose primary function was reconnaissance.[6] Warren was clearly frustrated with the dearth of warships on station and the impossibility of performing his duty without vast additions to the fleet. The friction between Warren and the Admiralty went both ways. Warren's lack of immediate success against the American navy and the paucity of his communications, both in number and content, produced much consternation among the Lords Commissioner.[7]

In November 1812, Croker promised to send three additional line-of-battle ships, twenty-one frigates, twenty-nine sloops, and fifteen smaller vessels to the North America station.[8] Melville incorrectly calculated that the American coast would now be home to one-seventh of the seagoing vessels in the navy at the time.[9] Moreover, only a fraction of these promised vessels actually appeared on station by January 1813. Forty-two ships of all sizes, including six line-of-battle ships, fifteen frigates, large and small, and nineteen sloops and brigs made up the bulk of this still undersized force.

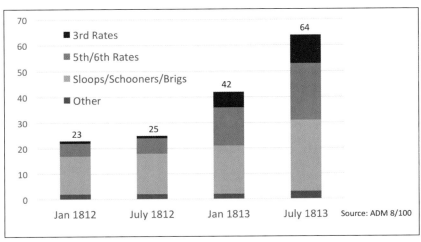

Graph 1: Vessels in the North America Station, January 1812–July 1813.

Despite the Admiralty's belief that the commander-in-chief possessed a fleet more than 'adequate to the duties to be executed', fears over Warren's lack of progress saw Melville agreeing to send an additional thirty frigates in March, which, according to his creative mathematics, would bring the total number of vessels on station to 120.[10] The proposed increase was evidence of the Admiralty's desire to halt the success of the American frigates and American privateers by enforcing a 'complete and vigorous blockade'.[11] It also reflected an abandonment of efforts at negotiation and a full commitment to war.

By July 1813, Warren was in command of sixty-four warships, including eleven third rates, twenty-two frigates, and twenty-eight sloops and schooners. It would be December of that year before the number of vessels even approached the promised proportion of one-seventh of the fleet, when the Admiralty assigned seventy-three vessels, including forty-four fifth and sixth rates, to manage the demands. It should be noted that the North America Station never saw anything like the 120 warships Melville had once considered necessary for the job.

Melville's rapid response to overhauling North American command versus the lag in his response to sending ships reflected circumstances in which a surplus of senior personnel existed alongside a dearth of naval vessels. The start of a new war strained limited resources of ships and seamen, especially at a time when the naval and military movements of Napoleon's forces in the Low Countries and Russia demanded the prioritisation of finite British naval resources.

By the summer of 1812, Wellington's forces on the Peninsula may have gained the upper hand, although the ongoing construction of Napoleon's second invasion fleet at Antwerp was of great concern to Liverpool's government. The failure of the Walcheren Expedition in 1809 dashed ambitions to seal off the mouth of the Scheldt Estuary and destroy the French fleet. This, combined with the fact that that it was impossible for Royal Navy patrols to see far enough into the Scheldt Estuary to assess the French fleet's readiness, meant that intelligence reports were vital to naval planning. A report to the Foreign Office in July 1811 announced Bonaparte's intention to construct '150 ships of the line . . . such is the state of the Empire that we shall shortly have that number'.[12] This represented one and a half times the number of line-of-battle ships then in service in the Royal Navy and a potentially devastating threat. While hindsight allows a dismissive view of Napoleon's naval ambitions, contemporaries had no such luxury. The necessity of maintaining a substantial fleet off Texel and the Scheldt, and a Channel Fleet in full readiness to defend the home islands, meant few vessels could be spared to reinforce Warren's command.

Evidence of the level of concern centred on the Scheldt was visible in July

SHIPS (all rates)	Jul 1812	Jan 1813	Jul 1813
North America	25	42	60
Leeward Islands	27	31	39
Jamaica	19	18	17
Newfoundland	12	7	13
Mediterranean	90	92	91
Baltic	39	15	45
Channel/Ports	68	67	51
Texel/Scheldt	53	34	30
Unappropriated	23	70	23
Other	251	233	255
TOTAL	607	609	624

Source: ADM 8/100

Table 1: RN Ships in Service by Station, July 1812–July 1813.

1812, when fifty-three warships and nearly 20,000 men (15 per cent of the total manpower of the navy) were stationed off Texel, a force 30 per cent larger than that of the Channel Fleet. A large proportion of ships and men were, at the same time, assigned to blockade Baltic ports (thirty-nine vessels and nearly 10,000 men). By the start of 1813, the number of vessels on station at Texel dropped from fifty-three to thirty-four, suggesting a seasonal draw down and an understanding that the French ships would be beached for the winter, thus posing little danger. With the spring, the threat from the Antwerp fleet renewed, although it is surprising to see that in July 1813, the number of ships and men at Texel was reduced again, by another 10 per cent overall. The reduction, however, may be explained by the presence of a Russian fleet, now working with the Royal Navy, which assumed blockading duties off the Scheldt in the spring/summer of 1813.[13] Their presence relieved some pressure on demands for British warships and enabled the reassignment of a number of vessels to North America. The redeployment, however, took time. Nearly all vessels stopped for refits at British ports before crossing the Atlantic. A few 74s were even razed to better compete with the American frigates.

The Russians were also a party to another major consideration preventing an immediate redistribution of the fleet in the summer of 1812. The start of Napoleon's Russian campaign brought much uncertainty. By 1810 the failure of the Continental System was clear to all involved and Tsar Alexander reopened Russian ports to neutral shipping. The subsequent breakdown of the Tilsit agreement in early 1811 allowed Britain a measure of cautious optimism. Resumption of trade with Russia meant access to vital naval supplies and the

MANNING	July 1812	Jan 1813	July 1813	
North America	3557	9369	14300	
Leeward Islands	3507	4713	6402	
Jamaica	3176	2583	3183	
Newfoundland	1860	989	2531	
Mediterranean	29277	29233	29135	
Baltic	9327	1884	8151	
Channel/Ports	19456	21462	16903	
Texel/Scheldt	19378	10203	9002	
Unappropriated	6518	18890	13271	
Other	35548	30801	33011	
TOTAL	131,604	130,127	135,889	Source: ADM 8/100

Table 2: RN Manpower by Station, July 1812–July 1813.

reestablishment of lucrative markets.[14] The problem, however, remained one of French military superiority and the possibility, even probability, that Alexander's armies would be defeated. Since October 1812 (and the end of the Anglo-Russian War that summer), Russian naval ships had been sent to winter in British ports and confidence in Russian intentions to take an active role in the destruction of Napoleonic forces was high.[15] But a French victory in Moscow would, at best, see a resumption of trade restrictions. At worst, it might see the strength of the Russian fleet added to French naval build-up, a situation that would require a sizeable investment of British naval power to contain the threat.

Only in December 1812 did the extent of the French failure in Russia become clear and evidence of the Royal Navy's reaction to the change of circumstances was apparent in the redistribution of vessels and manpower. By January 1813, the Baltic fleet saw drastic cuts with the number of warships reduced to fifteen vessels from thirty-nine just six months earlier. Similarly, the number of men on station dropped from 9,327 to just 1,884. The fall-off, however, was short lived. By July 1813 the Baltic Station regained its strength with forty-five vessels and more than 8,000 men, in consequence of the new war being fought by the Sixth Coalition in the German states.

Overall, the movement of ships and men suggests that a gradual draw down of vessels in the Texel and Channel Fleets between January and July 1813 resulted in the strengthening of the North America Station, which more than doubled (twenty-five to sixty-four vessels and 3,557 to 14,300 men) during this time. Other major theatres such as the Mediterranean, Leeward Islands, and

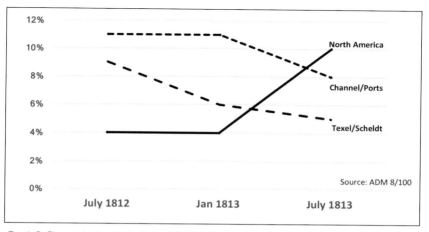

Graph 2: Changes in the distribution of RN Ships as a percentage of the Fleet, July 1812–July 1813.

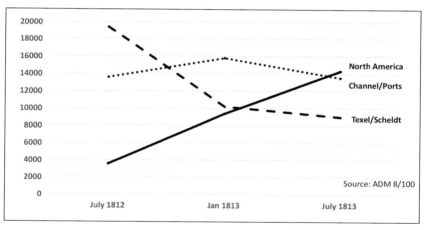

Graph 3: Changes in distribution of RN Manpower as percentage of the Fleet, July 1812–July 1813.

Jamaica stations remained relatively static during the same period.[16] As the total number of ships and men in service during the year changed little (609 vessels and 131,087 men in July 1812 compared with 606 vessels and 130,127 men in July 1813) the inverse relationship of movement between the Texel/Channel and North American fleets demonstrated an understanding of the need to divert more resources to meet the American threat. Dwindling faith in Warren's ability to subdue US frigates and protect British merchantmen contributed to a sense of urgency and explained why he received significant reinforcements by mid-1813, while requests for reinforcements from other vital commands, like the Mediterranean, were met with pert denials from the Admiralty: 'the exigencies of public service [being] at this time so great.'[17]

It must be acknowledged that factors at home including the Luddite riots, political instability in the wake of Spencer Perceval's assassination, and the economic strain of the Peninsular Campaign, which nearly quadrupled costs, from £3 million to £11 million between 1809 and 1811, affected the pace of government reactions to war with America. When it came to Admiralty decision-making, however, the most immediate considerations in June 1812 were the perceived military threats from the French fleet at Antwerp and the repercussions of a possible Russian defeat.[18] It is worth noting that in terms of naval expenditure a net increase of more than £2 million from 1812 to 1813 was evidence of the financial pressure exerted by the new war in North America and the demands it placed on naval logistics.[19]

While Liverpool's government did not welcome a war with the United States, the nation was fully geared for an active conflict; her navy controlled the oceans and therefore held the whip hand over neutral merchants in the service of Britain. A war would allow her to check US territorial ambitions in Canada and the economic expansion of American merchants, whose dominance of British markets in the West Indies was a cause for concern among colonial elites and mercantilist Britons alike.[20] For Melville's Admiralty, a new naval war brought significant logistical problems as it faced shortages of ships, seamen and supplies. The apparent slowness of the navy to react to the outbreak of war in 1812 did not reflect a dismissal of the American challenge but spoke to the problem of limited naval resources relative to immediate, existential threats on Britain's doorstep. As the United States upped the ante in late 1812, the Admiralty was forced to reassess its distribution of naval assets, albeit at the expense of its European theatres of operations.

Contributors' Biographies

Anthony Bruce was formerly a director at Universities UK and is now a higher education consultant. His first book (based on his doctorate) was on the purchase system in the British Army (1980). It was followed by *An Illustrated Companion to the First World War* (1989) and *The Last Crusade* (2002) on the war in Palestine, 1914–18. His *Encyclopaedia of Naval History* (1989) covers the period from the sixteenth century. Revised editions of *The Encyclopaedia* and *The Last Crusade* were published in 2013. He is currently working on research on the Royal Navy in the early Stuart period.

Sam Cavell, Ph.D. is the Assistant Professor in Military History at Southeastern Louisiana University, Hammond, Louisiana, and recipient of the Distinguished Teaching Endowed Professorship in the Humanities. She received her doctorate in naval and maritime history from the University of Exeter in the UK, where she received the Exeter Research Fellowship. Her publications include *Midshipmen and Quarterdeck Boys in the British Navy*, chapter contributions to *The Battle of New Orleans Reconsidered,* and *USNA's New Interpretations in Naval History.*

Chris Coelho was born in Buenos Aires and raised in New York City. He studied economics at Lafayette College in Easton, Pennsylvania, and became a history writer. He published *Pirates in Uniform: The Conspiracy to Invade Buenos Aires that Triggered a War* (2019) and *Timothy Matlack: Scribe of the Declaration of Independence* (2013). His recent book tells the unknown story of Sir Home Popham's brazen raid on Buenos Aires in 1806. In the Archivo General in Buenos Aires, Coelho located the untouched papers of Popham's co-conspirator, an American named William Porter White.

Linda Collison has enjoyed a composite career as a registered nurse, skydiving instructor, freelance writer, and novelist. Her three weeks as a voyage crewmember aboard the HM Bark *Endeavour* replica inspired the historical novel *Star-Crossed,* followed by the Patricia MacPherson Nautical Adventure trilogy. With her husband, Robert Russell, she has sailed many nautical miles aboard *Topaz*, a Cheoy Lee Luders 36 sloop.

Charles Fremantle is a direct descendant of Vice Admiral Sir Thomas Francis Fremantle via his eldest son Thomas, the First Lord Cottesloe, and also of the third and fourth Fremantle Admirals, Edmund, and Sydney. He is also descended from Wellington's ADC John Fremantle, who served at Waterloo and in the Peninsular Campaign. Charles entered Britannia Royal Naval College Dartmouth in 1951, and completed his service in 1991. He specialised as a Seaman Officer (Executive) with expertise in Anti-Submarine Warfare. He served on exchange at the Fleet ASW Centre, Norfolk, Virginia, from 1975 to 1977. He wrote the biography of Thomas Fremantle for 'The Trafalgar Captains' and has assisted the authors of the books *Nelson's Right Hand Man*, *Wellington's Voice*, and *Nelson's Band of Brothers*. He has been writing articles for the *Trafalgar Chronicle* and *Kedge Anchor* since 2008 using the Family Archives on loan to Buckinghamshire County from his cousin Lord Cottesloe. His family can boast of 214 years of unbroken Royal Navy service.

Lisa L. Heuvel, Ed.D. directed the Center for Teaching, Learning & Leadership at the Colonial Williamsburg Foundation. An adjunct faculty member with Christopher Newport University's Department of Leadership & American Studies, she also taught at The College of William and Mary and for the University of North Carolina's 'Learn NC' programme. Dr Heuvel earned her Ed.D. at The College of William and Mary, where she also obtained an M.A. and a B.A. She formerly managed programme development initiatives in educational media at Colonial Williamsburg and was an executive producer of its award-winning electronic field trip series. The author of over 100 articles on Virginia history and education, she lives in Williamsburg, Virginia.

Sean M. Heuvel, Ph.D. is a faculty member in the Department of Leadership and American Studies at Christopher Newport University in Newport News, Virginia. He holds a B.A., M.Ed., and Ph.D. from The College of William and Mary and an M.A. in History from the University of Richmond. A military historian, Dr Heuvel has authored multiple naval history publications and is an active member of The 1805 Club. He co-founded the Williamsburg-Yorktown American Revolution Roundtable in 2013 and now serves as a president *emeritus* on its executive board. Dr Heuvel and his family live in Williamsburg, Virginia. He is co-author/editor of *From Across the Sea: North Americans in Nelson's Navy* (2020).

Gerald Holland is an eight-year veteran of the United States Coast Guard, where he has served in operations dealing with Search and Rescue, Vessel Traffic Control, Communications, Counter-Drug, and Alien/Migrant Interdictions. He earned his M.A. in Military History with a concentration in the American Revolution from American Military University and his B.A. in History from Christopher Newport University. Presently, he is pursuing a Ph.D. in History at Liberty University. In 2014, along with Dr Sean Heuvel, he helped found the Williamsburg-Yorktown American Revolution Round Table.

Barry Jolly is a Trustee of Milford-on-Sea Historical Record Society (MoSHRS) and Editor of the Society's *Occasional Magazine*. His research on the admirals of Milford has been published in a number of national journals and underpinned the recent exhibition at St Barbe Museum and Art Gallery (Lymington, UK), 'Command of the Seas – The Navy and the New Forest Against Napoleon'. He was presented with a Personal Achievement Award for Local Historians by the British Association for Local History in June 2020.

A graduate in History and a former Lieutenant Commander in the Royal Navy, he has researched a number of personal histories over the past decade and a half, including Rear Admiral John Peyton in *The Trafalgar Chronicle* (2019) and Admiral Cornwallis in *Hampshire Studies* (2019) and *MoSHRS* (2011 & 2019).

Chipp Reid is a former award-winning reporter, a licensed ship captain, and a twice wounded US Marine Corps veteran. He is the author of *Intrepid Sailors: The Legacy of Preble's Boys and the Tripoli Campaign* and *Walls of Derne: William Eaton, the Tripoli Coup and the End of the First Barbary War* and the co-author of *Lion in the Bay: The British Invasion of the Chesapeake, 1813– 1814*. He is currently on his fourth book for the US Naval Institute, a biography of Captain James Lawrence. He works in Washington and lives in Annapolis, Maryland.

Captain John Rodgaard, USN (Ret) has over forty-one years with the naval service of the United States, to include twelve years as a petty officer and twenty-nine years of commissioned service as a naval intelligence officer. He is also a published author and a contributor to several Discovery Channel *Unsolved History* television programmes. Captain Rodgaard co-authored *A Call To The Sea: Captain Charles Stewart of The USS Constitution* (2005), and authored two editions of *A Hard Fought Ship: The Story of HMS Venomous* (2010 and 2017) and co-author/editor of *From Across the Sea: North Americans in Nelson's Navy* (2020). He is the recipient of the Naval Institute's History Author of the Year for the year 1999. He is a contributor and frequent reviewer to the Naval Institute's *Naval History Magazine*, the Society for Nautical Research quarterly, the *Mariner's Mirror*, and the Naval History Foundation's

Naval History Book Reviews. Captain Rodgaard holds an A.B. in History and Political Science; an M.A. in Political Science, and is also a graduate of the US Naval War College. He is the North American Secretary for The 1805 Club.

Captain Gerald Stulc, MD, FACS (Ret), FICS, MFA, MC, USN, Ret is a retired cancer and trauma surgeon who served in the US Navy Medical Corps. Thereafter, he obtained an M.F.A. degree in Creative Writing, publishing a historical fiction novel based on the Napoleonic Wars. He has presented papers at the WWI Military Medicine Conference in San Antonio, and the McMullen Symposium on Naval History at the US Naval Academy, Annapolis. He is currently writing a book on the history of military medicine, from antiquity to the present.

Lily Style is Founder and Chair of the Emma Hamilton Society. She has a passion for history and genealogy, and writes regularly for The 1805 Club's *Kedge Anchor*. This is her second *Trafalgar Chronicle* article. She is a direct descendant of Lord Nelson and Emma Hamilton. She appeared in the 2020 French documentary *Splendeur et Déchéance de Lady Hamilton.*

Peter Turner was a design engineer, specialising in lighting and elevators. When he retired in 2005 he created his AB&OS cartoon strip, in realisation of a childhood ambition to be a cartoonist, combining it with an interest in naval history; particularly the sailing navy. This led to his joining The 1805 Club, where, under the guidance of author Peter Hore (Captain, RN, Rtd. and former editor of *The Trafalgar Chronicle*) he also learned to become a writer. Consequently, he is now the editor of *Kedge Anchor*, the magazine of The 1805 Club. His other main enthusiasms are Woodbridge Tide Mill (a working mill in Suffolk), near his home, and his cats, of course.

Andrew Venn is a young naval historian from Portsmouth. He is currently studying a postgraduate degree in Naval History at the University of Portsmouth and works as a visitor guide on board HMS *Victory*. Having graduated with a First Class Honours degree in Film Production from Portsmouth, Andrew has combined his passions of film and history to focus his studies on the portrayal of the Georgian Navy in film, television and the wider media. He regularly enjoys presenting the history of HMS *Victory* to visitors of the ship, using his youthful perspective to deliver fresh perceptions of the past.

Notes

Representations of Horatio Nelson in the Visual Arts: Heroic Portraiture Versus Historical Reality from a Medical Perspective

1   Sabine De Brabandere, 'Human Body Ratios: A project that measures up', *Scientific American*, 16 March 2017, Newsletter.

2   Good, W., 'Admiral Lord Nelson's neurological illnesses', *Proceedings of the Royal Society of Medicine,* 1970 March 63:3, pp299–306.

3   Christopher Lloyd and Jack Coulter, *Medicine and the Navy, Vol. III, 1714–1815.* (Edinburgh and London: E&S Livingstone Ltd, 1961), Chapter 12, 'Nelson and the surgeons', pp139–157.

4   www.aboutnelson.co.uk/health.htm (accessed 17 March 2020).

5   Lloyd and Coulter.

6   Lloyd and Coulter.

7   B. T. Miller, D. K. Nakayama, 'In Close Combat: Vice-Admiral Lord Horatio Nelson's Injuries in the Napoleonic Wars', *American Surgeon.* 2019 Nov 1:85(11): pp.1304–1307.

8   Colin White, *Nelson* (Stroud, Gloucestershire: The History Press, 2005).

9   Colin White, 'The Battle of Cape St Vincent, 14 February 1797'. The 1805 Club, *Trafalgar Chronicle*, No. 7, 1997, p54.

10 Courtesy of M. K. H. Crumplin, Log: 'At the Private Court of Examiners holden at their House in Lincolns Inn Fields the 12th of October 1797', examination of Rear Admiral Sir Horatio Nelson.

11 Courtesy of M. K. H. Crumplin, Log, 'At the Private Court of Examiners holden at their House in Lincolns Inn Fields the 1st day of March 1798', Admiral Sir Horatio Nelson—examined …

12 Keynes, Milo. 'Horatio Nelson Never was Blind: His Woundings and His Frequent Ill-Health'. *Journal of Medical Biology*, Vol. 6, No. 5, 1998, pp114–119.

13 *The Times,* 10 April 1804.

14 Lloyd and Coulter.

15 Lloyd and Coulter.

16 Courtesy of M. K. H. Crumplin.

17 Harold Ellis, *Operations that made History,* (Cambridge: Cambridge University Press, 1996), pp89–90.

18 Lloyd and Coulter.

19 S. K. Khan, I. Saeed, and M. D. Brinsden. 'Thomas Eshelby (1769–1811), Nelson's Surgeon'. *Journal of Medical Biology*, Vol. 24, No. 3, 2016, pp363–271.

20 Courtesy of M. K. H. Crumplin, Surgeon Thomas Eshelby's Operative Record, 24 July 1797, HMS *Theseus.*

21 Ellis.

22 Brad Smith, 'Lord Nelson's Phantom Arm and The Battle of Tenerife', 26 September 2016, *The Vintage News*.

23 Lloyd and Coulter.

24 Horatio Nelson: The Dispatches and Letters of Lord Nelson: September 1799–December 1801 Vol. 4, (Barnsley, UK: Greenhill Books, 10 February 2006).

25 James F. Zender, 'Lord Nelson's Traumatic Brain Injury, Accomplishment in the face of disabilities', *Psychology Today*, 2 December 2016.

26 *Evening Mail*, Admiral Nelson's Jason Daley, 'New Portrait of Lord Nelson Found, Scars and All', *Smartnews, Smithsonianmag.com* 17 November 2017.

27 Horatio Nelson, *Letters to Lady Hamilton*, Franklin Classics, 14 October 2018, *The Letters of Lord Nelson to Lady Hamilton, Vol. II. With A Supplement Of Interesting Letters By Distinguished Characters,* Tradition Classics, 25 November 2011, p85.

28 Andy Bowen, Letter to Lord Kingsmill in 'Nelson's eyepatch and other famous falsehoods', https://nelsonandnorfolk.wordpress.com/2017/08/02

29 William Beatty, *Authentic Narrative of the Death of Lord Nelson. With Circumstances preceding, attending and subsequent to, that Event,* (London: Cadell and Davies, 1807).

30 'Artwork of the Month, October 2005', *National Museums, Liverpool,* www.liverpoolmuseums.org.uk/picture-of-month/displaypicture.aspx?id=274.

William Beatty, Arthur Devis and the Death of Lord Nelson in Early Nineteenth-Century Literature and Art

1 William Beatty, *Authentic Narrative of the Death of Lord Nelson* (London: Cadell and Davies, 1807).

2 Arthur Devis, *The Death of Nelson, 21 October 1805*, Oil on Canvas (Greenwich: National Maritime Museum, 1807).

3 Laurence Brockliss, John Cardwell and Michael Moss, *Nelson's Surgeon: William Beatty, Naval Medicine and the Battle of Trafalgar* (New York: Oxford University Press, 2005), pviii.

4 William Beatty, *Authentic Narrative of the Death of Lord Nelson* (London: Cadell and Davies, 1807; repr. Great Britain: CreateSpace Independent Publishing Platform, 2013), p3. Further references to this text will be from the 2013 edition.

5 Beatty, p14. (Many other examples of this exist throughout the text).

6 Beatty, pp39–40.

7 Warrant Officer John Scott was killed in the opening exchanges of cannon fire at the Battle of Trafalgar, prior to the wounding of Nelson.

8 Beatty, pp13–14.

9 Marianne Czisnik, *Horatio Nelson: A Controversial Hero* (London: Hodder Education, 2005), p78.

10 Beatty, pp22–30.

11 Brockliss, p156.

12 Czisnik, p77.

13 Beatty, p53. (In endnote)

14   'The Last Moments of Lord Nelson (From an Officer who was with him)', *Morning Chronicle,* 9 December 1805.

15   Brockliss, p136.

16   'Lord Nelson', *Morning Chronicle*, 10 December 1805. Also in A. Y. Mann, *The Last Moments and Principal Events Relative to the Ever to be Lamented Death of Lord Viscount Nelson* (London: H. D. Symonds, Cole and Dale, 1806), p7.

17   'Lord Nelson', *Morning Chronicle*, 28 December 1805. Also in *Naval Chronicle,* Vol. XV (30 June 1806), p38.

18   *Recollections of the Life of the Rev A.J. Scott, D. D.: Lord Nelson's Chaplain* (London: Saunders and Otley, 1842), pp187–190.

19   James Harrison, *The Life of the Right Honourable Horatio Lord Viscount Nelson, Volume II* (London: Stanhope and Tilling, 1806).

20   Czisnik, p97.

21   Benjamin West, *The Death of General Wolfe,* Oil on Canvas (Ottawa: National Gallery of Canada, 1770).

22   Geoffrey Quilley, 'The Battle of the Pictures: Painting the history of Trafalgar', in *Trafalgar in History: A Battle and its Aftermath*, ed. by David Cannadine (Basingstoke: Palgrave Macmillan, 2006), pp121–138 (pp122–123).

23   Benjamin West, *The Death of Nelson*, Oil on Canvas (Liverpool: Walker Art Gallery, 1806).

24   Andrew Lambert, *Nelson: Britannia's God of War* (London: Faber and Faber, 2004), p318.

25   Brockliss, pp133–134.

26   Arthur Devis, *Sir William Beatty, circa 1770–1842*, oil on canvas (Greenwich: National Maritime Museum, 1806).

27   Czisnik, p103.

28   Benjamin West, *The Death of Lord Nelson in the Cockpit of the Ship 'Victory'*, oil on canvas (Greenwich: National Maritime Museum, 1808).

29   Benjamin West, *The Immortality of Nelson,* oil on canvas (Greenwich: National Maritime Museum, 1807).

30   Czisnik, p101.

Nelson in Caricature and Cartoon

1   James Davey and Richard Johns, *Broadsides: Caricatures and the Navy 1756–1815* (Barnsley, UK: Seaforth Publishing, 2012).

2   National Maritime Museum and the Queen's House, Greenwich, London, England; *The Exhibition List*: https://theexhibitionlist.wordpress.com/2013/01/20/national-maritime-museum-and-the-queens-house-greenwich-london-england/ (accessed 4 March 2020).

3   Information on this artist can be found at blashygallows.com.

4   This content is available to members only at the US Naval Institute, *Naval History Blog*, https://www.usni.org/people/eric-smith (accessed 4 March 2020).

5   Cartoon Stock, Lord Nelson by Cartoonist Gary Brown. https://www.cartoonstock.com/cartoonview.asp?catref=gbrn163&ANDkeyword=&N

OTkeyword=&TITLEkeyword=&categories=All+Categories&artists=452&main (accessed 4 March 2020).

6   Paul Bommer, 'Full Fathom Five limited edition delft tiles', *Salmagundy* (blog) https://paulbommerarchive.blogspot.com/2012/ (accessed 4 March 2020).

7   Here is an image from the Seaway China website: https://www.seawaychina.com/product/lord-nelson-db365-royal-doulton-bunnykins/ (accessed 4 March 2020).

Tobias Smollett and the Early Georgian Navy

1   Tobias Smollett, *The adventures of Roderick Random* (Athens, Georgia: The University of Georgia Press, 2012). Chapters 24 to 37 describe Roderick's naval experiences.

2   George Orwell, 'Tobias Smollett: Scotland's best novelist', *Tribune*, 22 September 1944.

3   See, for example, Michael Lewis, *England's sea officers: The story of the naval profession* (London: Allen & Unwin, 1939).

4   Edward Ward, *The wooden world dissected in the character of a ship of war. By a Lover of the Mathematicks* (London: R. Bragge, 1707).

5   Nathan Comfort Starr, 'Smollett's sailors', *American Neptune* 32 (1972), pp81–99, discusses the naval characters in *Peregrine Pickle* and *The life and adventures of Sir Launcelot Greaves* (1760) as well as *Roderick Random*.

6   Lewis M. Knapp, *Tobias Smollett: Doctor of men and manners* (Princeton, New Jersey: Princeton University Press, 1949); Claude E. Jones, 'Tobias Smollett (1721–1771) – The doctor as man of letters', *Journal of the History of Medicine and Allied Sciences*, Vol. 12 (1957), pp337–348; W. G. P[errin], 'Tobias George Smollett', *The Mariner's Mirror*, Vol. 10 (1924), p94.

7   Perrin.

8   Richard Harding, *Amphibious warfare in the eighteenth century: The British expedition to the West Indies, 1740–1742* (Woodbridge: Royal Historical Society, 1991); Julián de Zulueta, 'Health and military factors in Vernon's failure at Cartagena', *The Mariner's Mirror*, Vol. 78 (1992), pp127–141.

9   George M. Kahrl, *Tobias Smollett: Traveler-Novelist* (Chicago: Chicago University Press, 1948), p4.

10   de Zulueta, p134.

11   Tobias Smollett, *A compendium of authentic and entertaining voyages*, Second edition (London: W Strahan, 1766), Chapter V, pp313–342. Smollett also wrote a brief summary of the campaign in *A complete history of England: from the descent of Julius Caesar, to the Treaty of Aix la Chapelle, 1748*. Second edition (London: Richard Baldwin, 1760), p11, pp78–85.

12   Charles Knowles, *An account of the expedition to Carthagena, with explanatory notes and observations* (London: M. Cooper, 1743).

13   *Critical Review* V (May 1758), pp438–439; Paul-Gabriel Boucé, 'Smollett and the expedition against Rochefort (1757)', *Modern Philology* Vol. 65 (1967), pp33–38.

14   Louis L. Martz, 'Smollett and the expedition to Cartagena', *Publications of the*

Modern Language Association of America Vol. 56 (1941), pp428–446.

15   *A journal of the expedition to Carthagena, with notes. In answer to a late pamphlet; entitled, An account of the expedition to Carthagena* (London: J. Roberts, 1744).

16   Smollett, *Roderick Random,* p86.

17   Smollett, *Roderick Random*, p92.

18   Daniel J. Ennis, 'Naval impressment in Tobias Smollett's *Roderick Random*', *Albion: A Quarterly Journal Concerned with British Studies*, Vol. 32 (2000), pp232–247.

19   Nicholas Rogers, *The press gang: Naval impressment and its opponents in Georgian Britain* (New York: Continuum, 2007).

20   Smollett, *Roderick Random*, p127.

21   Tom Scott, 'The note of protest in Smollett's novels', in *Smollett: Author of the first distinction*, ed. by Alan Bold (London: Vision, 1982), p111.

22   Smollett, *Roderick Random*, p. 128.

23   Claude E. Jones, *Smollett Studies* (New York: Phaeton Press, 1970), p55.

24   Smollett, *Roderick Random*, p168.

25   Smollett, *Roderick Random*, p130.

26   Smollett, *Roderick Random*, p131.

27   Smollett, *Roderick Random*, p134.

28   Smollett, *Roderick Random*, p137.

29   Smollett, *Roderick Random*, p135.

30   Smollett, *Roderick Random*, pp135–136.

31   Charles N. Robinson, *The British tar in fact and fiction: The poetry, pathos, and humour of the sailor's life* (New York: Harper, 1911), p268.

32   Smollett, *Roderick Random*, p141.

33   Smollett, *Roderick Random*, p141.

34   Smollett, *Roderick Random*, p143.

35   Smollett, *Roderick Random*, p145.

36   Smollett, *Roderick Random*, p148.

37   Smollett, *Roderick Random*, p157.

38   Smollett, *Roderick Random*, p159.

39   Smollett, *Roderick Random*, p160.

40   Smollett, *Roderick Random*, p162. A purser's quart refers to a quart that was less than a full measure because of pursers' dishonesty.

41   Smollett, *Roderick Random*.

42   James Lind, *A treatise of the scurvy. In three parts. Containing an inquiry into the nature, causes, and cure, of that disease*, Second revised edition (London: A. Millar, 1757), p.8.

43   Smollett, *Roderick Random*, p163.

44   Smollett, *Roderick Random*.

45   Frank R. Lewis, 'John Morris and the Cartagena expedition, 1739–1740', *The Mariner's Mirror* 26 (1940), p263.

46   Jeremy Lewis, *Tobias Smollett* (London: Jonathan Cape, 2003), p47.

47   Smollett, *Roderick Random*, p194.

48   Kahrl, p15.

49   Robert Chambers, *Smollett: His life and a selection from his writings* (London: W. & R. Chambers, 1867), p40.

50   Thomas Carlyle, *History of Friedrich II of Prussia, called Frederick the Great* (London: Chapman and Hall, 1898), Chapter IV, pp187–188.

51   Tobias Smollett, *The letters of Tobias Smollett,* ed. by Lewis M. Knapp (Oxford: Clarendon Press 1970), p112.

52   Two journals kept by Lieutenant Robert Watkins of *Chichester*, which cover the period from October 1741 to January 1742 (National Register of Archives ADM 51/4147), provide an eyewitness account of the voyage, although they make no reference to Smollett.

53   Lewis M. Knapp, 'The naval scenes in Roderick Random', *Publications of the Modern Language Association of America,* 49 (1934), pp593–598.

54   Knapp, p597.

55   Ennis, p246.

56   Sir John Pringle, *A discourse upon some late improvements of the means for preserving the health of mariners* (London: Royal Society, 1776), p5.

57   Jeremy Lewis, *Tobias Smollett*, p32.

58   N. A. M. Rodger, *The command of the ocean, A naval history of Britain 1649–1815* (London: Allen Lane, 2004), p320.

59   Kahrl, p25.

60   Kelly Kathleen Chaves, 'From hells afloat to happy ships: Naval fiction's influence upon the history of the Royal Navy during the Georgian era', *The Northern Mariner* 18 (2008), pp1–21.

61   Chaves, p9.

62   N. A. M. Roger, *The wooden world: an anatomy of the Georgian navy* (London: Collins, 1986), p14.

Beyond Lady Barbara: Women as Portrayed in British Naval Fiction

1   Frederick Marryat, *Poor Jack* (Gutenberg.org. Electronic edition, 1840) end of Chapter 1.

2   Tobias Smollett (1721–71) was one of England's earliest novelists. In *The Adventures of Roderick Random* (1748), Smollett drew on his own naval service as a surgeon's mate to produce the first significant fictional account of life on board an English warship.

3   Elliot Engel and Margaret F. King quoting Joseph Conrad in the book, *Victorian Novel Before Victoria; British Fiction during the Reign of William IV, 1830–37* (New York: MacMillan Press, 1984), p27.

4   John Peck, *Maritime Fiction; Sailors and the Sea in British and American Novels, 1719–1917* (Palgrave, 2001.), p64.

5   'Hypermom', A reader's review of C. Northcote Parkinson, *The Life and Times of Horatio Hornblower; A biography of C. S. Forester's Famous Naval Hero* (Ithica, New York: McBooks Press, Inc. 2005).

6   Andreas Mügge, 'The Romantic Side of Hornblower', Lüdinghausen: August 2018, Source: C. S. Forester Society, csforester.files.wordpress.com 2018/11 (accessed 21 February 2020).

7   C. S. Forester, *Beat to Quarters* (New York: Little, Brown and Company, 1937), pp299–301.

8   Dudley Pope (1925–97) was a renowned British novelist, who is well-known for historical fiction and nautical fiction. His background included work as a merchant mariner and newspaper reporter. Book Series in Order https://www.bookseriesinorder.com/dudley-pope/ (accessed 21 February 2020).

9   Douglas Reeman (1924–2017) was a British novelist who wrote historic novels about the Royal Navy of the Napoleonic Wars and of the Second World War. Under the pen name Alexander Kent he wrote about two characters: Richard and Adam Bolitho. Douglas Reeman https://www.douglasreeman.com (accessed 21 February 2020).

10 David Donachie, a Scottish historic naval novelist born in 1944, also writes under the pen names Tom Connery, Jack Ludlow and Jack Cole. His novels have been published from 1991 to the present. Source: Wikipedia, 'David Donachie', https://en.wikipedia.org/wiki/David_Donachie (accessed January 2020).

11 Julian Stockwin was born in 1944 in England. He has published historical naval novels from 2001 to the present. Julian Stockwin https://julianstockwin.com/ (accessed 21 February 2020).

12 Richard Woodman, born in England in 1944, retired in 1997 from a thirty-seven-year nautical career to write historic naval novels. Wikipedia, 'Richard Woodman', https://en.wikipedia.org/wiki/Richard_Woodman (accessed January 2020).

13 Margaret Muir, a British author, lives in Tasmania and is a member of the Tasmanian Sail Training Association. Historic Naval Fiction, https://www.historicnavalfiction.com/authors-a-z/margaret-muir (accessed February 2020).

14 Eva V. Ulett, an American author and book reviewer, is a member of the National Book Critics Circle and the Historical Novel Society. https://www.historicnavalfiction.com/authors-a-z/v-e-ulett (accessed February 2020).

15 Dewey Lambdin, born 1945, is an American novelist who writes historical nautical fiction. MacMillan Publishers https://us.macmillan.com/author/deweylambdin/ (accessed 21 February 2020).

16 John Cleland (1709–89) was an English novelist best known for his bawdy novel *Fanny Hill.*

17 Dewey Lambdin, *The King's Commission* (New York: St Martin's Press, 1996, electronic edition), Chapter 7.

18 Julian Stockwin, born 1944, is an English author of historical action-adventure fiction. Julian Stockwin https://julianstockwin.com/ (accessed 21 February 2020).

19 Julian Stockwin, *Tenacious: A Kydd Sea Adventure* (Ithaca, New York: McBooks Press, 2007, electronic edition), pp201–214.

20 Alaric Bond is a British author born in 1957 who writes books on fighting sail. His publications range from 2008 to present. Book Series in Order https://www.bookseriesinorder.com/alaric-bond (accessed January 2020).

21 Antoine Vanner, author of *The Dawlish Chronicles*, spent many years traveling in the international oil industry prior to becoming a naval historic author. *The Dawlish Chronicles*, https://dawlishchronicles.com (accessed January 2020).

22   Forester, p209.

23   Forester, p252.

24   Thomas Fremantle drew upon his family's Georgian-era naval history in his independently published 2020 novel, *From Norfolk to Trafalgar*.

25   Anne Fremantle, *The Wynne Diaries; The Adventures of Two Sisters in Napoleonic Europe* (Oxford: Oxford University Press, 1982), pp217–19.

26   Fremantle, p268.

27   Fremantle, p277.

28   Mary Ann Parker, *A Voyage Round the World in the Gorgon Man of War* (New York: Cambridge University Press, 2010), pp144–145.

29   W. B. Rowbotham, 'Soldiers' and Seamen's Wives and Children in H.M. Ships,' *The Mariner's Mirror*, Vol. 47, 1961, Issue 1, pp42–48.

30   Eyre, Lucy. 'Why Patrick O'Brian is Jane Austen at Sea', *The Guardian*, 28 November 2014 https://www.theguardian.com/books/2014/nov/28/why-patrick-obrian-is-jane-austen-at-sea (accessed 10 January 2020).

31   Sheila Kindred is a contemporary historian who writes about the novels of Jane Austen. https://www.sheilajohnsonkindred.com/ (accessed 21 February 2020).

32   Sheila Johnson Kindred, *Jane Austen's Transatlantic Sister; the life and letters of Fanny Palmer Austen* (Montreal and Kingston: McGill-Queen's University Press, 2017).

33   Patrick O'Brian, *The Hundred Days* (New York: Norton, 1999), p15.

34   Contemporary author Chris Durbin, who grew up in Wales, spent twenty-four years as a warfare officer in the Royal Navy before becoming a novelist writing about the eighteenth-century navy. https://www.goodreads.com/author/show/522092.Chris_Durbin (accessed 21 February 2020).

35   Private correspondence with Chris Durbin, author of *Perilous Shore* (No location: Old Salt Press, 2019).

36   O'Brian, pp48–53.

37   Dudley Pope, quoting the deposition of John Mason, former carpenter's mate in the frigate *Hermione*, on the title page of electronic edition of *The Black Ship* (Barnsley, UK: Pen & Sword Maritime, 2009).

38   N. A. M. Rodger, *The Command of the Ocean; a naval history of Britain, 1649–1815* (London: Norton, 2004), p407, pp505–506.

39   Spencer Childers, ed., *A Mariner of England; an account of the career of William Richardson from cabin boy in the merchant service to warrant officer in the Royal Navy (1780–1819) as told by himself* (London: John Murray, 1908), p. 110: Admiral Lord Cornwallis.

40   Childers, pp225–226.

41   Christopher Lloyd, quoting Admiral Hawkins, 'Statement of Certain Immoral Practices in H.M. Ships' in *The British Seaman* (London: Granada, 1968), pp224–225.

42   Rowbotham, p43.

43   Roy Adkins and Lesley Adkins, *The War for all the Oceans; from Nelson at the Nile to Napoleon at Waterloo* (New York: Penguin, 2008), pp179–180.

44 N. A. M. Rodger, *The Wooden World; an anatomy of the Georgian Navy* (London, New York: Norton, 1986), p151.

45 Alaric Bond, *True Colours* (Fireship Press: Tucson, Arizona, 2010), p20.

46 Vincent McInerney, (ed.) *Landsman Hay: the memoirs of Robert Hay* (Barnsley, UK: Seaforth, 2010), pp50–52.

47 Childers, pp169–170.

48 Tim Flannery, (ed.), *The Life and Adventures of John Nicol, Mariner* (New York: Grove Press, 1997), p37.

49 Flannery, pp121–122.

50 Flannery, pp174–175.

51 Adkins and Adkins, pp32–33.

52 Roy Adkins, quoting from *The Times* (13 May 1863); *Nelson's Trafalgar; The battle that changed the world* (New York: Penguin, 2006), pp79–81.

53 O'Brian, p281.

The Rise of the Fouled Anchor: The Visual Codification of the Royal Navy during the 1700s

1 'The fouled anchor button', *Historic Dockyard Chatham*, https://collection.thedockyard.co.uk/objects/9028.

2 W. G. Perrin, *British flags, their early history, and their development at sea; with an account of the origin of the flag as a national device* (Cambridge University Press, 1922), p82.

3 P. Kemp, *Oxford Companion to Ships and the Sea* (Oxford University Press, 1976) quoted in P, Lindfield and C, Margrave, *Rule Britannia?: Britain and Britishness 1707–1901* (Cambridge Scholars Publishing, 2015), p8.

4 'George Anson, 1st Baron Anson' *Wikipedia* https://en.wikipedia.org/wiki/George_Anson,_1st_Baron_Anson (accessed March 2020).

5 B. Wilson, *Empire of the Deep: The Rise and Fall of the British Navy* (London: Hatchette, 2013), Chapters 27 and 28.

6 J. Barrow, *The Life of George, Lord Anson, Admiral of the Fleet, Vice-admiral of Great Britain, and First Lord Commissioner of the Admiralty, Previous To, and During, the Seven Years' War* (London: J. Murray, 1839), p150.

7 Barrow.

8 Historic Dockyard Chatham, 'the fouled anchor button', online article https://collection.thedockyard.co.uk/objects/9028 (accessed January 2020).

9 *Public Advertiser*, 27 May 1772.

10 *Hampshire Chronicle*, 13 June 1774, p3.

11 Wilson.

12 Wilson.

13 *Derby Mercury*, 1 June 1786.

14 Kate Williams, *England's Mistress* (New York: Random House; UK: Hutchinson, 2006), p205.

15 Sylvia K. Robinson, 'In Defense of Emma: Scheming Adventuress or Radiant Presence?' (UK: CPI Books, 2016), p167.

16   BADA Ltd. website. https://www.bada.org/object/admiral-lord-nelsons-birthday-service-1798 (accessed January 2020).

17   Barrow.

18   Jason M. Juergens, *CPO leadership: unique and innovative leadership characteristics of senior enlisted that sustain Naval operations.* (Thesis and Dissertation Collection, 2010–03), p20.

19   'This is why the saltiest sailors wear a "fouled anchor"', *We Are the Mighty* https://www.wearethemighty.com/history/this-is-why-the-saltiest-sailors-wear-a-fouled-anchor (accessed March 2020).

20   'Foul (nautical)', *Wikipedia*, https://en.wikipedia.org/wiki/Foul_(nautical) (accessed March 2020).

Spain and American Independence: The Best-Kept Secret of the Georgian Age

1   William S. Maltby, *The Black Legend in England* (Durham, North Carolina: Duke University Press, 1971), pp19–20.

2   Hermenegildo Franco Castanon, *La razón de Trafalgar: La Campania naval de 1805, Un análisis critico* (Valladolid, Spain: AF Editories de Historia Militiae, 2005), p10.

3   John D. Harbron, *Trafalgar and the Spanish Navy* (London: Conway Maritime Press Ltd, 1988), pp98–112.

4   Charles Ramirez-Berg, *Latino Images in Film: Stereotypes, Subversion and Resistance* (Austin, Texas: University of Texas Press, 2002), pp14–15.

5   Maltby, p5.

6   Douglas T. Peck, 'Revival of the Spanish "Black Legend": The American Repudiation of Their Spanish Heritage'. *Revista De Historia De América*, No. 128 (2001), pp26–29.

7   David Greenberg, 'Agit Prof: Howard Zinn's Influential Mutilations of American History,' *The New Republic*, 19 March 2013.

8   Howard Zinn, *A People's History of the United States* (New York: Harper Perennial, 2003), p1.

9   Zinn, p2.

10   Peck, pp30–39.

11   Zinn, p2.

12   Eduardo Gonzalez, 'Stereotypical Depictions of Latino Criminality: U.S. Latinos in the Media during the MAGA Campaign'. *Democratic Communique*, Vol. 28, No. 1 (2019), pp50–53.

13   Frank de Verona, 'Spain and Hispanic America: Forgotten Allies of the American Revolution', *Hispanic Presence in the United States: Historical Beginnings* (Miami, Florida: The National Hispanic Quincentennial Commission, Mnemosyne Publishing Company, 1999), p24.

14   Orders of Alexandre Marie Eleonor of Saint-Mauris, Prince of Montbarrey to Jean Baptiste Donatien de Vimeur, Comte de Rochambeau, 1 March 1780, Henri Doniol, *Historie de la Participation de la France a l'Establissement des Etats Unice d'Amerique: Correspondance Diplomatique et Documents* (Paris: Imprimerie Nationale, 1892), Vol. 5, pp326–329.

15 Guillermo and Gregorio Callejo Leal, *Galvez y Espana en la Guerra de Independencia de los Estados Unidos* (Valencia, Spain: Albatros Ediciones, 2016), p152.

16 Felipe Fondesviela y Ondeano to Antonio Bucareli, 25 April 1777, Archivos General de Indias, Seccion Gobierno, Adiencia de Mexico, Legajo 1,214 (AGI), Sevilla, Spain.

17 Thomas E. Chavez, *Spain and the Independence of the United States: An Intrinsic Gift* (Albuquerque, New Mexico: University of New Mexico Press, 2002), p202.

18 Carlos Jose Gutierrez del Rios, Conde de Frenan-Nunez, *La Vida de Carlos III* (Madrid: Librería de Fernando Fe, 1898).

19 Antonio Ferrer Del Rio, *La Historia de la Reinada de Carlos III* (Madrid: Matute y Compagni, 1858), Vol. 3, pp252–256.

20 Harbron, pp102–105.

21 Herbert W. Wilson, *The Downfall of Spain, A Naval History of the Spanish-American War* (London: Sampson, Low, Marston and Company, 1900), pp78–79.

22 Ian Cobain, 'Exocet Missile: How the Sinking of HMS *Sheffield* made it Famous', *The Guardian*, (15 October 2017), p22. 'The British public became fascinated by the Exocet missile after one sunk HMS *Sheffield* shortly after the outbreak of the Falklands war in 1982.'

23 Harbron, p84.

24 Prince of Montbarrey to Comte de Rochambeau, 1 March 1780, Doniol, *Historie*, Vol. 5, pp326–329.

25 Gerard de Reyneval to Prince of Montbarrey, 12 April 1780, Papers of Jean Baptiste Donatien de Vimeur, Comte de Rochambeau, Box 15, Reel 4, Library of Congress Manuscript Division, Washington DC (RPLC).

26 George Washington to Mesheck Ware quoted in Stephen Bonsal, *When the French Were Here: A Narrative of the Sojourn of the French Forces in America and Their Contribution to the Yorktown Campaign, Drawn from Unpublished Reports and Letters of Participants in the National Archives of France and the Manuscript Division of the Library Congress* (Garden City, New York: Doubleday, Doran and Company, Inc., 1945), p108.

27 Bonsal, p111.

28 Rochambeau to Washington, 20 August 1780, Doniol, *Historie*, Vol. 5, pp367–369; Rochambeau to Washington, 17 May 1781, Doniol, Vol. 5, p474; Rochambeau to de Grasse, 28 May 1781, Doniol, *Historie*, Vol. 5, pp475–476.

29 Bonsal, pp103–115.

30 See George Washington's correspondence with Major General Nathaniel Greene, Robert Morris, Rochambeau, Marquis de Lafayette, and others in *The Papers of George Washington* (Charlottesville, Virginia: University of Virginia Press, 1968).

31 De Grasse to Rochambeau, 29 March 1781, Doniol, Vol. 5, p488.

32 Francisco Saavedra Sagronis, *The Journals of Don Francisco Saavedra de Sagronis*, Francisco Morales Padron, ed. (Gainesville, Florida: University of Florida Press, 1989), ppv–xxxii.

33 Bonsal, pp118–121.

34 Rochambeau to de Grasse, 1 June 1781, Doniol Vol. 5, p481.

35 Rochambeau to Prince de Montbarrey, 18 September 1780, RPLC, Box 3, Reel 2.
36 Rochambeau to de Grasse, 18 June 1781, Doniol, Vol. 5, p495.
37 Saavedra, 31 July 1781, p208.
38 Saavedra, 1 August 1781, p209.
39 Saavedra, 27 July, 28 July, 30 July 1781, pp204–207.
40 Saavedra, 28 July 1781, pp206–207; Doniol, Vol. 4, p649.
41 Saavedra, 15 August 1781, p211.
42 Saavedra, 16 August 1781, p211.
43 For a complete examination of the genesis and history of the myth of the 'Ladies of Havana,' see Jose Ramon Fernandez Alvarez, *Las Damas de Habana y Sus Joyas: Un Mito Persistente en la Historia de Cuba* (Miami, Florida: Ediciones Universal, 2015).
44 The merchants did not donate the money outright. Instead, they purchased subscriptions in future deliveries of American agricultural exports, principally wheat and rice, which they could sell in other Spanish colonies as well as those of France and Holland and in Europe. See Alvarez, pp106–109.
45 Saavedra, 16 August 1781, p211.
46 Bonsal.

Sir Andrew Pellet Green: Vice Admiral Sir Thomas Fremantle's Protégé

1 E. J. Hounslow, *Nelson's Right Hand Man* (The History Press, Cheltenham, UK, 2016), p52.
2 Hounslow, p60.
3 E. Jurien de la Graviere, *Guerres Maritimes Tome Premier* (Paris, G. Charpentier), p86.
4 E. J. de la Graviere, p84.
5 E. J. de la Graviere, p96.
6 Andrew Pellet Green, *His Notebook* (Green Family Papers).
7 Battle of Jean-Rabel; Off Haiti. Destruction of French frigate *Harmonie*, eleven merchant ships captured.
8 Vice Admiral Hyde Parker Biography. *Wikipedia*: https://en.wikipedia.org/wiki/Hyde_Parker_(Royal_Navy_officer,_born_1739 (accessed 15 Jan 2020).
9 Anne Fremantle, *The Wynne Diaries, Volume 111* (Oxford University Press, 1940), p41.
10 Charles Fremantle, *Rear Admiral Thomas Fremantle and the Adriatic Campaign*, *The Trafalgar Chronicle, Yearbook of The 1805 Club, No. 18* (Barnsley, UK: Seaforth Publishing, 2008), pp193–202.
11 Hounslow, p177.
12 O'Bryne's *Naval Biographic Dictionary, 1849;* Green Kt KCH KSS Captain 1814.
13 K. M. Green, *Andrew Pellet Green: A biography* (Green Family Papers).
14 Nigel Foxell, *Travels in the Two Sicilies 1817–1820* (Book Depository, UK: Mailer Press, 2007), pp26–27.
15 Charles Fremantle, 'A Boy in Battle', *The Trafalgar Chronicle NS 1* (Barnsley, UK, Seaforth Publishing, 2016), pp59–70.
16 Gareth Glover, *Wellington's Voice* (Barnsley, UK, Frontline Books, 2012), p318.

Commander Sir James Pearl

1   Donald L. Hutchens and Lilla Ross, *Pearl: The Man and the Place* (St John's, Newfoundland: SeaFlow Publishing, 2007), p3.
2   Hutchens and Ross, pp3–4.
3   Hutchens and Ross, p4. The children were David, 1771; Eunice, 1773; Abigail, 1775; Mary, 1779; Hannah, 1781, and Ruth, 1784; John Marshall, *Royal Naval Biography; or Memoirs of the Services of all the Flag Officers, Superannuated Rear-Admirals, Retired-Captains, Post-Captains, and Commanders, Addenda to Flag Officers and Post Captains; Commanders*, Vol. IV, Part II (London: Longman, Hurst, Rees, Orme, Brown, and Green, 1835), pp275–276.
4   Marshall, p5.
5   Marshall, p5. Papers for his lieutenant's examination, The National Archives, Kew, London, ADM 107/35/423, indicate that he was born in St Paul, Connecticut, on 27 September 1783 but his obituaries published in 1840 claimed that he was fifty years old at that time, thus making a 1790 birth year more likely.
6   Marshall, p7.
7   Hutchens and Ross, pp. 7–9; J. R. Campbell, *A History of the County of Yarmouth, Nova Scotia* (St John's, Newfoundland: J. & A. McMillan, 1876), p64.
8   Hutchens and Ross, p7.
9   Hutchens and Ross, pp8–9.
10 Marshall, p274; Hutchens and Ross, pp11–14. During this period, by virtue of Pearl's age he was likely not at sea constantly, but rather in a more sporadic fashion.
11 Hutchens and Ross, p12.
12 Andrew Lambert, *Nelson: Britannia's God of War* (London: Faber & Faber, 2004), p277.
13 Lambert, p15; 'Commander Sir James Pearl Obituary,' *Oxford Journal* (Oxford, UK), 29 February 1840.
14 Hutchens and Ross, p15.
15 Hutchens and Ross, p16.
16 Hutchens and Ross, p17.
17 Lambert, p303.
18 Lambert, p17.
19 Lambert, p17.
20 'Commander Sir James Pearl Obituary', *The Royal Gazette* (Hamilton, Bermuda), 14 January 1840.
21 Hutchens and Ross, p19.
22 Hutchens and Ross, p19.
23 *Mediator*'s actual captain was Blamey: see 'Marshall' in *Wikipedia*, https://en.wikisource.org/wiki/Royal_Naval_Biography/Blamey,_George_William
24 'Marshall' in *Wikipedia*, pp19–20; John Marshall, pp243–244.
25 Marshall, pp19–20; Pearl Obituary, *The Royal* Gazette, 14 January 1840; Pearl Obituary, *Oxford Journal*, 29 February 1840.
26 Marshall, pp20–21.
27 Marshall, pp20–21.

28   Marshall, pp20–21.
29   Marshall, p21; *Oxford Journal*.
30   Marshall, pp20–21.
31   Marshall, pp20–21.
32   Marshall, pp20–21.
33   Marshall, pp20–21.
34   Marshall, p22.
35   Marshall, p23.
36   Marshall, p23.
37   Marshall, pp23–25.
38   Marshall, pp23–25; *Oxford Journal*.
39   Marshall, pp26–27.
40   Marshall, p27.
41   Marshall, p29.
42   Marshall, p29.
43   Marshall, p31.
44   Marshall, p31.
45   *Oxford Journal*.
46   Hutchens and Ross, p31.
47   Hutchens and Ross, p31. The Duke of Clarence later went on to rule Great Britain as King William IV from 1830 to 1837.
48   Hutchens and Ross, pp118–119.
49   Hutchens and Ross, p32.
50   Hutchens and Ross, p33.
51   Hutchens and Ross, pp33–34. Prior to leaving England, Pearl also proposed to the Royal Navy a method for improving rigging on vessels, which included the replacement of shrouds and stays with iron bands or collars (National Archives, Kew, London, ADM 1/2366/39).
52   Hutchens and Ross, pp35–36.
53   Hutchens and Ross. The 1,000-acre land grant (awarded in July 1828) was located in the town of Kentville, Shelbourne (now Kings County, Nova Scotia), and consisted of three lots on the banks of the Trusket River. A major problem with the grant (and a source of frustration to Pearl) was that the acreage was not all congruent, making development of the land more difficult.
54   Hutchens and Ross, p38.
55   Hutchens and Ross, p41.
56   Hutchens and Ross, p57. The Royal Guelphic (or Hanoverian) Order is a Hanoverian order of chivalry instituted by the Prince Regent in 1815. King William IV often used it to reward old navy friends and associates. The Royal Guelphic Order has not been conferred by the British Crown since 1837, when the personal union of the United Kingdom and Hanover ended following King William IV's death.
57   Hutchens and Ross, p57. Since the Royal Guelphic Order was technically a foreign order, King William IV usually conferred simultaneous knighthood (as knight bachelor) on honorees, thus allowing them to use the accolade, 'Sir', in British

society. In the case of Pearl, Queen Victoria may have continued this practice with knights of the Royal Guelphic Order who were appointed shortly before King William IV's death.

58 Robert Bigsby, *Memoir of the Illustrious and Sovereign Order of St John of Jerusalem, From the Capitulation of Malta to the Present Period* (Derby, UK: Richard Keene, Irongate, 1869), p210. The Order of St John of Jerusalem was a charity-based organisation in Great Britain that evolved from a faction of the Order of Malta in the 1830s. It was later constituted as a Royal Order of Chivalry by Queen Victoria in 1888.

59 Hutchens and Ross, p57.
60 Hutchens and Ross, p57.
61 Hutchens and Ross, p59.
62 Hutchens and Ross, pp59–60.
63 Hutchens and Ross, p61.

Captain John Houlton Marshall

1 David Armstrong, 'William James Marshall RN', Nova Scotia-L Archives, 10 August 2003, *Ancestry*: http://archiver.rootsweb.ancestry.com/th/read/NOVA-SCOTIA/2003-08/1060487869.

2 Armstrong. 'Careening' was the process of beaching and listing a ship on her side for hull maintenance.

3 David Armstrong, *Memorandum of the Services of Captain John Houlton Marshall, RN*. Mr Armstrong, who provided this document, is a direct descendant of John Marshall.

4 J. J. Colledge and Ben Warlow, *Ships of the Royal Navy: The Complete Record of all Fighting Ships of the Royal Navy from the Fifteenth Century to the Present* (London: Chatham Publishing, 2006), p8.

5 Colledge and Warlow.
6 Colledge and Warlow.
7 Armstrong, *Memorandum*.
8 Phyllis R. Blakeley, Hughes, Sir Richard in *Dictionary of Canadian Biography*, www.biograpPhyhi.ca/en/bio.php?id_nbr=2468 (accessed January 2020).
9 Armstrong, *Memorandum*.
10 Armstrong, *Memorandum*.
11 The three colonies would be unified by the British as British Guiana in 1831.
12 Colledge and Warlow, p312.
13 Colledge and Warlow, p238.
14 This capture is considered the greatest haul of prize money of any single action in Royal Navy history.
15 The annatto is an orange-red product derived from the achiote tree. Annatto is used as a colouring agent for clothing and for food. Most likely the annatto found on board the *Santa-Brigida* was in a powder or paste form. https://en.wikipedia.org/wiki/Annatto.
16 Or the equivalent of 100 years' pay ... 'HMS *Naiad* (1797)' *Wikipedia*, https://en.wikipedia.org/wiki/HMS_Naiad_(1797); David Armstrong, 'William James

Marshall RN'; *Royal Naval Biography, or, Memoirs of the Services of all Flag-Officers, Superannuated Rear-Admirals, Retired-Captains, Post-Captains, and Commanders*, Vol. III, Part II, (London: Rees, Orme, Brown, and Green, Paternoster Row, 1832), p402, http://bit.ly/29rJ5SC.

17 *London Gazette* No. 15197, pp1094–1095, 22 October 1799.

18 *Royal Naval Biography.*

19 Armstrong, *Memorandum*. Currently, no record is available to show Marshall's service from that time through July 1804.

20 John Christian Schetky, Loss of the Magnificent 25 March 1804, National Maritime Museum, Greenwich, UK, http://prints.rmg.co.uk/art/521575/loss-of-the-magnificent-25-march-1804. Commanded by Captain W. H. Jervis (formerly Ricketts), the ship was one of twenty sailing ships of the line blockading the French fleet in Brest, Brittany. She foundered after striking uncharted rocks near the Pierres Noir (Black Rocks). In Schetky's rendering the ship lies on its side with waves crashing over it and the ensign at the stern turned upside-down, a traditional distress signal. Read more at http://prints.rmg.co.uk/art/521575/loss-of-the-magnificent-25-march-1804#oCpRagORvtqviVjQ.99

21 'R.C.N. Greets R.N. on Trafalgar Day', *Montreal Gazette*, 22 October 1942. Marshall is mentioned in the article as *Britannia*'s first lieutenant during the Battle of Trafalgar.

22 Edward Fraser, 'Old Ironsides' in *Champions of the Fleet* (London and New York: John Lane, 1908), p272.

23 Nicholas Tracy, (ed.), *The Naval Chronicle: The Contemporary Record of the Royal Navy at War*, Volume III 1804–1806, (Chatham Publishing, 1999), p222. Northesk's account is widely discredited; *Britannia* lagged at the rear of the windward line and Northesk fell into an argument with his captain, who wanted him to bring her into action.

24 Keith Mercer, 'Lord Nelson on the Mind: Naval Victories and Cultural Memory in Nova Scotia', *The Trafalgar Chronicle*, Vol. 22 (2012), p179. pdf. www.keithmercer.com/uploads/1/7/6/7/17679083/tc2012_mercer

25 Keith Mercer, 'Trafalgar Veterans from Atlantic Canada', 21 October 2013. pdf. www.keithmercer.com/blog/trafalar-veterans-from-atlantic-canada; 'Atlantic Canada', https://en.wikipedia.org/wiki/Atlantic_Canada

26 Mercer, 'Trafalgar Veterans'.

27 Colledge and Warlow, p24.

28 Armstrong, *Memorandum*.

29 'HMS *Halcyon* (1813)', *Wikipedia*, https://en.wikipedia.org/wiki/HMS_Halcyon_(1813); *Royal Naval Biography*, p402.

30 Mercer, 'Lord Nelson on the Mind', p179.

31 'John Houlton Marshall', *Wikipedia*, https://en.wikipedia.org/wiki/John_Houlton_Marshall (accessed January 2020).

Captain Ralph Willett Miller

1 Nathaniel Philbrick. *Mayflower: A Story of Courage, Community, and War.* (New York: Penguin Books, 2006), p200.

2   David Howarth and Stephen Howarth, *Lord Nelson: The Immortal Memory* (New York: Viking, 1988), p189.
3   Peter Hore, *Nelson's Band of Brothers: Lives and Memorials* (South Yorkshire, Uk: Seaforth Publishing, 2015), p30.
4   Alfred Thayer Mahan, *The Life of Nelson: The Embodiment of the Great Sea Power of Great Britain* (Boston: Little & Brown, 1899), p233.
5   Hore, p31.
6   Hore, p32.
7   Oliver Warner, *Nelson's Battles* (New York: The Macmillan Company, 1965), pp69–70.
8   The Battle of the Nile, Nelson Society, www.nelson-society.com
9   Thomas J. Pettigrew, *Memoirs of the Life of Vice-Admiral Lord Viscount Nelson* (London: T. & W. Boone, 1849), pp98–99.
10   Pettigrew, pp98–99.
11   Mahan, p526.
12   Pettigrew, p99.

The Popham Code Controversy

1   Fletcher Wilkie, 'Recollections of the British Army in the Late Revolutionary Wars', *United Services Journal*, Vol. 1 (1836), p485.
2   Hugh Popham, *A Damned Cunning Fellow* (Cornwall: Old Ferry Press, 1991), p224.
3   For more about Popham's signal book see *Royal Museums Blog:* www.rmg.co.uk/discover/behind-the-scenes/blog/hol17-signal-book-1760 (Accessed 7 February 2020).
4   Sir Home Popham, *Telegraphic Signals or Marine Vocabulary* (London, 1803), p3.
5   William G. Perrin, *British Flags; Their Early History, and Their Development at Sea* (Cambridge: Cambridge University Press, 1922), p178.
6   Popham, p3; *Annual Register* Vol. 4 (London: 1762), p130.
7   Papers respecting the Ship *L'Estrusco*, Parliamentary Papers, (London: 1808), px.
8   Thomas Carson Hansard, *The Parliamentary Debates from the year 1803 to the Present Time*, Vol. 11, pp721–763 (31 May 1808).
9   Hansard.
10   Popham purchased the *President Washington* from Thomas Willing Francis of Philadelphia, representing Brown & Francis of Rhode Island, for one lakh (100,000 rupees) plus 20,000 rupees or about 78,000 Spanish dollars or about £20,000 (£2,100,000 in 2013). Popham added a false bill of sale that named his new flag captain, Giacomo Pons, as the buyer. When Pons fell ill at Canton, Popham replaced him with the ship's Venetian surgeon, Balthazar Georgi. Like Coppi and Pons before him, Georgi's role was to act as commander and owner of the ship.
11   Hansard, p731.
12   Hansard, p729.
13   Hansard, p735.
14   Hugh Popham, p87.
15   Hugh Popham, p44.
16   Hugh Popham, p47, From B. T. Esq., Late Secretary of the Admiralty, British Library.

17   Hugh Popham, p48.
18   Cyril Northcote Parkinson, edit. Samuel Walters, Lieutenant R.N: His Memoirs (Liverpool; Liverpool University Press, 1949), p139.
19   Parkinson.
20   *Nautical Economy; or Forecastle Recollections of Events during the Last War By a Sailor politely called by the Officers of the Navy, Jack Nasty-face* (London: 1836), p43: 'It has been the generally received opinion that this memorable Signal was, "England expects every man to do his duty," but an extract from the Log-book of the Victory, will shew it correctly.' According to this source the message was the more personal **253** ENGLAND **269** EXPECTS **238** EACH **471** MAN **958** WILL **220** DO **370** HIS **4** D **21** U **19** T **24** Y. See also *The Monthly Review from September to December Inclusive* 1836, p144. The version 'England expects that every man will do his duty' is unlikely, considering that Popham's instructions stated, 'prepositions and articles will be used as seldom as possible'.
21   *Corbett's Political Register*, Vol. 8 (London: 1805), pp909–910.
22   *Corbett's*.
23   *Publications of the Navy Records Society*, Vol. 59 (London: NRS, 1924), p127.
24   The idea of a monopoly on coffee had originated with David Scott, the Director and Chairman of the East India Company. Popham said Scott had 'most particularly urged this point'.
25   Edward Ingram, *In Defence of British India: Great Britain in the Middle East, 1775–1842* (London: Frank Cass, 1984) pp37–39. St Vincent and John Blankett both served under Admiral Augustus Keppel.
26   *Observations on a pamphlet which has been privately circulated, said to be 'A concise statement of facts, and the treatment experienced by Sir Home Popham, since his return from the Red Sea', to which is added, a copy of the report made by the Navy-Board to the Admiralty, on investigating the account of expenditure for the Romney and Sensible, at Calcutta, in 1801, whilst under the orders of Sir Home Popham* (London: 1805), pp48–56.
27   *Chronological arrangement of the accounts and papers printed by order of the House of Commons in February, March and April, 1805, respecting the repairs of the Romney and others of His Majesty's ships belonging to the squadron lately under the command of Sir Home Popham: with their material contents and some few cursory remarks in elucidation*, (London: 1805), p7.
28   Hugh Popham, p108.
29   *Continuation of a concise statement of facts, relative to the treatment experienced by Sir Home Popham, since his return from the Red Sea* (London: 1804).
30   Waite, p108 from Nelson to Lady Hamilton; *Despatches of Lord Nelson*, V, p184.
31   Richard Hall Gower, *A Treatise on the Theory and Practice of Seamanship: Containing General Rules for Manoeuvring Vessels, with a Moveable Figure of a Ship, So Planned that the Sails, Rudder, and Hull May be Made to Perform the Manoeuvres According to the Rule Laid Down. To the Above is Added a Miscellaneous Chapter on the Various Contrivances Against Accidents, and a System of Naval Signals, the Whole Forming a Useful Compendium to the Officer, to Instruct*

Him when Young, and to Remind Him when Old. Second edition (London: 1796). The first edition was published in 1793.

32 Richard Hall Gower, *A Treatise on the Theory and Practice of Buenos Ayres July 2, 1806* (London: 1806).

33 'Seamanship, Together with a System of Naval Signals,' *The Gentleman's Magazine*, 3rd Edition (London: 1808), p206. Gower also published 'A Treatise on Signals' in *The Naval Chronicle*, Vol. V (London: 1801) p22. Popham published his *Telegraphic Signals on Marine Vocabulary* in 1803. He dated his dedication: Romney, Sheerness, 2 May 1803; His introduction: Romney, Sheerness, 1 November 1800.

34 Perrin, p176.

35 *Naval Sketch Book: Second Series* Vol. I (1834), p166.

36 *The Gentleman's Magazine*, Vol. 90 (London: 1820), p276. Robert Dundas, the 2nd Viscount Melville, was First Lord of the Admiralty for many years.

37 Michael H. Styles, *Captain Hogan: Seaman, Merchant, Diplomat on Six Continents*, (Fairfax Station, Virginia: Six Continent Horizons, 2003), p131.

38 Martyn Downer, *Nelson's Purse* (London: Corgi, 2005), p359. Relative value of money calculated using measuringworth.com.

39 Sir Home Popham and Lady Popham are buried at St Michael's Church in Sunninghill. Popham's monument shows the names of four battles: Copenhagen, Cape of Good Hope, North of Spain, and Buenos Ayres.

40 Martyn Downer, *Nelson's Purse*. (London: Bantam Press, 2004), p279.

41 *Morning Post*, 15 September 1806.

42 J. Fairbourn, *An Authentic and Interesting Description of the City of Buenos Ayres including an Account of the Capture of Buenos Ayres July 2, 1806*, (London: 1806).

43 *A Full and Correct Report of the Trial of Sir Home Popham, Second Edit* (London: 1807), p97.

44 *A Full and Correct Report*, p224.

45 *The Gentleman's Magazine and Historical Chronicle for the Year 1808* Vol. LXXVIII (London: 1809), p81.

Cornwallis, a Woman Named Cuba, and the Caribbean

1 G Cornwallis-West, *The Life and Letters of Admiral Cornwallis* (London: Holden, 1927), p130.

2 Barry Jolly, 'The Three Admirals Window receives full military honours', *The Glazier, (a publication of The Worshipful Company of Glaziers and Painters on Glass) No. 60* (Summer 2019).

3 Barry Jolly, 'Cornwallis and Hampshire', *Hampshire Studies – Proceedings of the Hampshire Field Club & Archaeological Society*. No. 74 (2019), pp137–152. Milford-on-Sea Historical Record Society also published a special commemorative edition of its *Occasional Magazine*.

4 Richardson was a sailor who had risen to be a warrant officer by the time his naval career ended in 1819.

5 For example, James Davey, *In Nelson's Wake* (London and New York: National Maritime Museum and Yale University Press, 2015), p138; Barry Jolly, 'Admiral Sir

William Cornwallis – Aspects of a Life' *Milford-on-Sea Historical Record Society Occasional Magazine,* NS 6 (2019), pp40–42.

6   Colonel Spencer Childers (ed.), *A mariner of England; an account of the career of William Richardson from cabin boy in the merchant service to warrant officer in the Royal Navy (1780 to 1819) as told by himself* (London: John Murray, 1908), p110.

7   Rev N. B. Cryer, *The Cornwallis Family History 1225–2006* (York: 2006), p222.

8   The Parish register shows the name Mercella, but Crier apparently misspelled it as Marcella.

9   Jamaica (Bishop's) Transcripts – 'Jamaica, Church of England Parish Register Transcripts, 1664–1880' database with images, *FamilySearch* (https://familysearch.org/ark:/61903/1:1: … : 9 August 2017), Port Royal, Jamaica, Registrar General's Department, Spanish Town; FHL microfilm 1,291,769.

10   Jamaica transcripts commentary https://www.familysearch.org/wiki/en/Jamaica,_Church_of_England_Parish_Register _Transcripts_(FamilySearch_Historical_Records) ; Jamaica Transcripts, 1664–1880.

11   Cornwallis-West, pp19–20.

12   Cornwallis-West, p27.

13   Maitland family history: www.antonymaitland.com/captfred.htm

14   Clan Maitland: https://clanmaitland.uk/history/century-18th/15-frederick-lewis-maitland-of-rankeillour/57-frederick-lewis-maitland-part-I

15   Born 13 March, baptised 2 May 1760.

16   John, son of John Maude, baptised 27 April 1771.

17   Jo Stanley, 'Questing for Cuba Cornwallis, Nelson's Afro-Caribbean Nurse', *Trafalgar Chronicle,* NS 3 (2018), pp24–33.

18   Letter to Captain Looker of 23 January 1780 in Sir Nicholas Harris Nicolas (ed.), *The Dispatches and Letters of Vice Admiral Lord Viscount Nelson Vol. 1 January 1798 to August 1799* (London: Henry Colburn, 1844), p33.

19   Variously written as Coubah, Couba, Cooba or Cuba.

20   Cornwallis-West, p45.

21   Jamaica Transcripts, 1664–1880. Johanna Smith, 20 October 1799, Christening p50.

22   Will dated 11 December 1815, The National Archives, Kew, London: Prob 11/1818.

23   See Barry Jolly, *Mrs Whitby's Locket*, Milford-on-Sea Historical Record Society (2011).

A Second Naval War: The Immediate Effects of the American War on Royal Navy Operations, June 1812–July 1813

1   Andrew Lambert, *The Challenge: Britain Against America in the Naval War of 1812* (London: Faber and Faber, 2012), pp83–85; Bradford Perkins, *Prologue to War: England and the United States 1805–1812* (Berkley: University of California Press, 1961), pp418–419.

2   Admiral Sir William Young quoted in Roger Knight, *Pursuit of Victory: The Life and Achievement of Horatio Nelson* (New York: Basic Books, 2005), p676.

3   Croker to Warren, 10 February 1813, The National Archives, Kew, London, ADM 2/1376, ff73–74.

4   N. A. M. Rodger, *The Command of the Ocean, A Naval History of Britain, 1649–1815* (New York: Norton & Norton, 2015), p567.

5   House of Commons, Debates, 18 Feb 1813, XXIV, pp642–649.

6   The National Archives, Kew, London, ADM 8/100, Admiralty List Books, January 1812–July 1813.

7   Kevin McCranie, *Utmost Gallantry, the US and Royal Navies at Sea in the War of 1812* (Annapolis, Maryland: Naval Institute Press, 2001), pp88–89.

8   Croker to Warren, 18 November 1812, The National Archives, Kew, London, ADM 2/1375, f252.

9   Melville to Warren, 3 December 1812, National Maritime Museum, Greenwich, UK (NMM), WAR/82, f18. The true proportion was half that.

10   The National Archives, Kew, London, ADM 2/1376; WAR/82, ff18–20.

11   Melville to Warren, 26 December 1812, The National Archives, Kew, London, ADM 2/1375.

12   Report, 11 July 1811, The National Archives, Kew, London, ADM 1/3976.

13   Melville to Wellington, 28 July 1813, in Wellington, *Supplementary Dispatches and Correspondence of Arthur, Duke of Wellington, 1813–1814*, VIII (London: John Murray, 1861), pp144–145.

14   Dominic Lieven, *Russia against Napoleon: The True Story of the Campaigns of War and Peace* (New York: 2009), pp67–70; Lambert, pp126–127.

15   Naval Intelligence Papers, 1811–1834, The National Archives, Kew, London, ADM 1/3976. Russia also sent fifteen ships of the line and seven frigates to augment the Royal Navy's Mediterranean Fleet in December 1812.

16   The National Archives, Kew, London, ADM 8/100.

17   Croker to Pellew, 12 February 1813, The National Archives, Kew, London, ADM 2/926.

18   Rodger, p564.

19   House of Commons, 1868–1869 (366) XXV, pp1177–1179.

20   Russel and Lord Castlereagh, Aug to Sept 1812, The National Archives, Kew, London, FO 5/91; Troy Bickham, *The Weight of Vengeance, The United States, the British Empire and the War of 1812* (Oxford, 2012), pp76–101; Rodger, pp563–574; Brian Arthur, *How Britain won the War of 1812, The Royal Navy's Blockades of the United States, 1812–1815* (Woodbridge, Uk: Boydell Press, 2011), p51, pp61–62.

The 1805 Club

President: Admiral Sir Jonathon Band GCB DL
Chairman: Bill White

The 1805 Club is a registered charity no. 1071871

The 1805 Club was established in 1990, and as of 2020, celebrating its thirty years of dedication toward commemorating and conserving the history and heritage of the Royal Navy and the merchant service during the era of the Georgian sailing navy.

No other organisation is so dedicated in its efforts to conserve artefacts, graves, memorials, and monuments, and support to scholastic research of the Georgian era, as exhibited in such a publication as *The Trafalgar Chronicle*

For thirty years, the members of The Club have demonstrated their enthusiasm for all aspects of the sailing navy of the Georgian era, and through the partnership of Seaforth Publishing, *The Trafalgar Chronicle* represents such a singular endeavour.

To join the 1805 Club go to www.1805club.org
and download the membership application form.